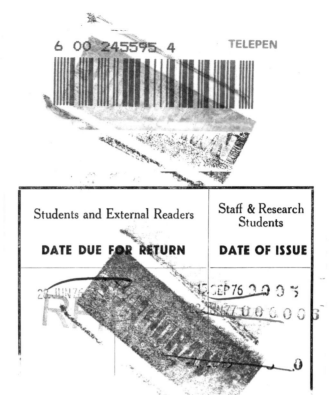

**Long Term Projections of Power:
Political, Economic, and Military
Forecasting**

Some of this research was sponsored by the Office of Naval Research, Navy Analysis Programs at Mathematica, Inc.

Long Term Projections of Power:

Political, Economic, and Military Forecasting

Klaus P. Heiss
Klaus Knorr
Oskar Morgenstern

Ballinger Publishing Company • Cambridge, Mass.
A Subsidiary of J.B. Lippincott Company

International Standard Book Number: 0-88410-008-1

Printed in the United States of America

Library of Congress Catalog Card Number: 73-12393

Library of Congress Cataloging in Publication Data

Heiss, Klaus P.
  Long term projections of power.

  Research sponsored by the Office of Naval Research; ONR contract number, N0014-72-C-0341; task number, NR 277-077.
  Bibliography: p.
  1. Technological forecasting. 2. Economic forecasting. 3. Power (Social sciences) I. Knorr, Klaus Eugen, 1911-   joint author. II. Morgenstern, Oskar, 1902-   joint author. III. Title.
T174.H44   301.5   73-12392
ISBN 0-88410-008-1

Contents

List of Figures

List of Tables

Foreword

This book presents a critique of forecasting techniques with particular emphasis on forecasts of future technology and related changes in the structure of international power.

Our review of representative forecasting techniques is limited to a few approaches and areas of application that have received widespread attention in recent years. Our selection includes technological forecasts, quantitative-analytical techniques, simulation, time-series analysis, and the so-called "prospective" approach. In terms of areas of application, we have emphasized forecasting work on "The Limits to Growth" and the impending energy crisis; and we have paid special attention to international configurations of power involving the United States, the Soviet Union, China, Japan and Western Europe.

Our work has impressed us with the inherent difficulties of forecasting although we realize that objects of forecasting vary greatly in their conjecturability. But the resulting skepticism regarding particular and, more or less, all forecasting methods, does not lead us to the conclusion that the attempt to forecast is worthless. As long as forecasting results are presented and used with adequate caution, planners can learn something, even if nothing really solid, in their attempts to shape future developments. Indeed, we believe that, whenever feasible, multiple techniques should be employed, if only in order to keep us from attaching excessive confidence in the results derived from any one mode of analysis.

We should warn the reader that the authors were unable to reach complete agreement on forecasts of the industrial development of China though they did agree that the policies of China's political leadership will probably play a major role in her ability to industrialize with speed and continuity.

Finally, we wish to acknowledge that this book resulted in large part from work which the authors undertook for the Office of Naval Research from 1970 to 1973 and which was undertaken at Mathematica, Inc.

Klaus Heiss   **Klaus Knorr**   **Oskar Morgenstern**

Princeton, October 1973

Preface

In March 1970 we completed an evaluation of long term forecasting techniques of power for the Office of Naval Research. A second report, a revised and broadened edition of the March 1970 report, was submitted in January 1973. The work published here contains considerable additional material. In our review of forecasting techniques we, in addition, looked for empirical evidence supporting the work of one or another group, tried to develop a constructive approach within the limits of operationally useful forecasting efforts, and applied some of the techniques and evaluation to the long term outlook of major world regions.

In our review of forecasting techniques we tried to limit ourselves to a few major approaches and areas. Obviously this selection involved value judgments of our own. In the evaluation we included Technological Forecasts, Quantitative Analytic Approaches, Simulation, Time Series Analyses, and the "Prospective" movement.

In quantitative empirical work we demonstrate the extent and impact of price changes, income changes, and research development work on sectors of the economy. The empirical findings suggest to us that these mechanisms and options are underestimated by "operators" of long term forecasting work. At the same time these findings are the inherent reason for difficulties in reliable long term forecasting and in the identification of critical variables affecting the power of nations and regions in the long term.

Based on the evaluation of the approaches used and our empirical findings, we recommend a "mixed strategy" of approaches and work. The inherent difficulties of long term economic, technical, and social forecasts make such an approach—and skepticism—necessary. The three major analytic approaches we propose, in addition to any of the discussed techniques, are (1) the dynamic simultaneous equation approach for empirical, data oriented work; (2) a check for predictive compatibilities in sector by sector, and country by country forecasts; and (3) an investigation of the compressibility of economic systems, or economic sectors. The energy problem is given particular attention since it seems the single most important physical variable that may have significant repercussions on the future power of major world regions.

Five regions are considered: the United States, the Soviet Union, Western Europe (EEC), China, and Japan. For two regions, Japan and Western Europe, severe outside energy source dependencies are shown to exist, with adverse implications as to the future power of these two regions.

Although our evaluation of long term forecasting efforts is rather reserved, our work leads us to a rather positive evaluation of the overall outlook of the major world regions for precisely the same reasons that make useful forecasts so difficult: the price-market mechanism, income elasticities, and, most important, the response of production systems and sectors to scientific and technical innovation—i.e., research and development.

On China, considerable discussions among the authors led to the views presented here: on one side positive trends in the economic and technological development of China were recognized in the March 1970 report and are reconfirmed here; on the other side, the authors agree that the principal, most important variable affecting China's development in the next ten to twenty years will be the political will and persistence in the effort needed to achieve and continue economic and technical change experienced in China since 1949. Whether this political will can be sustained for such an extended time is the question.

Introduction

This is a study of the way various authors have made projections of the future, to approximately the year 2000 and beyond. It examines how these projections may be relevant for guiding research and development. While the assignment is fairly concrete, the subject matter is diffuse and uncertain, making the applicability of our conclusions appear less specific than may be hoped for. It does, however, become clear—in spite of all doubts connected with specific forecasts of the world's general future and its technological development—that certain changes are likely to affect the position and relative importance of the military in the new environment. As the destructive power of weapons increases, they will no longer be acceptable means for settling disputes. Rather they will exercise, as they have since 1945, a paralyzing influence upon the emergence of large scale conflicts, especially between the large "advanced" countries.

There is strong evidence of change throughout the world pointing towards famine, perhaps large scale starvation, exhaustion of natural resources, and ruination of the ecological environment man needs for survival. If these crises actually occur, military power in any conventional sense loses much of its meaning, for none of these problems could be settled by its use. Such "power" as exemplified by the existence of weapons, men under arms, missiles ready to be fired, submarines prowling the seas, etc., will still be with us by 2000—but their function as "problem solvers," as part of rational politics, will have diminished. If the United States and the Soviet Union recognize this, they may cooperate in preserving the world from the dangers that threaten them as well as Western Europe, China, and Japan.

Transformations such as those predicted by the various authors examined cannot possibly occur without great political changes. We have not attempted to analyze these transformations, since that would involve going far beyond our task. For example, the Soviet Union or China are more likely to break apart into a number of nation states than is the United States. Should this occur, there would be a transformation of the political and military map of the world which has not been contemplated by any of our authors. Yet we believe that even if this momentous event were to occur, it would lessen neither the pressure from population increase in India, Egypt, South America, etc., nor the spread of technology with its insatiable hunger for more and more resources. (To give an idea of the magnitude, the United States during the last 30 years has consumed more minerals than the whole world has mined since the beginning of human history! Much of it came from abroad.)

This study focuses on the problem, and particularly on methods, for projecting, or conjecturing about, the future of technology in the next couple of decades. Anticipating this future (if, and to the extent that, such anticipation is feasible) should be an important basis for planning in the United States from two distinct points of view.

First, the knowledge of what kinds of technological opportunities are likely to develop with varying degrees of probability would give us an invaluable basis for guiding long range R & D. It would help us in charting R & D to encourage these—or some of these—new technological opportunities to become available, and to use these opportunities to the best political and military effect. From this point of view, the location of technological advance is of secondary importance, except when it occurs in the Communist world. Whether advances occur in the United States, Western Europe, or Japan (non-Communist areas which are the most likely to advance technologically) does not much matter. New technology created anywhere in the non-Communist world will probably be available to the United States, which has great capacity for absorbing new foreign technologies. Even if technological advance occurs in the Communist world, where the Soviet Union is a dominant technological power now, it may advance technology elsewhere—if only because the knowledge that something can be done is a great advantage in learning how to do the same thing. But technological knowledge created in the Communist world is likely to be diffused only with considerable, and perhaps critical, delay.

Second, United States planning would also be notably assisted if, or to the extent that, we could predict the technological capacity of particular states and regions over the next decade or two. National technological capacity is a crucial determinant of the political, economic, and military potential of countries and regions. At present this capacity is highly concentrated in a handful of states ranking far ahead of the rest, with most of the remaining states possessing only a negligible capacity. As past performance indicates, however, it is unlikely that this capacity of states will grow equally, or in proportion to current levels. In other words, there may occur significant changes in the relative technological capacity of states and regions. It is precisely for this reason that forecasting the future technological capacity of nations and regions becomes interesting to the planner.

Part I is concerned with methods of predicting or projecting the technological future. Part II is an evaluation of representative literature on whether and how it is possible to conjecture about the future technological capacity of states and regions. Part III is an outline of the major problems that have to be dealt with in a meaningful conjecture and prediction of the power and technologies of nations. Part IV gives suggestions on a constructive approach to forecasting and its relevance to R & D efforts; and Part V presents some final conclusions.

A bibliography is attached. It is, of course, highly selective. The literature that might have to be considered is truly enormous and many writings are repetitious. We aim at focusing on principal problems and methods used in the various approaches toward prediction in the given field. We are not dealing with the profound philosophical questions underlying prediction. Some of these have occupied the human mind since the dawn of civilization, an indication of the deep-seated urge to learn about the future. One might hope that the progress of science in all fields would also have extended to prediction. But we shall see that, though we can make better forecasts of the weather and many other natural, notoriously unstable phenomena, our predictive powers in the political field are still exceedingly limited and may remain so for an indefinite future.

Part I

Chapter One

The Content of Future Technology

If we are interested in attempts at predicting in some sense the content or shape of technology ten or more years ahead, it is useful to recognize differences in the conjecturability of technological advances.

First, there are marginal improvements in known technologies; for instance, improvements in the efficiency of coal-burning plants for generating electricity, or the life capacity of aircraft with a given propulsion system, or the accuracy of ballistic missile guidance. Various enterprises are continuously engaged in bringing about such marginal upgrading, and people knowledgeable about these efforts should be able to make fair predictions of what might be achieved, especially in the near future.

Second, there is the combined application of known and improvable technologies in order to do something never done before. The NASA plan to put man on the moon within a definite number of years is an example. Though various inventions were needed to place man on the moon, these were known to be within the evolving state of the art and would be achieved by a massive application of resources. Such future technologies are planned and not too difficult to predict, though there may be a question about the exact timing of such achievements. Surprise would result only if it turned out that the planned technology proved infeasible as a result of unknown factors, at least at a given level of financial and intellectual effort.

Third, new technologies are desired because of the great benefits they promise. For the invention of these technologies a large amount of resources may be devoted—for example, a drug to cure cancer, or the thermo-nuclear generation of electric power. Even if one is confident that these technologies will be invented, it is much more difficult than in the first two cases to conjecture that they will be part of available technology in five, ten, fifteen, or even fifty years. Among such new technologies to be invented in order to achieve particular economic, military, and social goals, adequate scientific support may or may not exist at the time when the need is identified. For example, increasingly large energy deficits in some regions such as Europe and Japan make the development of new large scale economic energy sources mandatory, including new technologies such as magnetohydrodynamics, fuel cells, nuclear breeder reactors, controlled fusion, and solar energy.

Finally, there are future technologies about which we know nothing now, for which there exists no identified need (ex-ante), and hence will come with true surprise. The only examples we can mention here are those of the past, such as jet propulsion for aircraft, or the nuclear bomb from the vantage point of 1930, aspirin in 1900, lasers in 1950. The question here is whether improved forecasting methods can reduce the number of surprises.

Furthermore, in technological forecasting, two situations indicate some of the underlying difficulties of such attempts. These are: (a) forecasting from existing technology, using existing theory and scientific laws and principles, and (b) forecasting a *new* law of physics or of social managerial content with the attendant technological possibilities according to (a). The following comments are in order.

Ad (a): Forecasting under these conditions is feasible to some extent, but there is generally no accounting in advance whether, when or how known effects will actually be used. The case of DDT having been known for decades prior to its use is well known. An even more important and telling example is the development of radar. In 1887 Hertz observed the reflection of radio waves by solid objects and he proposed the idea of using this effect for detection. Hulsmeyer patented a device in 1904 for preventing collisions based on radio echoing. Guglielmo Marconi proposed in 1922 a return radiation device to detect ships in fog or thick weather. In 1925 Breit and Tuve employed, experimentally, radio pulse echoes to examine the ionosphere. Yet it was only in 1939 that the United States Navy tested a radar set in battle maneuvers on the *USS New York* and the first military use of radar occurred on December 19, 1939 in antiaircraft defense by Germany against Britain (a Freya-device).[1] Thus there existed a period of *over 50 years* between the first formulation of an idea and its implementation in an area of utmost military and technical importance. There are countless other such illustrations.

Sometimes a known effect, compound, device, etc., cannot be used before other technological developments have occurred (e.g., the motorcar had no future before air-filled tires became available). A good example of "having to wait for the right time" is information theory, which has been proven of tremendous importance for modern communication devices. The kernel of the theory is contained in some work by Ludwig Boltzmann (1844-1906), but it was left to Claude Shannon to rediscover it and to establish in the 1940s the fundamental theorem on which the technology depends.[2] Thus there was a lengthy lag before the intellectual readiness appeared to develop Boltzmann's ideas further, to the culmination of the theory, and its application to communication.

The best illustration of a deliberate creation of a host of new technologies is the Manhattan project. Here a firmly established physical effect—fission—with tremendous implications, military as well as civilian, was used as the sole narrow basis for a large scale engineering and enormous investment effort whose success could be predicted within a certain time span. In the course of the development, a great number of new inventions became necessary and were made. Wartime pressure accounted for the speed with which all was accomplished. But success does not always come in this manner: fusion is also a well understood physical principle, but *controlled* fusion has so far eluded the considerable efforts made in that direction by several countries. It may be achieved in a few years, in thirty years, or not for a long time. Yet it is clear that if it happens, a worldwide change in the availability of energy will eventually take place, profoundly affecting the entire picture of fossil fuel supplies and all forecasts will be falsified that are based on the assumption that they will remain the chief source to satisfy an ever increasing worldwide demand for energy.

Similar illustrations can be obtained from other fields, but perhaps none is as striking as the above. A time may be right for some new technological or scientific breakthrough; however, the reverse dependency often holds between available technological knowledge and its implementation in an economic system or in military hardware. Many of the most advanced technological innovations, known and implemented in developed countries, are meaningless for most of the rest of mankind—the developing countries—as their economic base is inadequate to take advantage of and implement such innovations. Some important recent examples are Large Scale Integration (LSI) in electronics (for computer memory circuits), the development of metal-oxide semiconductors,[3] or problems and solutions to aircraft noise and pollution. Or, going further back in history: Greek culture and science knew most of the principles necessary for a mechanical-industrial society that developed in eighteenth century Europe. Nevertheless, the social and economic base of Greece at that time was inadequate to take advantage of the existing technological and scientific knowledge.

Ad (b): Before a new law or effect is discovered, no statement about it is possible. After the event, the discovery may appear "natural," "logical," "necessary," or whatever the phrase might be. This is usually cheap ex post facto rationalization, of no help in prediction (which would have to come from the current basis of knowledge). There is no evidence, as far as we are aware, where such projections were made, or indeed were possible. Why was Galileo the first to look at the moon with a telescope, invented earlier by Huyghens? Why did not Leonardo da Vinci, the great inventor, discover lenses, build microscopes, telescopes? Decades had to go by before this happened after his death. Why did Leonardo, the masterful student of light in painting, not develop Newton's theory of light? The idea that a situation has to be "ripe" for recognition or invention is still true. What are the present discoveries that are *not* being made, but which are now possible as later developments will surely show?

Chance, then, as well as conditions which we do not yet fully understand, rule discovery and historical events in general to a far greater extent than is often realized, although for chance to happen, the scientist must place himself in a position where it can touch him. A great deal of humility is necessary. Quasars and pulsars were never suspected, yet they may change our entire view of the universe.

The experience of occasional examples of past successes with prediction are rather puzzling, particularly when long term forecasts were involved. Were they themselves more than chance events? In times of change and innovation, at a scale unprecedented in human history, such forecasts are particularly hazardous, if at all meaningful.[4] Vast clouds ("vast" in an astro-nomical sense) of formaldehyde and other complex molecules discovered in stellar space were a recent surprise of unimaginable consequences. Whether any of this will affect technology in the next 30 to 50 years, or only in 1000 years, or ever, is impossible to say. If it should, there will be consequences which we can guess now just as little as anybody 40 to 50 years ago could have guessed that only the understanding of solar processes would lead us to have great laboratories in which we hope to sustain controlled fusion to use that hoped-for laboratory result industrially.

Such results could mean a vast industrial upheaval all over the world. Similarly, there are other developments in the offing. Once the role of enzymes in the chemical reaction in the human body is understood, as will surely happen, it will be possible to transform radically our chemical industry. That industry at present uses tremendous quantities of energy and materials not directly con-nected with the desired chemical reactions. In addition, these processes take a long time. The body, on the other hand, builds the most complicated com-pounds rapidly with negligible use of energy. We are bound to comprehend these processes some day. As a consequence, anything said in this study regarding shortages of certain raw materials and energy may prove wrong. When this will happen, no one can foresee.

Many other similar observations are possible. They all point in the same direction—engineering prediction on the basis of *present* science is possible within wide bounds of error regarding timing and cost. But prediction of the far more decisive *scientific* developments is not. Yet it is precisely the latter which produce the fundamentally new situations that affect our life more profoundly than the extension of currently available engineering technology.

Of course, the two areas are not sharply divided. There is a gray zone of fresh scientific matter that has not yet found its way into the engineering world. It is possible to abbreviate time lags by modern devices of communica-tion, but this should not be overestimated. Chance will still rule supreme.

In order to illuminate this element of chance, we observe the following: a new discovery is made on the basis of existing knowledge and technology. It is well known that more scientists are alive today than have ever lived before, and this statement will remain true for a long time to come. At the same time, technology is fairly evenly spread among the advanced countries. For example, laboratories for electronics in the United States, the Soviet Union, Japan, and Europe will in general be similarly equipped. In all these countries, the problems confronting scientists and engineers are virtually identical, which is a sign of the maturity of the physical sciences. When there were few scientists, the chance of a new discovery was obviously much smaller than now. But at present, if it is made in one country, it may equally be made in another *simultaneously*. The fact that discoveries and inventions are made at the same time will become more common than is already true. We might say that *chance now has a better chance to operate*.

At a given moment of time the discovery of A, B, or C may be possible. If there are few scientists, only one may occur, say B. This discovery may have important practical applications which may be recognized and used soon. But if there are many scientists working in the same area, as described above, A and C may also be discovered, some of them simultaneously in different countries. This then explains the rapidity of scientific-technological change and its generally even distribution among the advanced countries. It shows the hopelessness and undesirability of some nations' attempts to keep new knowledge secret. If the discovery A is made in the first country, it will surely be made eventually in the second and third, since there are many scientists monitoring developments everywhere. When there were few scientists, they were fully occupied by whatever chance discovery was made by them.

These examples apply to the physical and life sciences, but a similar development began in the social sciences in the last 25 or 30 years and will be intensified rapidly. This is very important for the purpose of this study, as the following illustration will show. Largely influenced by mathematics, game theory, and management science, operations research has unified thinking in many countries, and has overcome traditional, ideologically anchored, and antiquated techniques of governing and planning. By necessity these new concepts are used in politically different states for describing and directing social activities. In these areas, too, there are more scientists at work now than ever before, unified in many ways in their thinking and experience. They are bound to make further discoveries in a problem area of unbelievable complexity.

To illustrate, we refer to some notions of great military and political importance. There is no question that the concern with game theory, both in the United States and the Soviet Union, has led to identical definitions and evaluations of "deterrence," "threat," "bluff," etc., as is evidenced by the virtual synonymity of writings in these fields (e.g., the books and papers by Sokholovsky, Zakarov, etc.). While this development is not sufficient to immediately stabilize relations between the two super powers, they generate similar modes of problem solving based on international science rather than national ideology. Further *simultaneous* discoveries undoubtedly will be made in these fields, well beyond the present limits. They will affect the question of human survival in the face of population increases and ensuing pollution, exhaustion of resources, etc. We may soon see new ideas and techniques applied to such issues as arms control, mutual inspection, peacekeeping, and the like.

In light of these observations, it is striking that the various predictions examined in our work are completely oblivious of the more abstract relations here described. This means a grave restriction concerning the use of these predictions in their present form. What is needed is the development of techniques that can deal with anticipated crises. Such new techniques, however, are part of the projected future and can influence only that part of the future which follows their discovery and introduction. In other words, this poses the classical question of the "falsification" of the forecasts, because it is in our power to improve the use of forecasting. We do not have to sit back and accept the new predicted course of events; we can try to modify them—as our interests demand—and we can adjust our intervention when we see our true interests more clearly. This is a form of dynamic programming (see below, pages 143-181).

The true problem in this area of predictions is to find out what the times scales are—first in which crises situations will develop, and second in which remedial (preferably anticipating) actions are possible. The closer the two are to the present, the more certain a crisis will emerge. Third, measures deemed effective against a crisis also take time before their effect is produced. Thus, there are three time segments to consider. If the first two coincide, there is inevitability. The same is true when they differ, but only if the third—the time needed for remedies to work themselves out—is too long for actions to become effective.

For example, consider population growth. If a certain future population is critically undesirable, it may be possible to see that birth control could prevent that event. But for reasons of lack of acceptance of the means, and of biological nature, the composite time may be so long that the desired halt in population growth would come only *after* the predicted onset of crisis. In this manner, after development of the proper mathematical models, each set of interdependent variables should be examined for the most important geographical areas affected. Then the resultant new set of integrated variables should be examined to find the one which will yield the most realistic picture.

The literature on the future does not contain much analysis of this type. It should be expanded because progress in this direction would yield results not only of scientific interest but also of great practical value. The work by Forrester and Meadows, discussed in Chapter 4, is an attempt in this direction, but is subject to severe flaws and limitations.

After scanning the literature on forecasting the future content of technology, we analyze the work by Gordon and Helmer of 1964 and its development since then. The work by Kahn and Wiener, examined in Chapter 4, is also in part addressed to the forecasting of the shape of future technology; the work by Wilhelm Fucks is concerned more implicitly with the spatial spreading of existing technologies to other regions. Fucks is less concerned with technological innovations than with the possible developments of power relations from the present over the next one and two generations. Also included is a review and critique of the limits to growth literature originated by Forrester and Meadows. We comment on other writers (e.g., Gaston Berger), but we do not survey the entire literature, which is immensely repetitive. We have identified certain approaches and methods, and examine their validity and promise. In doing so we analyze empirically (using the U.S. communications sector) the responses of economic and social systems to research and development efforts, to price changes, and to changes in other economic and social policy parameters. The results shed new light on the flexibility of economic and social systems to respond to most challenges.

Part II

Review and Evaluation of Representative Literature

Chapter Two

Technological Forecasting

The field of technological forecasting has rapidly developed in the past decade and the bibliography to this book reflects some of the more representative works. As far as these forecasting efforts reflect quantitative techniques developed previously in other disciplines (econometrics, statistics, mathematical economics), we will deal with those techniques separately, not under the heading of technological forecasting. The single most noteworthy contribution to forecasting techniques made within the field of technological forecasting is the Delphi method. We therefore will restrict ourselves in this part to an evaluation of Delphi, although many other quantitative and intuitive techniques are used within this area.

OVERVIEW OF APPROACHES

A brief overview of forecasting approaches and their classification is given here. Ian I. Mitroff and Murray Turoff recently studied the underlying philosophies motivating investigations of this type. We would like to classify the forecasting approaches in a very similar way, albeit somewhat differently. Five broad approaches exist to (technological) forecasting.

Experimental—Empirical

Specific technical developments are forecast based on an empirical evaluation of existing data. Quantitative analyses developed in statistics, econometrics, and opinion survey sampling are used to document the factual sources of the forecasts made. These approaches are reviewed in this book in the section on Time Series Analyses (Chapter 4), and further demonstrated in Appendix A.

Analytical

The basis for approaches in this category is a well defined theoretical model trying to explain interrelationships between a few, or many, variables.

13

These variables can be endogenous, i.e., explained within the model, or exogenous, i.e., inputs to the model that are historically given or inputs under the control of policy makers.

Such models, typically, are not formulated with a view towards the availability of quantitative data; rather, some relationships are based on the subjective (intuitive) judgment of the model builder, while other relationships may be explained based on empirical data. Typical forecasting techniques are simulation, correlation analyses, and substitution analyses. Approaches of this type are reviewed or demonstrated in Chapter 4 in the Limits To Growth Model, and in Chapter 5 in "Problems of Predicting the Scale and Structure of Technological Capacity."

Mixed Analytic-Empirical

Approaches of this type consider the availability of data or experiments supporting the hypotheses of the theoretical model in the formulation of the forecasting model. Sometimes the process is reversed: given the available empirical evidence (data, experimental results, historical record), a theoretic model is formulated to best explain the observed data and occurrences. The ability of the theoretical model to forecast is judged by its ability to explain the past and present events. Approaches of this type are reviewed in this book in Chapter 3, on the Fucks forecast (a quantitative analytic approach) and, importantly, in Chapter 7, The Dynamic Simultaneous Equation Approach, by Sector.

Teleological (Goal Oriented)

Analyses of this type recognize explicitly the interaction between the forecasts made and what actually will come about. The world without the forecast made would be different from the world where a particular forecast is made. Thus any forecast has intrinsically to be goal oriented and recognizes the interplay between exploratory forecasts based on the existing assured basis of knowledge, and normative forecasts, which typically assess, first, future goals, needs, desires, missions, and then work back to the present. Typical techniques used within this area of technological forecasting (a better expression is "technology assessment") are benefit-cost analyses, normative "backcasts" (PERT and GERT analyses), and technical feasibility analyses. Approaches of this type are discussed in Chapter 4 on the "Prospective" Movement, and in Chapter 8, Predictive Compatibilities and The Compressibility of Economic Systems.

Dialectical

The underlying philosophy of approaches of this type to forecasting is that both history and the future are a sequence of conflicts, and the truth content of a system—or the events in the past and future—are the results of a

OVERVIEW
APPROACHES TO FORECASTING

DATA oriented (EMPIRICAL)	MODEL oriented (ANALYTICAL)	GOAL oriented (TELEOLOGICAL)	CONFLICT oriented (DIALECTICAL)

INTEGRATED
DATA ⟷ MODEL
(ITERATIVE)

USE OF ALTERNATIVE APPROACHES IN DIFFERENT PHASES OF FORECASTING PROBLEM

PHASES:

PROBLEM IDENTIFICATION (teleological, dialectical)	PROBLEM ANALYSIS (empirical, analytical)	PROBLEM SOLUTION
o LIST GOALS, OBJECTIVES	o DATA / MODELS } ITERATION	(1) THERE MAY BE NO PROBLEM
o MAIN ALTERNATIVE (1)	TECHNIQUES:	(2) PROBLEM MAY BE UNSOLVABLE
o MAIN COUNTER ALTERNATIVE (2)	o ECONOMETRICS	(3) DECISIONS UNDER UNCERTAINTY:
o OTHER ALTERNATIVES (3, 4, ... N)	o MATHEMATICAL ECONOMICS	o PURE STRATEGIES
o CREATE TRUE CONFLICT SITUATION	o STATISTICS	o MIXED STRATEGIES
	o SIMULATION	o PORTFOLIO AND RISK ANALYSES
	o INTUITION	

highly complicated process that depends on the existence of both a plan or working hypothesis and a diametrically opposed counterplan or set of counter interests. These strongly divergent and opposing concepts bracket a whole range of other, alternative outcomes, and the conflict resolution will, if successful, identify a best plan or alternative, which can include either of the original opposing theses, or a compromise (mutually agreeable) new plan (alternative).

A credible forecast has to be the result of such an honest conflict definition and resolution, as only such a conflict will expose the assumptions underlying an expert's point of view that are often suppressed when experts agree beforehand.[1] Methods typically used for conflict resolution are game theory, the Delphi Method, scenario approaches, and some types of benefit-cost analyses. Approaches of this type are reviewed in Chapter 2 in The Delphi Method, Chapter 4 in Kahn-Wiener: The Year 2000, and implicitly in Parts IV and V.

These different approaches are certainly not mutually exclusive. In the preceding chart a brief scheme of the approaches just listed is given and a possible framework on where and how each of these approaches may be used in different phases of forecasting problems, technological or otherwise.

THE DELPHI METHOD

Nature of the Work

The report by Gordon and Helmer[2] describes and analyzes an experiment in trend predicting and forecasting ten to fifty years ahead in six broad areas, including "scientific breakthroughs," automation, space progress, and future weapon systems. The experiment used a variety of the Delphi techniques involving a sequence of questionnaires to elicit predictions from individual experts in the areas concerned. A summary of responses from each round of questionnaires was fed back to the respondents before they executed each succeeding round of questionnaires. Essentially, a group of experts made forecasts which were formulated separately (i.e., shunning the committee method), revised by them in the light of responses of other panelists, and roughly aggregated by the directors of the forecasting enterprise.

Claims, Admission of Limitations, Suggestions for Improvement of the Technique

The report makes no claims "for the reliability of the predictions obtained" (Part VI) and its authors were aware that they would not "through some miracle be able to remove the veil of uncertainty from the future" (pp. 2-3). However, they claim that predictions such as these "should lessen the chance of surprise and provide a sounder basis for long range decision making than do purely implicit, unarticulated, intuitive judgments" (Part VI). They believe that the findings "represent a beginning in the process of sifting the likely from the unlikely among the contingencies of the future . . . "(p. 2).

There are some flaws in the method and in this particular experiment. Some of these will not be discussed because they are plain and remediable. These are instability of panel membership, considerable time lapse between questionnaire rounds, and ambiguous phrasing of questions. Helmer and Gordon also discuss a possible drawback of the application of the technique, namely the possibility of self-fulfilling and self-defeating prophecies. They deal with this problem modestly. There are two reported limitations, however, to which we will return in the critique. These are problems connected with the competence of the panel members and with the establishment of experts' consensus by "undue averaging."

The authors mention the following feasible improvements in this forecasting method: reasonably stable panel membership, reduced time lapse between questionnaires, more careful phrasing of questions, enough rounds for adequate feedback, improvements in the selection of experts, search for schemes eliciting self-appraisals of competence from panel members, development of techniques for the formulation of sequential questions that would probe more systematically into the underlying reasons for the respondents' opinions, etc. (see pp. 68-69 loc. cit.).

Critique

We discovered no type of limitation of this forecasting method which the report does not itself identify and discuss. However, we see reasons for being more critical of some of these limitations than the report is, and we are convinced that this criticism is essential to a realistic evaluation of the technique.

1. The report claims that the forecasting method used makes the future more surprise free. It can do so, however, only to a very limited degree. The report admits that the method in question "cannot hope to uncover the unexpected, spectacular, unanticipated breakthrough, but must concentrate on narrowing down the dates and circumstances of occurrences which can be extrapolated from the present" (p. 2). The best the method can hope to achieve is to increase the probability that presently available knowledge plus judgment are employed toward forecasting what is in fact predictable. Only to this extent can the method hope to assist us in preventing surprise in the future.

The value of the method—for purposes of human problem solving, especially long range planning—depends on whether the unexpected and unpredictable are "spectacular," that is, of crucial consequence or not. But this in itself seems to us unpredictable. One could examine the past in order to ascertain whether, over certain periods of time, predictable or unpredictable events dominated the outcome of problem solving. This would not be easy to do, and it would be difficult to secure agreement. But even if we could derive compelling conclusions about this matter in the past, we could not be sure that the past would repeat itself in this respect in the future.

Another problem demanding clarification is how one should draw the dividing line between the predictable and the unpredictable future in technology. The inventions predicted by the panelists of the Gordon-Helmer experiment seem to be the expected ones—those which people are recognizably working on or towards. We can predict this kind of future correctly (unless something unexpected intervenes) because we are planning and working deliberately to bring it about. In a sense, these technologies are already invented.

This suggests that the unpredictable events are those which we are unable to imagine, or which we at present have no way of bringing about. It is fair to assume that in the mid 1930s no panel of experts like the Gordon-Helmer panel would have predicted atomic bombs, jet aircraft, or the transistor. Yet scientists were then doing things which eventually led to these inventions, just as scientists and engineers are now doing things which will lead to the now unpredictable technologies. To some extent, the unpredictable will happen because we will, as has often happened in the past, stumble on a new discovery. This is the fruit of serendipity. To some extent, also, unexpected and unpredictable events depend upon planned progress along many seemingly unrelated paths, the possible joining of which we are unable to foresee at this time. In that case we are unable to perceive or evaluate the implications of some of the things which we are now doing or planning to invent. In either case, the future is unpredictable because it is not expected.

Of course, there is no sharp dividing line between predictable and unpredictable future technology. There presumably is a boundary area which men who combine intuitive imagination with expert knowledge are more or less, but not reliably, able to penetrate. For example, this combination of competence must have been present to a high degree when the small Tizard Committee in Britain, charged in 1935 with considering "how far advances in scientific and technical knowledge can be used to strengthen the present methods of defense against hostile aircraft," decided very expeditiously that radar was the technology which would make a difference and which should be developed. One wonders how many committees would have arrived at the same forecast, for at the time this forecast was made, the device did not exist. The only thing which preceded the forecast were basic theory and some preliminary experiments.[3]

2. The value of the results obtained by the Gordon-Helmer method depends clearly and crucially on the competence of the panelists. The technique attempts to obtain the "intuitive judgment as systematically as possible from persons who are recognized experts in the area of concern" (p. 4). The competence in question evidently has two components: *substantive expertise* in the area of technology, and *"intuitive judgment."*

This raises the important question of how we recognize excellence in these two abilities. For instance, which criterion or criteria should be used for measuring substantive expertise in a scientific or technological area? If one chooses reputation, one raises such questions as reputation among which group or groups? The many or the few? Among people who themselves have a high reputation? Among older or younger experts? To what extent is reputation earned or unearned, and to what extent obsolete or not? Criteria other than reputation, such as certain kinds of achievements (e.g., inventions, publications), raise similar problems of ambiguity.

An interesting idea in the Gordon-Helmer Report refers to the future use of self-appraisal by the experts. Self-appraisal by experts will presumably enter in any case, since some individuals requested to participate will refuse on the ground that they do not feel sufficiently qualified. But the report suggests that self-appraisal might also be solicited to be exercised by panelists regarding any particular question in the questionnaires. This idea deserves experimentation. It also has limitations. In the first place, panelists might be too eager or too reluctant, for various reasons, to admit incompetence. They might be reluctant because they are ignorant or biased in judging their expertise; or they might be eager to escape from a difficult job. Second, if self-exemption was widespread, some questions might elicit very few responses, one answer, or no answer. If few answers are forthcoming, the result is very sensitive to the expertise of the remaining respondents or respondent.

There is also the very critical question regarding the range of expertise being sought. The identification of expertise will be facilitated if the range is narrowly limited. But this also entails a serious drawback. Such limitation would seem to render a group of experts less equipped for forecasting technologies that derive from advances in different and, in terms of the adopted organization of expertise, quite separate fields.

But if the recognition of expertise raises difficult problems, this is even more the case with the recognition of intuitive judgment. The problems are the same; but they are more severe since true indicators of the kind of "judgment" here in demand are more elusive than true indicators of expertise. How do we recognize good judgment which defies replicability?

These difficulties lead to the conclusion that the result of this forecasting method is very dependent on the judgment and resources of those in charge of applying it, that is, on the judgment of the Gordons and Helmers. If they work by hearsay in assembling their panelists, how good is their hearsay, and how good are they in evaluating it? Whether or not maximum consensus among the producers of hearsay promises good results remains an open question for the reasons we have presented. Furthermore, most methods of selection are apt to be costly in terms of effort and time, and this raises the possibility that opportunism will limit and perhaps degrade the search for the best panelists.

Even if all these problems could be solved satisfactorily, there is the question of whether the top people identified can be persuaded to participate in an effort which is rather demanding in terms of time and intellectual application. If there is a large supply of people highly qualified in expertise and judgment, there would, of course, be several or many equal substitutes for any person who is chosen but denies participation. The results of the method are highly sensitive to the quality of personnel inputs, and only exceptionally qualified people promise good results. Yet, such people are not only hard to identify but also hard to recruit. It is doubtful that Einstein, Bohr, Pauli, Planck, von Neumann, Dirac, Weyl, and many others would have agreed to serve as panelists. Yet *their* discoveries and influence decisively changed the "future."

This last difficulty is compounded by a further technical short-coming of Delphi. In order to come to a consensus of opinions, a number of time-consuming rounds (iterations) are required; as all panel members start with their own subjective projections, it will take a number of such iterations and considerable time to come up with a Delphi forecast. Also, some acceptable method has to be found in advance by which to terminate the feedback of information for new rounds. Finally, the acceptable refinement of the projection will depend upon the purpose for which the projections are made—e.g., long term policy planning versus investment planning, R & D planning, etc.

3. Our next question goes to the very heart of the group character of the Delphi forecast: In what way are the forecasts of a group superior to those of an individual? The group tends to be superior to the individual in bringing to bear relevant knowledge about what is going on—that is, in the matter of expertise. Expertise is additive. It is questionable that this advantage extends to that part of forecasting which depends on imaginative judgment. The report recognizes this problem implicitly when it deals with the objection that the emphasis it places "on the median as a descriptor of the group opinion and in the quartile range as a measure of degree of consensus biases the outcome unduly against the far-out predictor, whose judgment may after all prove to be right while the majority opinion may be wrong" (p. 65).

The majority opinion may indeed be "wrong," but we must ask why this is so. An exceptional capability for imaginative judgment, which is needed for penetrating the borderline area between the expected and the unpredictable, is by definition rarer than high level technical expertise. Since such capability is not easily identified, and people possessing it not easily recruited, any group of panelists probably will vary considerably in intuition or even lack it completely.

In the first case, any majority forecast is likely to be deficient in this quality and the best forecasts come from a minority or a single "predictor." In the second case, any minority or single forecast also lacks merit. It follows that one should expect majority forecasts, regarding matters depending on imaginative judgment, to be of low value, while minority or single forecasts can be of low, high, or perhaps indeterminate value. "Averaging" of forecasts would then have nothing to commend itself. The value of using a group would simply be that of the probability that one person or some persons of exceptional intuitive ability are included, identified, and given a weighted hearing.

The panelists do not receive only one round of questionnaires. The results of the first round are fed back and additional responses are invited. Moreover, "Some of the questions directed to the respondents may, for instance, inquire into the 'reasons' for previously expressed opinions, and a collection of such reasons may then be presented to each respondent in the group, together with an invitation to reconsider and possibly revise his earlier estimates" (p. 5).

In view of the difficulty of distinguishing excellent from mediocre intuitive judgment, this seems to be a commendable practice. Unfortunately (perhaps for economic reasons) Gordon and Helmer followed it only *selectively*. They describe the procedure used with the panel on "Scientific Breakthroughs." The report states: "Collation and pairing of the responses led to a list of 49 items." Whether or not something of value slipped through the fingers of Messrs. Gordon and Helmer at this stage depends on their judgment. Regarding a subsequent stage, the report states: "On the basis of findings such as these, it was judged that for 10 of the 49 items there existed a reasonable consensus among the respondents. . . . As for the remaining 39 items, on which an insufficient consensus had been observed, the experimenters at this point used their discretion in singling out a subset of 17 items which they thought to be deserving of further exploration. These were presented once more to the panel . . . " (p. 8).

Again, the outcome of the exercise depended on the judgment of the directors. It seems that the enterprise was excessively concerned with consensus. Although consensus is valuable to the extent that forecasting requires a pooling of knowledge of expected new inventions or events, it is of little or no value when it comes to applying intuitive judgment. The value of majority response to feedback, then, is to expose those "far-out" predictions which are based on ignorance, fallacy, etc. The failure of the majority to follow the *good* "far-out" judgment, however, only proves that its members lack in intuitive judgment.

The report remarks: "Thus a far-out opinion is in principle only rejected if its proponent fails to justify it before the rest of the panel" (p. 66). But, aside from the fact that since "far-out" conjectures have been quietly dropped by the directors of the enterprise, "justification" is not a good method for sifting minority forecasts. We are all aware of the fact that the possessor of good intuitive judgment is often unable to explain how he came to his "judgment." According to Webster, intuition is " . . . the knowledge obtained, without recourse to inference or reasoning. . . . " To the extent, then, that forecasting becomes imaginative and depends on intuitive judgment, the reasoning may not do justice to the value of the forecast, and the majority of the panelists may be unable to follow along because they lack adequate judgment. Regarding the truly enterprising part of forecasting, the emphasis on the convergence of panel opinions is hardly virtue.

4. A major drawback in the application of the Delphi method since 1964 has been the inherent tendency to solicit from *all* group members expert opinions in fields where at most one or two are experts. This leads to situations where after several rounds, panelists are asked to give expert judgments on projections completely outside their fields of competence, leaving them only two equally unpalatable choices: (a) abstaining from judgments, which defeats the purposes of Delphi, or (b) giving a layman's view, which then leads to a mingling of possibly good individual judgment with badly founded opinion (see paragraph 3 above). This again defeats the goals of Delphi. Ways must be found to combine judgments based on consensus with expert individual judgment.

5. In order to summarize the findings of experts, the method relies on "objective" coding of the items on the questionnaire. This permits a quick, easy, and "objective" measurement of range and convergence in the replies. This is a stultifying procedure in a forecasting technique which attempts to collect the "wisdom" and insights of the participants.

To the participating expert the questions are often ambiguous or distorting, but he cannot question the questions and must answer them as they are. If experts interpret a question differently, the different responses do not reflect differences in judgment about the question which the designer had in mind. Also, box-checking types of questions are not only often irritating because of perceived ambiguities, but also invite a quick, impatient, facile response. Although this is probably an unavoidable defect, it also can substantially degrade the ultimate output.

6. Depending on how the panel or group of panels is set up and used, it will still be necessary for a coordinating panel or the director(s) of the project to examine the various forecasts as to their possible interdependence—positive, by making progress in other projected fields more likely, or negative, by similar (human, material) resource requirements under limited endowment. Finally, the technical projections should be subject to an evaluation of their social, economic, and military desirability. Only with these additions can Delphi aspire to make worthwhile contributions to planning.

We do not wish to make too much of the difficulties inherent in this application of the Delphi technique for forecasting. When applied judiciously, the technique can be useful if the consumer of the results is fully aware of its severe limitations. Its usefulness could be increased somewhat if the problems recognized in the Gordon-Helmer report and examined in this critique lead to improvement where this is feasible, and to further caution in the evaluation of results where it is not.

The Gordon-Helmer report remarks: "One must judge the merits or promise of an approach such as this in terms of the alternatives available" (p. 6).

This is true, but only barely. The implication of the statement is that one could not do without an "approach." But the fact that one needs or wants to do something does not always mean that it can be done. Thus, a bad method or "approach" is still bad, even though available alternatives are worse. The value of the Delphi approach to forecasting is, in our opinion, generally low. However, it is a variable.

Forecasting by this means is easier in some subject areas than in others, and usually easier for the short range than for the long range future. By replacing open discussion and committee activity, Delphi reduces the influence of the following psychological effects of face-to-face confrontations: persuasion by irrelevant factors (e.g., pompousness of one or two members), hesitation to abandon past erroneous opinions, undue influence by majority opinion. The initial independent forecast by each panel member "from scratch," and the reasoning that goes into it, seems of particular appeal. The independence of these forecasts makes it more likely that (at least in the early rounds) one or two important points of detail may arise to which other panel members did not give due consideration.

These original and new issues may not emerge if panel participants start with submitted projections and conjectures (as proposed in some later version of Delphi), since they may lead all participants astray (the SEER technique).[4] The quality of the results are clearly sensitive to the care and ingenuity with which the method is employed. The value of forecasts to the consumer depends on his full awareness of the limitations inherent in the method and on the variable incidence of these limitations.

EXPERIENCE, MODIFICATION, AND USE OF DELPHI SINCE 1964

Helmer reports on a further experiment in using the Delphi technique for "systematizing" the use of expert judgment.[5] He reports that if the respondents of "extreme" opinions are made to justify their estimates, and this information is fed back to the other respondents in subsequent questionnaire rounds, considerable convergence (i.e., movement toward the median) of opinions is usually achieved. (Sometimes, however, opinion becomes polarized.)

There is no further justification by Helmer of the value of convergence. He continues to regard the method as one for extracting "information" which a group possesses collectively. But he recognizes no distinction between information derived from expertise and information that results from expert *judgment*. The emphasis on consensus is rooted in the assumption that—especially after a series of feedbacks—one man's judgment is as good as another's.

It is understandable why directors of Delphi forecasting exercises desire convergence. What are they to do if the forecasts are widely dispersed?

Are they to pick one? If so, on what basis? And if not, how useful is the outcome to the consumer who wants forecasts? Throwing out the extremes could be sacrificing what will be known, in retrospect, as the best prediction. And what if responses cluster in a bipolar pattern? Surely, averaging is then most likely wrong. Unfortunately the desirability of convergence—of essentially one forecast—does not make it happen, and to bring it about artificially is apt to nullify the value of the method.

Among ideas expressed for varying the forecasting method, Helmer mentions the possibility of attributing different weight to the opinions of different experts in calculating the consensus. "Clearly, if it were easy to measure the relative trustworthiness of different experts, we would give greatest weight to the opinions of those who are more trustworthy. In the absence of objective measurements to this effect, we have examined the possibility of relying instead on the experts' subjective self-appraisal of their own competence, and found this quite promising" (p. 7). The logic of the first sentence is peculiar. Surely, if it were easy to measure the trustworthiness of experts, there would be no need to give greater weight to the more trustworthy. In that case one would simply throw out the less trustworthy. Employing the experts' self-appraisal (whatever their trustworthiness) seems to us promising in the case of forecasts in which expertise is much more important than judgment in arriving at reasonably good results (e.g., forecasting the general state of the economy or the flow of tax revenue for the following year). But for the reasons we have already given, the self-appraisal of experts is of dubious value when it comes to forecasting enterprises involving highly speculative matters.

Besides the 1967 modifications of Delphi by Helmer, several other developments of Delphi took place. H.Q. North tried to apply Delphi for forecasts in industrial technological developments for TRW in 1966[6] and 1968,[7] and in addition to Helmer's and Gordon's continued work on Delphi[8] the technique was also further developed by B. Brown[9] and N.C. Dalkey,[10] and in particular by G.B. Bernstein and M.J. Cetron[11] (SEER: Systems for Event Evaluation and Review). SEER was developed for NAVSUP (Naval Supply Systems Command) to give a fifteen-year forecast of information processing technology. The technique used is a variant of Delphi, but more goal and policy oriented than work previously done. In particular, SEER and its forecasts are designed to: (a) highlight unexploited capabilities, (b) identify gaps and/or deficiencies in the state of the art, (c) enable the establishment of long range capabilities and standardization goals, and (d) facilitate research and development planning and resource allocation through identification of alternative short, medium, and long range goals and the (desirable or necessary) supporting events. Several modifications were made which meet some of the shortcomings and increase the usefulness of Delphi. In SEER there exist now only two rounds. The first round is designed to come up with technical forecasts from experts in that field of technology, and the second round, consisting of different participants from industry, government, and universities, is designed to fit the policy goal orientation of SEER. In limiting SEER to only two rounds, several compromises had to be made. These are:

1. Panel members of Round 1 were presented a list of potential events developed from secondary sources and interviews to provide a starting point. Depending on the purpose of the project, this could be a serious drawback in case Delphi should generate new, heretofore unconsidered potential developments.

2. The feedback in successive rounds among participants of the same panel was lost, thereby giving up one of the major aims of Delphi—that is, to form a consensus. Though much more operational than the original Delphi technique, it is still open to the major criticisms advanced above. Still, some positive results were achieved in terms of generating useful information from industry and scientists.

Other applications of Delphi were made by J. Martino,[12] H. Hayward (with Gordon),[13] A.D. Bender, A.E. Strack, G.W. Ebright, and G. von Haunalter,[14] C.A. Bjerrum[15] and others. However, despite the modifications of Delphi made since 1964, technological forecasting using Delphi methods remains a very costly enterprise. This results mainly from the lengthy time requirements and the cost of high-quality panelists: the initial setup cost of PATTERN was betweeen $250,000 and $300,000, with an annual maintenance cost of $50,000.[16] PROBE II used inputs from 140 experts[17]; the Navy technological forecast cost at least $1.9 million.[18]

We conclude that, although experience has led to improvements in the Delphi method of forecasting, it remains largely subject to the flaws we evaluated in our criticism of the original report by Gordon and Helmer. The technique has limited value provided expectations are modest and the results are used with a proper dose of skepticism. Indeed, the identified defects are in toto so considerable that one wonders whether, despite its well known weaknesses, the committee method is not, after all, better than this replacement.

Gordon and Helmer were, of course, quite right in their criticism of face-to-face meetings. But Delphi has great inherent weaknesses of its own, and is very costly to boot. Essentially, elimination of the intrusion of personality factors has been bought at the expense of losing the intellectual stimulus which committee meetings often produce: it is so often that a remark made by one member touches off a new thought in another.

Even if one wants to avoid the face-to-face meeting for ascertaining the intelligent judgment and guesswork of experts, there is *the alternative of intensive interviewing*, which is worth further experimentation. If the interviewer himself is intelligent, misunderstanding can be minimized, and individuals' subtlety of thought becomes capturable. This alternative procedure would clearly also require judgment in the aggregation of responses. Indeed, this kind of aggregation would not have the deceptive aura of hardness which the use of computers is apt to engender. But that may be an advantage.

Chapter Three

Quantitative Analytic Approaches: The Fucks Forecast

The book by Wilhelm Fucks, *Formeln zur Macht*[1](roughly translated, "The Equations of Power") was widely acclaimed in Europe when it appeared in 1965. The major reason for interest in the book arises from the fact that it was written by a well known physicist instead of a social scientist. The author is professor of theoretical physics and director of the physics department at the Aachen Institute of Technology and the Institute of Plasma-Physics in Julich. This explains the completely uninhibited and in some ways novel and fresh approach to the analysis of potential developments of nations. It also led to the use of scientific methods which a physicist is accustomed to: simplification to a few but essential variables and, based on the derived formulas which explain the present state, very uninhibited and far-reaching extrapolations. We will first describe the theories and results, then perform sensitivity analyses of his extrapolations, and later we will give a critique of the methodology used.

Fucks deals with the size and evolution of state power from the present right into the next century. Based on Volterra's analysis of the evolution of biological species in a restricted environment, and given the present phase of industrialization of various countries, Fucks comes to one overwhelming result: a startling development of expected Chinese power to an uncontestably first place. The initial values of power as calculated for 1960/63 are of interest in themselves, and show at least the importance of getting some quantitative estimates of existing power relations. Such factors are all too often neglected in basic political, military, and economic decisions, as Fucks demonstrated retrospectively in the analysis of 1938 figures for Japan, the United States, and others.

THE MATHEMATICAL MODEL OF FUCKS'S ANALYSIS[2]

The physicist Fucks assumes, in analogy to physical and biological processes, that differences in social systems tend to be eroded and overcome, particularly where these differences are due to technological and organizational skills. Fucks's thinking is further influenced by observations on the logistic growth of biological cultures in a closed environment: a small number of a species will first grow at increasing rates when introduced into a new culture on which it feeds; this growth will subside when the population is reaching the long term limit that the given resources can sustain.

Fucks observes the large differences in today's technological know-how, aggregate and per capita production levels, and production efficiency. These differences are due to past historical developments and technical-cultural shocks ("quantum jump") which gradually spread to all countries, especially those where the social and political motivations exist to acquire this technology.

The growth of a single biological species (and economic sector) in an equally favorable or hostile environment will be determined mathematically by

$$\dot{P}_t = n\,P_t - m\,P_t = (n - m)P_t, \qquad (3.1)$$

where P_t is the population or product at time t, n the birth rate or gross rate of growth, m the mortality rate or rate of depreciation. Assuming n and m to be constant, Fucks assumes the growth in such an environment to be proportionate to the already achieved level of production or number of species existing. We have (for $\rho = n - m$)

$$\dot{P}_t = \rho\,P_t \qquad (3.2)$$

where ρ is the net rate of growth or decay. If P_o is the initial value we solve for P_t

$$P_t = P_o\,e^{\rho(t - t_o)} \qquad (3.3)$$

i.e., an exponential growth or decay. In case $n = m$, the population remains constant. If the species double within each time interval T, we have for ρ

$$e^{\rho T} = 2 \text{ and } \rho = \frac{\ln 2}{T} = \frac{0.693}{T} \qquad (3.4)$$

In case of decay, we substitute $1/2$ for 2 in Equation (3.4). Given, however, a constant resource endowment for the species, the growth of the species' technological knowledge will be limited by a certain level of saturation beyond which growth cannot expand. The rate of growth is therefore bound to decline the more the population reaches the level of saturation and, once reached, the population will stagnate. The growth of the population is therefore determined by (a) its present level and (b) its distance from the level of saturation. The larger P_t, the smaller that distance. We may approximate this decline in the rate of growth by $\rho - \gamma P_t$, where γ is a positive constant. The growth of the population at time t is now

$$\dot{P}_t = (\rho - \gamma P_t) P_t \qquad (3.5)$$

and

$$\rho \, dt = \frac{\rho dP_t}{P_t(\rho - \gamma P_t)} = \frac{dP_t}{P_t} + \frac{\gamma dP_t}{\rho - \gamma P_t} \qquad (3.6)$$

which gives, by integrating,

$$c \cdot e^{\rho t} = \frac{P_t}{\rho - \gamma P_t} \qquad (3.7)$$

where c is a constant. For P_t we have therefore

$$P_t = \frac{c \cdot \rho \cdot e^{\rho t}}{1 + c \cdot \gamma \cdot e^{\rho t}} \qquad (3.8)$$

The saturation level is given by

$$\lim_{t \to \infty} P_t = \overline{P} = \frac{\rho}{\gamma} \qquad (3.9)$$

which corresponds to our definitions of ρ and γ. Again, if P_o was our initial value for population (production) we have

$$c = \frac{P_o}{\rho - P_o \gamma} \quad \text{and} \qquad (3.10)$$

$$P_t = \frac{\rho \cdot P_o \cdot e^{\rho t}}{\rho + P_o \gamma (e^{\rho t} - 1)} \qquad (3.11)$$

where $P_o < P_t < \overline{P}$. The resulting growth path is also known as Pearl curve or Verhulst-Pearl effect (the logistic law of population growth).[3]

In case the distribution of the rate of growth over different time periods is known, we may write Equation (3.5) in a more general form as

$$\dot{P}_t = \rho_t \cdot P_t \qquad (3.5a)$$

Substituting for ρ_t the particular known or assumed distribution and integrating the differential equation yields again the desired values for P_t. Again we have $P_o < P_t < \bar{P}$.

In the case of population growth, particular interest has centered on the evolution of birth rates (n) which, by considering the aging process (process of intoxication of biological species), yields Volterra's second type of equation

$$N_t = N_{ot} + \int_o^t N(\tau)f(t-\tau)d\tau \qquad (3.12)$$

where N_{ot} are the expected numbers of births from the initial population, τ is the age of females, f the maternity function as composed by survival probability and probability of bearing a child at age τ for a newborn female at time $t - \tau$.[4] ρ_t is then again obtained as the difference between expected rates of birth and mortality.

In all this, the saturation level $\bar{P}$ itself may change through some evolutionary or revolutionary process. Historically, mankind has experienced up to now three such positive "shocks," which propagated to all regions: the change from nomad states to permanent settlements (beginning 6000 B.C.), the introduction of iron and agricultural techniques (beginning 1000 B.C.), and the industrial revolution from 1800 onward (science and technology).*

Recent economic and technological growth has not yet been diffused to all countries. Some, such as China, are just beginning to experience this evolution.

The Index of Power

The following indices are constructed by Fucks: (1) an index based on steel production and population, (2) an index based on energy production and population, and (3) an overall index as the average of these two indices. The choice of this last index has certain advantages. GNP in monetary values itself cannot be relied upon because price systems and types and quantities of goods produced differ too much between societies. Therefore, one has to substitute suitable physical quantities. Such are population and energy. Steel production is less suitable as an index since steel may sooner or later be partly replaced by other materials. We should, therefore, look at the development of steel production as part of the development of basic *material production*. In a later analysis we will look at a material production base including steel, cement and fertilizer production. For the moment, we assume steel production to give an accurate picture of the material basis of the main economic systems involved,

---

*Among others: E.A. Johnson, H.E. Striner, "The Quantitative Effect of Research and Development on National Economic Growth," *Proceedings of the Second International Conference on Operations Research*, New York, 1961, pp. 499ff.

though not for small nations. Energy consumption is clearly an important index of economic growth.

Fucks calculates a set of possible indices of power and finally selects the one that seems to correspond most closely to the power hierarchy of the leading nations as perceived (by him) in 1960/63 (column E of Tables 3-1 and 3-2), i.e., based on $M_s = P^{1/3} \cdot S$ and $M_e = P^{1/3} \cdot E$; these values are then normalized by setting the United States = 1,000.

Tables 3-3 and 3-4 show equivalent index numbers, but now based on 1970 data on energy and steel production. Were we to accept Fucks's 1960/63 index selection (column E), then a noticeable *narrowing* of the power of the nations shown would have taken place: the Soviet Union now ranks a close second to the United States; West Germany and France improved their relative position; and China ranks about equal to its 1960/63 position when compared to the United States.

Table 3-5 lists some of the major countries ranked by 1960/63 and by 1970 data, when one combines the energy and steel indices. The noticeable changes are the increase in the positions of Japan (to 322, a change of 179 points, or 125 percent); of the USSR (to 825, a change of 151 points or 22

Table 3-1. Possible Power Indices from: $M_s = P^a \cdot S^b$ (1960/63 Data, USA = 1000)

	A S^2P	B $S^{2/3}P$	C $S^{1/2}P$	D SP	E $SP^{1/3}$	F $SP^{1/2}$	G $SP^{2/3}$	H $SP^{3/2}$	I SP^2
United States	1000	1000	1000	1000	1000	1000	1000	1000	1000
Soviet Union	740	840	1060	935	840	860	916	1030	1120
China	54	129	1310	448	185	232	289	1200	1715
West Germany	28	50	158	89	205	167	135	45	25.4
France	7.7	18.4	105	44	110	88	69.6	21	11.5

P = Population, S = Steel Production, E = Energy Production

Table 3-2. Possible Power Indices from: $M_e = P^a \cdot E^b$ (1960/63 Data, USA = 1000)

	A E^2P	B $E^{3/2}P$	C $E^{1/2}P$	D EP	E $EP^{1/3}$	F $EP^{1/2}$	G $EP^{2/3}$	H $EP^{3/2}$	I EP^2
United States	1000	1000	1000	1000	1000	1000	1000	1000	1000
Soviet Union	275	395	820	570	508	516	537	621	677
China	127	296	1620	690	285	354	442	1330	2590
West Germany	5.4	14.6	108	39.5	89	73	59.4	21.6	11.7
France	0.7	3.0	57	13	31.8	25	20.2	6.35	3.2

P = Population, S = Steel Production, E = Energy Production

Table 3-3. Possible Power Indices from: $M_s = P^a \cdot S^b$ 1970 Data, USA = 1000)

	A S^2P	B $S^{2/3}P$	C $S^{1/2}P$	D SP	E $SP^{1/3}$	F $SP^{1/2}$	G $SP^{2/3}$	H $SP^{3/2}$	I SP^2
United States	1000	1000	1000	1000	1000	1000	1000	1000	1000
Soviet Union	1115	1159	1165	1148	1027	1056	1086	1248	1357
China	75	1009	1396	527	220	274	341	1013	1949
West Germany	41	151	178	109	250	203	165	59	32
France	10	84	110	49	125	99	78	24	12

P = Population, S = Steel Production, E = Energy Production

Table 3-4. Possible Power Indices from: $M_e = P^a \cdot E^b$ (1970 Data, USA = 1000)

	A E^2P	B $E^{2/3}P$	C $E^{1/2}P$	D EP	E $EP^{1/3}$	F $EP^{1/2}$	G $EP^{2/3}$	H $EP^{3/2}$	I EP^2
United States	1000	1000	1000	1000	1000	1000	1000	1000	1000
Soviet Union	412	834	908	698	624	638	660	759	825
China	155	1288	1673	757	317	386	490	1456	2800
West Germany	2	56	85	25	56	45	37	13	7
France	.2	23	42	7	18	16	11	4	2

P = Population, S = Steel Production, E = Energy Production

percent); and the EEC (six countries, to 510, a change of 47 points or 10 percent), where the United States is ranked at 1000 points.

Expected Population Growth

For each of the main countries the expected population growth was calculated by Fucks according to the model set forth above. Rates of birth and mortality were calculated separately and assumed to reach some constant value in the long run. The values of ρ_t as calculated by Fucks are represented in Figure 3-1 (p. 34), where the dotted curve represents the ρ_t for Europe from 1740 to 2020 and the other curves expected or assumed ρ_t for China. Curve A was calculated under the assumption that the decay of ρ_t of China will occur in a way similar to the European one (skewed to the left); the Curve B was computed under the assumption that the areas enclosed to the left and right of the maximum of ρ_t were equal. Fuck's predictions are based on an average of these two curves. Curves C and D give ρ_t under our additional assumption that China's population growth will be immediately cut to those constant rates (1.0 percent[a] and 0.5 percent). In addition, while Fucks assumed China's population to be 700

---

[a]A population growth of 1.0 percent per annum is the presently stated long term goal of China.

Table 3-5. Indices of Power for 1960/63 and 1970, USA = 1000, Based on Energy and Steel Outputs and Population

1960/63		*1970*	
United States	1000	United States	1000
Soviet Union	674	Soviet Union	825
EEC, (6)	463	EEC, (6)	510
Germany & France	274	Japan	322
China	250	Germany & France	281
Germany, (W)	174	China	269
Japan	143	Germany, (W)	153
Great Britain	120	Great Britain	103
France	71	France	72
India	67	India	66
Poland	43	Italy	50
Italy	37	Poland	48
Canada	31	Canada	46
CSSR	26	CSSR	28
Germany, (E)	20	Belgium	20
Belgium	16	Germany, (E)	17

million in 1960, we assume that this level was reached only in 1965.[5] The expected population of the United States, Soviet Union, and China are then as shown in Table 3-6 (p. 35).

Expected Steel Production

The growth of steel production, based on the mathematical model of Fucks described above, depends on the level of output already achieved and the distance from its saturation level. Per capita consumption levels are accordingly calculated for different countries at different levels of saturation related to per capita production one generation and two generations hence. While per capita production levels are already 600 kg in the United States, 350 kg in the Soviet Union, and between these levels or above the United States level in all major European countries, Fucks predicts that steel production (or material production) in China will reach the Soviet Union standard in about 25 years (1995) and the 600 kg level in another generation. Considering the population at each time, we then calculate the expected development of steel output, based on the various initial values. The results of the calculations are shown in Figure 3-2 (p. 35).

Expected Energy Production

An analogous approach is made to compute the expected energy productions of various countries. The levels of per capita production in 1960

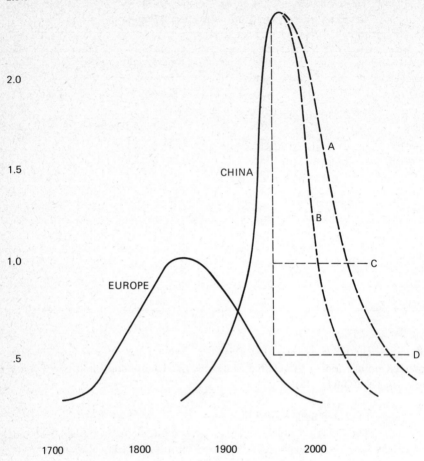

Figure 3-1. Population Growth Rates $\rho_t = n_t - m_t$ Europe–China

were 65 Mega Watt hours (MWh) in the United States, 38 MWh in Great Britain, 30 MWh in Germany, and 23 MWh in the Soviet Union. Assuming the achievable levels of per capita energy production in China to be 15 MWh around 2000 and 35 MWh around 2040, we can again calculate expected Chinese energy production with reference to various population estimates.

Corresponding production levels are computed for the other nations, given their initial values and saturation levels. The results are again plotted in Figure 3-3. The economic implications of such a potential growth are analyzed separately in a later section.

Table 3-6. **Expected Size of Population of Three Regions**

	1960	*1965*	*2000*	*2040*
United States	180	195	245	280
Soviet Union	220	231	300	335
China	700	750	1700	2700 (Fucks)
Assumption C	680	700	992	1476 (1 percent)
Assumption D	690	700	833	1000 (0.5 percent)

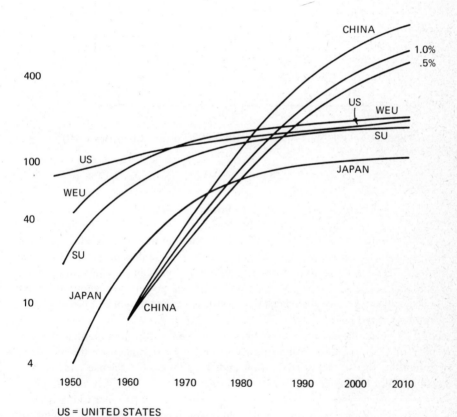

US = UNITED STATES
SU = SOVIET UNION
WEU = WESTERN EUROPEAN UNION

Figure 3-2. Projected Steel Production 1950-2010, 10^6 Metric Tons

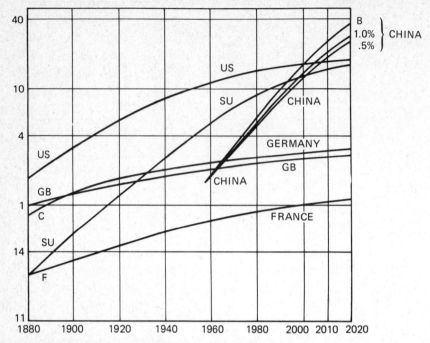

Figure 3-3. Energy Production 1880-2020 of Six Countries in 10^9 MWh

The Expected Evolution of Power

The index constructed by Fucks, i.e., $M_t = ((M_s)_t + (M_e)_t)^{1/2}$, is applied to the expected values of population figures, steel production, and energy output. The resulting development is represented in Figure 3-4. It is interesting to analyze how different hypotheses on China's population growth would affect the expected break-even points of power throughout the next decades. The results of such an analysis, within the assumption of Fucks's model, are summarized in Table 3-7.

As the figures suggest, in the next generation the potential development of Chinese power will be nearly exclusively determined by the industrial revolution—that is, the introduction and development of science and modern technology. In this process *mere adaptation to levels already achieved earlier elsewhere* is necessary to bring about this evolution. The sooner China reaches the frontier of modern science and technology, the more likely is her industrial progress. This process in itself will be a revolutionary event, since never before has a 700-800 million society reached that frontier. Its political and economic implications should be pondered even now, though these may be far less "menacing" than is generally feared.

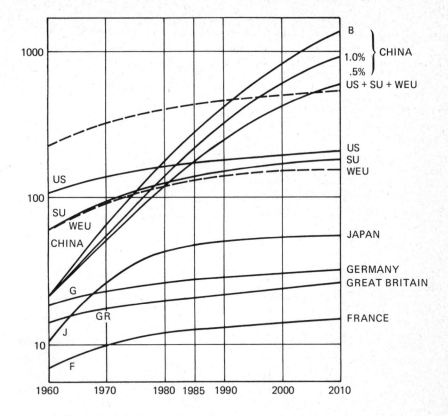

Figure 3-4. Projected Power Index of Fucks: M_t

One of the main criticisms of Fucks's approach might be his estimate of a future Chinese population of 2.7 billion for the year 2040. This estimate itself is not as unrealistic as it might seem. But in order to eliminate a possible upward distortion, we reduced China's population growth drastically to 1.0 and, alternatively, 0.5 percent. The results are not influenced significantly by different growth rates in population over the next generation for China. As to the counter argument that a large population and extended population growth may hinder rather than further economic growth, we would have to analyze extensively China's actual conditions and potential over the next generation.

Basically, we believe that such an analysis would show the fallacy of this argument for China. One is too readily impressed by China's 700 or 800 million population, if one does not relate this figure to the resources and area of that country. China is slightly larger in area than the United States (including Alaska), is richly endowed with all major natural resources, and has a highly industrious population whose technological skill is now being developed extensively. In comparison, India and Pakistan together have nearly the same

Table 3-7.   Break-Even Points of Alternative Indices

i) Break-Even Points in Steel Production

Between	*Fucks*	*1.0%*	*0.5%*
China-Japan	1974	1978	1981
China-SU	1981	1985	1987
China-US	1982	1986	1988
China-WEU	1983	1987	1990
China-US + WEU	1990	1994	2000
US-SU	2030		

ii) Break-Even Points in Energy Production

Between	*Fucks*	*1.0%*	*0.5%*
China-SU	1996	1997	2000
China-US	2000	2001	2004
US-SU	2030		

iii) Break-Even Points in the Power Index

Between	*Fucks*	*1.0%*	*0.5%*
China-WEU	1976	1980	1981
China-SU	1977	1981	1983
China-US	1980	1984	1986
China-US + WEU	1987	1991	1995
US-SU	2030		

population as China, but less than half the area, just a fraction of the known natural resources, and none of the social discipline inculcated by China's culture.

By comparison, Western Europe, with a population of roughly 400 million, is about half the size of China and has fewer natural resources, but has a GNP of about $672 billion. Furthermore, all of Europe (to the Urals) compares to China in area and population (712 million vs. 800 million people), and had a combined GNP of about $1,344 billion in 1970, i.e., 34 percent higher than the United States GNP in 1970 ($990 billion). These comparisons demonstrate that the major restraint to China's development cannot be natural resources (as these are more abundant in China than in Europe), or population alone (equal or larger concentrations of population occur in many parts of the world, often combined with a high standard of living, e.g., Japan), but *technology and human capital.* And this is a variable that can be completely changed in one generation. This is the major thrust of our argument and is stimulated partly by Fucks's analysis.

CRITIQUE

Approach and method used by Fucks are of interest because they concern the gross economic-military potentials including industrial and technological capacity of major countries. If the method was complemented by an analysis of possible constraints, and its compatibility with technological constraints assured, it would be possible to project the comparative potential of large and presumably important countries and regions over 20, 30, or more years.

The Fucks method deals only with measurable physical things—population, steel, and energy production. It employs rigidly mechanical formulas and arrives at sets of figures comparing the power potential of countries and regions. The simplicity of the method and the quantitative nature of the results, however, should not deceive the reader into assuming that he can use these results without a great deal of qualitative interpretation. Some figures used in this forecasting have to be hypothetical, and even if they turn out to be right, they have uncertain consequences.

Within the narrow framework selected by Fucks, the influence of some parameters on the forecast of the next 20 to 30 years is negligible on the overall outlook, once we accept the few assumptions on which Fucks's theory is based. This is the case particularly for China's population: independent of its growth over the next generation, the development of China's economy and technology will be spectacular if she just adopts such known technological achievements as transistors, wireless communications, thermal and nuclear power plants, hybrid corn, wheat, and rice production, large scale fertilizer plants, flood control and irrigation, deep well oil drilling, off-shore oil and gas ventures, etc. Rapid development occurred in the last two decades (1949-1969) despite such major disruptions as the Korean War; the withdrawal of Soviet aid (technicians, repair and maintenance materials); and extremely bad weather from 1959 to 1962. The real question about China's population problem is: will it be possible for China to feed, educate, house, and clothe her growing population over the next generation and assure economic and military progress at the same time? The answer appears to be probably yes.

As a rule, the forecast of the power of nations in this model is sensitive to the expected rate of population growth, particularly in developed countries where forecasts of steel and energy production, for instance, refer to *per capita* output and saturation levels. The development of China's power index, however, is not significantly affected by her expected rate of population growth, except that the "parity of power" may be postponed for a few years, i.e., from 1985 to 1990. This is explained by the impact, in the early phase of the technological-economic takeoff, of the *absolute* as well as the per capita gap in economic and technological performance. Examples of such "adaptation growth," given the human and organizational capital, can be found in Western

Europe and Japan in the postwar periods from 1948 to the 1960s, although these areas were much more advanced industrially at the beginning of the time period than China is now.

Similar sensitivity analyses could be made to other assumptions in Fucks's analysis: can China—then with a population of between 1.0 and 1.7 billion—achieve by 1995 the level of material or energy production (per capita) of the Soviet Union in 1965? What are the possible constraints?

From the construction of the power index, it is evident that the assumptions in selecting the weight of population, steel, and energy affect the projection significantly. Fucks selects a formula which roughly fits the present distribution of power between various countries and regions. If we are confined to the choices presented in the previous tables, the E formula seems to us most realistic. But this formula may either understate or overstate the relative future power of China, depending on other, especially political and military, variables.

The figures obtained by strictly applying Fucks's model indicate that China will reach break-even points in steel and energy production with Japan, the United States, the Soviet Union, and other countries or regions the sooner, the higher is the chosen rate of Chinese population growth. This assumption conflicts with a large body of existing literature on economic development. But, as already indicated, we do not believe population growth to act as a major drag on China's industrial development. From this point of view, we see no reason why China should not witness a great expansion in her economic (and military) potential.

The overall power index by Fucks is based on forecasts of population, steel (or raw materials), and energy. But in this aggregate index, we do really need steel? The one major quantitative index in addition to population is certainly energy. Various empirical studies have shown a close correlation between energy production and growth of GNP. Does therefore the inclusion of steel production really add something indispensable to our forecasts? We have already noted the limited importance of steel by shifting its interpretation to a more general base-material index in this context. Energy clearly supplies the best single indicator of development.

There seems to be some value in varying Fucks's forecasting method; thus, even if we pick rather low rates of "adaptation" growth, China's power index will be about 500 by the year 2000 compared with computed values for other countries and regions shown in Figure 3-4, and it is conceivable that higher rates of "adaptation" will prevail. The interest in doing this originates in two factors: the huge size of the Chinese population at present, and the probability that this population will grow faster (in absolute numbers) than those of the Soviet Union, the United States, Japan, and Europe.

If any such forecasts are made, they must be used with great caution if the future military capacity of China is the focus of the enterprise. For the reasons presented earlier, it is important to recall first that different kinds of military conflict (e.g., strategic-nuclear, conventional, revolutionary) make different demands on economic and technological resources—different both qualitatively and quantitatively; and second, that the amount of military strength which can be derived from any given level of industrial and technological resources depends importantly on (a) administrative skill, and (b) political will.[6] The ability of China, with her still low level of development, to produce advanced nuclear armaments over the past several years emphasizes the importance of these factors.

As we have previously explained, *scale* of population and other resources is an important ingredient of military potential. In China, the scale is gigantic. If one notices that China has now an estimated per capita product of only $100-$130, one is focusing on the relatively low stage of her economic development. But one must not forget that a high GNP per capita is militarily significant only if associated with a fairly large population, and conversely, that a large population with a quite modest degree of economic development may nevertheless have a considerable military potential.

To put it differently, even at her present stage of economic and industrial development, China possesses highly trained scientists and engineers, a manufacturing capacity, and an energy base which, if they were associated with a fraction (say, one-twelfth) of her population, would make China an economic power about equal to France. It is the rate at which these key resources increase which will largely determine China's relative military potential over the next few decades. This is not to say that China's very large population is necessarily a liability from this point of view. On the contrary, this large mass of manpower gives her the opportunity to mitigate to some extent the shortage of real capital stock by using labor-intensive processes in lieu of other resources. That is to say, China can employ its labor resources to produce certain outputs (highways, dams, irrigation projects, even machine tool plants) that otherwise require considerable capital investments. Also China can build up considerable military capacity, which is denied to countries of much smaller population with higher levels of economic development. China's development is a "bootstrap" process—by now well under way.

This brings us to a last and most important issue not touched upon in Fucks's book, but which ultimately shows whether Fucks's projections are realistic: Are the implied economic growth rates possible economically and does there exist historic precedence for such an expansion? What has the actual performance of China been in the past two decades under socialist rule? Has China in the past 20 years created a base of human capital which will allow it now to expand along this projected path? These are most relevant questions and, to our knowledge, they have not been addressed in a meaningful way.

To begin with, if one steps outside Fucks's formula, there is no way of forecasting high or low rates of growth for any of the variables with any high degree of confidence. As we will point out shortly, they depend on *political* as well as on economic constraints. Population growth is the least difficult to forecast. However, catastrophes such as large scale war could upset any trend resulting from the other factors. If the Chinese government maintains control over the population, population growth will be sensitive to any government policy in this matter. As past demographic forecasts on other societies have shown, public policy on population growth and resulting birth rates can undergo fairly swift changes. There are many indications that China has population growth, and the problems resulting from it, well under control. The Chinese population is in this respect far more disciplined than that of India or Egypt.

Increases in the production and the output capacity of material goods are similarly subject to changes in government policy and attitudes (e.g., attitudes toward work in the labor force, work days per week, etc.). The past economic growth of China reveals very large fluctuations. The extremely high rate of industrial expansion during much of the 1950s resulted not only from a high rate of public saving and investment, but also from an extraordinarily large scale infusion of advanced foreign technology from the Soviet Union. The abrupt cessation of Soviet aid combined with three years of catastrophic weather stunted economic growth much more than might have resulted from the wasteful response to the uncoordinated "great leap forward." Growth recovery, in large part, resumed at a considerable pace several years after the abandonment of the "great leap forward" strategy (1963 and later).

The Cultural Revolution in recent years is assumed to have again put a damper on economic expansion in 1967-68. The impact of these unique conditions was powerful. Could we have predicted these events in 1950? Can we predict similar events, or their absence, over the next 10, 20, or 50 years? There can only be a negative answer to these questions and this fact argues for organizing this sort of forecasting by resorting to a set of possible futures. Indeed, we regard this problem as so important that we examine it further in the following section.

A NOTE ON GNP

The data used in this study are the best one can obtain today. They ought not only to be better in quality, sharper in concept, and more plentiful; there ought also to be very different data. By this we mean that we concern ourselves exclusively—to the extent that we have numbers—with physical phenomena: so many people, so many tons of steel, oil, number of cars, etc., etc.; or we use monetary expressions to measure their sales. This is entirely along the conventional way of reporting on "economic" phenomena. Yet it ought to be clear that this description, no matter how extensive and detailed, is only part of the story. The economic processes are of a psychological character, involve decisions, attitudes, plans, expectations, and so on. When these change, the underlying physical entities mentioned above assume different meaning and significance, but that change is nowhere expressed or recorded. To give an example from the military field (to which the same observation applies) assume a nation to be in possession of nuclear weapons. If the nation is war-minded, these weapons mean one thing, but if in that nation a hostility toward the use of nuclear weapons develops, they mean something quite different. Yet statistics would only record the distribution of the physical weapons and would not be able to describe the changes in attitudes—which is the dominant fact. The same argument applies to economics. This clearly places a restriction on the correct and exhaustive interpretation of the data, even if otherwise they should be of excellent quality.

However, it is not possible to have data without errors. There are observations in physics with error components ranging from $\pm 50\%$ to 10^{-14}. The fact that errors of measurement are irreducible—in principle!—is much neglected in economics, giving economic arguments and deductions a much greater appearance of certainty than they actually possess. On the other hand, the presence even of considerable errors does not preclude the making of powerful theory: to wit Newton's Theory of Gravitation was based on data that had an error component of $\pm 8\%$.

With this caveat in mind, we point out another source of trouble. No measurement is worth anything unless guided by a sharp concept. It is fairly easy to determine the number of automobiles in the United States, to count the tons of steel produced in Japan, or the inhabitants of a country. (Is it? Consider China, or Chile, or Zambia!) But when we come to use aggregates, the matter is different.

We shall only point out one, which is freely used the world over: GNP (gross national product). It is used in this study too, though with misgivings and reservations. First, the measurement of so complex a phenomenon cannot be free of error, though one will look in vain for its disclosure. These errors will vary greatly from one country to another and for all of them over time. The main trouble with the GNP notion is, however, conceptual: GNP is supposed to measure all value added in transactions; therefore, it cannot distinguish between good and bad. The production and sale of food will be recorded as well as that of poison; the services of a doctor as well as those of a prison guard. Every traffic jam on the ground as in the air increases fuel consumption: up goes GNP, while in fact this is nothing but a malfunctioning of the system. When after a flood or fire, houses or whole cities have to be rebuilt, GNP rises. This list can be continued ad libitum.

We record here our misgivings and acknowledge our dilemma of either being purists in an enterprise in which conjecture, guesswork, and judgment dominate anyway, or of using some indicators which allow us to distinguish at least orders of magnitude—something a carefully and cautiously used GNP statistic may allow us to do. We have chosen the latter approach but we want to warn the reader that we are all treading on treacherous ground. He should also apply the same caution when he encounters GNP statistics elsewhere.

Finally, as a consequence, a word about growth rates, or any other rates of change. It should be obvious that rates of change are greatly affected by the reliability of the underlying figures from which they are computed. If the growth rate from successive *error-free* figures is 3%, when a +1%, +3% error in the first figure and none in the second is noted, we obtain a growth of 2% or 0% respectively. If the reverse is the case, the rate is 4.1% or 6.1% respectively (see Table 3-8). If the first figure has an error of only ± 1% and the second one of only +1%, we have a "growth" of 5.1% (instead of 3%). All this can of course be generalized, but having made our position clear, we shall not pursue this matter any further.[7]

Table 3-8. Apparent Rate of Growth for ±1, ±3, ±5 Percent Errors[a]

		Figure II						
	% Error	*−5*	*−3*	*−1*	*0*	*+1*	*+3*	*+5*
Figure I	−5	3.0	5.2	7.3	8.4	9.5	11.7	13.8
	−3	0.9	3.0	5.1	6.2	7.3	9.4	11.5
	−1	−1.2	0.9	3.0	4.1	5.1	7.2	9.2
	0	−2.2	−0.1	2.0	3.0	4.1	6.1	8.2
	+1	−3.1	−1.1	1.0	2.0	3.0	5.0	7.1
	+3	−5.0	−3.0	−1.0	0	1.0	3.0	5.0
	+5	−6.8	−4.8	−2.9	−1.9	−0.9	1.0	3.0

Error-free growth rate = 3%.

[a]*Source:* O. Morgenstern, Note 7, p. 288.

CHINA'S POLITICS AND ECONOMIC GROWTH

Forecasting models (for which Fucks's is a prototype) that focus wholly on quantitative data (e.g., demographic and economic) are attractive precisely because they permit the problem to be quantified, and because they yield apparently clear-cut results. However, as we have warned repeatedly, they are peculiarly subject to falsification because the continuation of observed trends assumes that everything else remains the same, and this assumption concerns importantly *political* conditions which can prove unsettling and possibly cause radical changes in a country's *economic* performance. Indeed, in the case of China, this sort of disruption has already occurred more than once during the last two decades. In the following, we therefore analyze the impact of unstable politics on China's economic growth and speculate a little, without much confidence, about this sort of impingement in the future.

The following conditions have tended to increase China's rate of economic growth in the past:

1. High rate of savings imposed by government
2. Creation of a highly industrious and disciplined labor force
3. Early massive technical aid from the Soviet Union

4. Spotty but very sizable prerevolutionary investments (especially in former treaty ports and in Manchuria, mostly dismantled by the Soviet Union)
5. Thin but top corps of scientists, many trained at the best foreign universities
6. Recognition of the need to develop foremost the agricultural sector of the economy

The following factors have tended to retard China's economic growth in the past:

1. Disruptive political drives (i.e., the Great Leap Forward and the Cultural Revolution); on the other side these same drives led to the motivation of vast social reforms
2. Need to provide minimal consumer needs at a level sustaining labor productivity
3. Expensive high priority projects in defense (especially nuclear development and missile program)
4. Bad crop years, especially 1959-1961
5. Absence of foreign technical aid since Soviet Union pulled out (1959) and since then doctrinal insistence on self-reliance
6. Relatively very small foreign trade. It grew from $1.5 billion to $4.3 billion between 1950 and 1960, but has grown very little since then. The volume is *very small* for a country with China's GNP
7. Unwillingness to go into foreign debt or accept economic aid. Again, the ideal of self-reliance. China's exports and imports are carefully kept in balance
8. Very considerable Chinese foreign aid and technical assistance especially recently (not only to North Vietnam)
9. Deficiencies in higher education, especially emphasis on political indoctrination, admixture of physical work by students (e.g., harvesting), deemphasis on research
10. Involvement in strain of international conflict (e.g., Sino-Indian conflict, Korean War, and Russian Border conflict) involving very substantial troop buildup
11. The repeated resurgence of rigid ideological commitments which conflict with using ordinary performance criteria in giving people productive incentives. To do so is apparently believed to undermine the true revolutionary spirit. But how long can one develop on the basis of enthusiasm?

We have identified these factors since they reveal conditions which are likely to influence the future Chinese growth rate. (There are, of course, *other* factors that could be important in the future, for example, large fossil fuel discoveries.) Though not exhaustive, the following observations are compelling:

1. What strikes one is the importance of policy decisions. Moreover, nearly all these political factors are among those retarding economic growth by our concepts. Can we speculate about their future impact? While China *might* oscillate between isolationism and foreign involvement, as in the past, it seems unlikely that China will greatly reduce her foreign involvement, thus the efforts of 3, 8, and 10 (above) will probably continue. On the other hand, it seems less likely that the Chinese government will over the long run forego the benefits of foreign borrowing and openness to foreign technical assistance; and China will probably also increase the ratio of foreign trade to GNP. She can do all this with Japan and the West, including the U.S., especially since the latter is abandoning its trade embargo policy. But we cannot rule out détente with the Soviet Union and increased economic transactions with that country. Any policy change in these areas could give an added boost to economic development.

2. More crucial, however, are the policies mentioned under 1, 9, and 11 (above). No radical change is likely as long as Mao is alive and functioning. But he is old and ailing; and the propensity of the Chinese Revolution to have its Thermidor has been clearly revealed in the years before the Cultural Revolution. Unless China turns out an absolutely unique case historically, a gradual return to a normal incentive system which rewards people for economic productivity in career and material terms is quite likely.

3. If both sets of policy changes occurred, it might well mean the difference between an economic growth rate of between 2 and 4 percent per annum, and one ranging between 8 and 10 percent or more. Given the magnitude of the base, the difference would be staggering over a 10- or 15-year period.

4. The political conditions of economic growth could be, of course, different and less conducive to growth. The past turmoil might repeat itself—or worse, there might be, at least temporarily, heavy disorders and a return to a new kind of war-lordism (loss of control by the center). But the bets seem against this.

5. We do not want to belittle the relevant factors on which economists usually focus when examining national growth prospects. For instance, the unsettling impact of crop failures is less likely in the future since China has undertaken enormous investments (immensely labor-intensive) in flood control and irrigation. All we are stressing is that the *political* conditions are extremely important.

Conclusion: There is no reason to assume that an order of political disturbance similar to those experienced in China could not happen elsewhere—

for instance in Japan, or the Soviet Union, or even the United States—over the lengthy time periods which are often involved in longer range attempts at forecasting. We are not referring to routine political fluctuations, but to events which have, in the jargon of Kahn and Wiener, the character of "turning points." In addition, major wars often have the profound consequences of a turning point. These kinds of events *usually* come as surprises; that is to say, they are virtually unpredictable, except perhaps when they are immediately imminent.

Chapter Four

Four Different Forecasting Approaches

1. THE SCENARIO APPROACH:
KAHN-WIENER—THE YEAR 2000

The Kahn-Wiener method[1] of forecasting is not explained systematically, concisely, or clearly. However, following pp. 5-12 (loc. cit.) on method, which are vague, some relevant statements are dispersed throughout the book. One infers that the authors absorbed or consulted a great deal of relevant material found in various massive literatures—that is, they greatly increased their base of relevant knowledge—and then applied their individual intuitive judgments to forecasting primarily by means of trend analysis, projection, and interpolation. Judgment was introduced especially in constructing multiple projects (i.e., sketching or pinpointing alternative futures) and in deciding on what seemed the most likely future. There was presumably feedback between the two authors and from various critical readers of parts of the evolving manuscript. The method is essentially a special variation of the Delphi technique of forecasting, though of course very informal.

The book is both very ambitious and quite modest. It is enormously ambitious in the vast range of conjecture about technology, economics, politics, ethics, and the arts in the United States and globally. Few people could command the skill or daring required by so vast a scope. At the same time, the book is modest, though sometimes rather mockingly, in that it does not claim to be predictive. It presents the authors' far-ranging speculations about the future (and the past). Since the quality of conjectures about the future is our main interest, *The Year 2000* will be reviewed only from this point of view regarding the future technology, economic capacity, and military potential of countries and regions.

Kahn and Wiener distinguish among the inherent conjecturability of different phenomena. "Aggregative phenomena (such as population, GNP, civilization) are easier to conjecture about than unique events, which are definitely unpredictable" (p. 2). They also say it is easier to conjecture about the near future than the more distant future (p. 12). They say, in a preceding statement, that it is easier to predict population (an aggregative phenomenon) over the next ten years than it is to predict which political party in the United States will win a presidential election (a unique event). Evidently uniqueness dominates over the time scale in rendering forecasting difficult. Although they observe that the rate of change has generally increased (p. 3), surprisingly they do not infer that conjecture has become more difficult as a result. This critical point is important. Although the authors concede that the absence of grave surprises or great crises is an untenable assumption beyond a decade, the book promptly projects to the year 2000, and sometimes even beyond!

The authors aim at elaborating various "surprise-free" futures or projections. Their definition of a "surprise-free" projection should be noted carefully. It is "one that *seems* no less surprising than any other specific possibility" (pp. 5-6, italics supplied)—simply the one most in line with current trends and expectations. It is definitely *not* the one which will spare us surprise in the future. The surprise-free assumptions may not be realized (p. 133). Indeed the authors stress that it "would be very surprising if in any thirty-three year period the real world did not produce many political and technological surprises" (p. 8). Kahn and Wiener say that "surprise-free projection" is similar in spirit to the "naïve projection" of the environment which assumes a continuation of current trends" (p. 8).

The authors say that the surprise-free projection is only *relatively* surprise-free, since it is difficult to imagine the future without taking current trends into account. Although they disclaim the implication that this projection is likely, they maintain: "It may, in fact, be the *most* likely of the various possible projections; that is to say that when contemplating a thousand things which could happen, the surprise-free projection may have a probability of much less than one in a hundred, yet be more probable than any of the other 999 possible occurrences. It could be 'most probable' and still be quite improbable" (p. 43, italics in the original).

Put in this way, it is hard to see much use in a conjecture which has less than one chance in 100 to turn out right. It is not a chance on which one would want to bet anything (even though all other available chances look worse) as long as one has the option of forgetting about the whole thing. In making this statement, Kahn and Wiener were probably carried away to unnecessary lengths by their endeavor to sell an enterprise which they know, and which they know that their readers know, is decidedly hazardous.

On the basis of past experience, the surprise-free projection will probably turn out to be wrong not only by a matter of degree, but extremely wrong because surprises have strikingly important consequences. The historical examples presented on pages 16-17 of their book—such as World Wars I and II, the rise of fascism in the 1930s, and the October Revolution in Russia—make this quite clear. Their surprise-free projection "assumes the continuation of the multifold trend, but excludes precisely the kinds of dramatic and/or surprising events that dominated the first two-thirds of the century" (p. 28). From experience, it is the "historical turning-points" which escape any projection (p. 13). The authors naturally do not include turning point events which will dominate the next 30 years or so in their surprise-free projection. They cannot know their nature and timing.

However, Kahn and Wiener do not entirely shrink from conjecturing about the kinds of events that, in our judgment, are of turning point character. For instance, the authors "tend increasingly to *feel* that, at least as far as the 'old nations' are concerned, the next thirty-three years will not be marked by as many politically and economically surprising and cataclysmic events as the first sixty-six years of this century. This seems to us quite *plausible*, despite much current anxiety about thermonuclear war . . . there seems to be a growing consensus that we are entering a period of general political and economic stability . . . " (p. 133, italics supplied). Of course, if a thermonuclear war *should* occur, all the projections about the future populations, GNP, etc., of the states involved would be worthless.

Kahn and Wiener could have dodged any conjecture about this kind of turning point event (which they admit belongs to the category of unpredictable phenomena) by simply saying that all their other projections are based on the *assumption* that no thermonuclear war or similarly cataclysmic event will occur. This would not have made their other predictions worthless since it is certainly possible that no such event will take place. But they did choose to conjecture about this class of events, and based the conjecture on their feeling and a "consensus" of other experts. Moreover, only two years after the book was published, the above-quoted passage looks already like a dubious assumption (or "prediction"). Certainly the United States has been subject recently to considerable convulsions as a result of public reactions to the war in Vietnam; and wherever we now look in the highly affluent societies—and especially at the attitudes and behavior of the young generation—one no longer has the impression that these societies are politically very stable, and that major surprises in this respect are extremely improbable.

The Kahn-Wiener conjectures are projections of current or recent trends. To start with such trends is indeed the first step of any person going intelligently about the business of forecasting. If they can be properly plotted at all, such trends are, or seem to be, something solid to go on. If it could be assumed that they would continue to shape reality, it would be easy to predict the future of important phenomena. This is not the case, however, because first, current trends are not easily identified and measured; and second, current trends may change just as past trends have changed under political, economic, and social forces. At any rate, a "trend" needs time to show up, and this makes the notion of "currentness" rather dubious in relation to trends.

Moreover, as the Kahn-Wiener study points out, identification and measurement of a current trend amounts to fixing "baselines" for purposes of projection (p. 5). The difficulty of doing this can be seen when referring to such quantifiable things as the growth of population or GNP for a country or region or the world. In considering the past economic growth of a country, it may make a great difference whether we look at the past three or four years, or at the past eight or ten. Growth may be substantially faster for the shorter period than for the longer period. Simple projection of both trends would lead to enormously different GNPs 30 years hence. But which base should we choose? Choosing the shorter period because it is closer to the future may be wrong because unusual factors during this period may have produced a very high rate of growth. If we choose the longer period, we neglect the possibility that some underlying factors have changed which, if continued, will place the country's economic growth on a higher plateau. The choice is a matter of judgment on which individuals may well differ without ability to demonstrate the necessary correctness of their choice.

Even if there were no problem about measuring "currently dominant" tendencies, Kahn and Wiener unhesitatingly admit that they may not remain dominant in the future. Straight-line trends, they say, are rare in history (p. 12), and they point to the belief of experts that, on matters of population growth, current trends are probably misleading (p. 41). Nevertheless, the two authors also say that they "depend very heavily on straight-extrapolations" (p. 39) as indeed they do. They are basically saying if "the basic trend continues, then such and such will happen" (p. 29). Is this prediction?

One reason why choosing a proper base for projection is difficult is that the recent past may have been affected, if only slightly, by emerging trends which may greatly alter the future. These emerging trends are obviously difficult to identify and to project.

In making their forecasts the authors use two methods: the "scenario," which is an exercise in the sequential plotting of events as they *could* happen (but need not); and the *alternative futures* (p. 6), which fundamentally project to a range rather than a point. The authors project a "standard world," in terms of political and cultural development, but also offer what they call "canonical variations." They pick three base values for various quantifiable phenomena and present projections of high, medium, and low; or they select two possibilities, high and low, which they believe will "bound" the "reasonable possibilities" (p. 129).

A great deal of judgment enters into the construction of even those alternative futures which can be quantified. For example, in order to arrive at a high and low forecast of the GNP of the United States for the year 2000, the authors face choices on the percentage of how much labor productivity will increase per hour, the size of the employed labor force, and the average number of hours worked by each member per year.

The authors realize that their judgment is an important element in making such selections. They do not claim that the future will fall within the range of their alternatives. "If we say that something should range between five and ten, we do not mean that it cannot be less than five or greater than ten. We simply mean that we would be willing to make a bet at say two-to-one, or five-to-one, or even 20-to-one odds, as the case may be, that the variable under discussion will, in fact, range between five and ten" (p. 42).

The reader must be careful in his interpretation of alternative futures. First, when high-low values are used, the differences of the projection over 30 or more years can be very great. For instance, using a very long term past base for projecting the United States GNP to the year 2000, the result is $6,750 billion; using a shorter base period, the result is $10,160 billion. The equivalent projections for Japan are $3,100 billion and $8,590 billion (p. 124). Are forecast ranges of this breadth useful?

Second, the reader must not assume that the median is the most likely value to be realized in the future. Third, facing a table giving high, medium, and low projections for a number of countries (p. 183), the reader may be tempted to conclude that whether all countries actually reach the high value or whether all reach the low value does not disturb inter-country relationships very much. This temptation must be resisted since it is quite possible that Country A will reach the low value, Country B the high, Country C a value beyond the high value, etc. Fourth, for reasons already indicated, the expected usefulness of such projections must decline with the length of the future period considered in the forecast. Thus, on Table 21 (p. 183), the values forecast for 1975 are worth more than those projected for 2000, let alone 2020. It is indeed questionable whether such projections beyond at most a 20-year period make any sense.

The results of Kahn-Wiener technology forecasts are similar to those of the Gordon-Helmer forecasts, but greatly exceed the latter in number. Like the Gordon-Helmer forecasts, the Kahn-Wiener forecasts include, simply, all things which are being thought by people *at present* as possible in the future. Kahn and Wiener admit that, as a number of important inventions and innovations came as a surprise in the past (e.g., atomic energy, the computer, radar, and jet propulsion (p. 72)), so it must be expected that their present list does not include some important surprises which the future will bring. They discuss synergism and serendipity as conditions which make many inventions unpredictable (p. 72). Some of the technological surprises undoubtedly will be of major consequence in that they will substantially affect such things as economic capacity and military power. This kind of unpredictability is unavoidable, and, in this respect, one wonders whether our present ability to forecast *technology* is unchanged from what it was in the 1930s.

It is regrettable that Kahn and Wiener do not go further than they do in tracing the implications of major foreseen inventions. They say that they count on these to sustain continued increases in labor productivity (p. 123), but they refrain from speculating how some new technologies (e.g., a really cheap method for deriving fresh water from seawater) could affect the relative economic growth of countries, or their raw materials needs, etc.

In order to make quantitative projections on the international power rankings of states, Kahn and Wiener use "three simple indices—population, gross national product, and GNP per capita" (p. 136). These projections invite four comments. First, the use of GNP data is subject to weighty objections, as was explained above. Second, it is unclear why GNP *per capita* is included. Apparently the authors wished to equate power in part with a nation's "surplus over and above subsistence," but they themselves point out (p. 137) that GNP per capita is a "poor measure of such surpluses." This is indeed true. "Subsistence" is not some sort of biological minimum; rather it is a variable which changes with GNP, urbanization, government policy, and many other things. The degree to which consumption is postponable is, to a considerable extent, a psychological factor. This postponement could be longer in North Vietnam (where the population is used to such calamities as crop failures and floods) than in the United States. In any case, the compressibility of consumption is highly dependent on situational factors (e.g., personal identification with a war emergency, etc.). It cannot therefore be listed and projected as a general—and at any one time invariable—property of a nation.

Third, even if one disregards GNP per capita, the power projections are no better than the projections of population and GNP; that is, they are unlikely to be worth much beyond a relatively short period ahead, and even short term projections suffer from the difficulties of evaluating GNPs comparatively.

Fourth, the power index can, at best, forecast no more than how economic potential can be mobilized for purposes of exerting power. As we pointed out in the introduction, actual power also depends upon the degree and skill of such mobilization. Furthermore, the relevance of economic potential varies with different types of power. And there are now, after all, types of military confrontation which are consummated too rapidly to make *potential* capacity relevant.

Despite the foregoing criticisms, we do not conclude that *The Year 2000* forecasts or the methods used producing them are worthless. It would be easy for a highly critical reader to grant them entertainment value, but nothing beyond that. In fact, studies like *The Year 2000* are valuable because they summarize conveniently, and interrelate interestingly, a great deal of current knowledge and expectation. In other words, they are informative about the bases from which we all start moving into the future. Moreover, such studies are helpful to policy planning in that they stretch the mind about the range of things that may be possible. As Kahn and Wiener point out, their work provides "a framework for speculation" (p. 31). We certainly agree that such long term conjecturing is "not entirely useless" (p. 13), and that in order to explore any predictions, one must make them up (p. 8).

But we must never forget that surprising things are bound to happen, and that if they do, many speculations may prove wrong. Beyond this, particular projections will vary in relative credibility. Credibility will tend to be higher for short term projections and for the projections of phenomena which can be expected to change slowly. Lower credibility can be expected for long term forecasts and more mercurial phenomena. Finally, one's own judgment about the Kahn-Wiener judgment—another variable no doubt—will affect the credibility of any of their forecasts.

2. SIMULATION: FORRESTER AND MEADOWS—THE LIMITS TO GROWTH

The Limits to Growth[2] is the report to the Club of Rome which aroused worldwide attention. It deserves some analysis here because it is an ambitious computerized effort at forecasting complex phenomena, and may well be a forerunner of many similar attempts in the future. It may be regarded as a prototype of distinct forecasting techniques.

The Limits to Growth (LTG) Model

The LTG model focuses on a family of five interdependent growth phenomena: population, industrial output, food production, depletion of non-renewable resources, and pollution of the environment. It projects their trends, as observable in recent decades, into the future on a globally aggregated basis, the time frame being from 1900 to 2100. All five quantities are presented as having grown and as still growing exponentially—that is, as increasing by a constant percentage. Such nonlinear growth leads to ever shorter periods of time within which the quantity will double.

Based on a prototype of "Systems Dynamics" developed earlier by Professor Jay W. Forrester at MIT, the model incorporates interaction among the five variables. Cross impacts are at the heart of the model. How does a change in one factor impinge on another? The model is essentially a complex system of interlocking feedback loops, both positive and negative. The conclusion is that a continuation of current trends will lead inevitably to catastrophic malfunctioning within the next 100 years since the system has a built-in tendency to "overshoot" and bring about "collapse" (p. 130). Indeed the chart which depicts and projects the "standard world"—in which all five variables continue to grow exponentially—suggests that growth would come to an end in 40 years or so. Diminution of natural resources will force industrial production to drop steeply, followed with some delay by similar declines in food output, population, and pollution (p. 129). Several modifications of the standard world produce similarly catastrophic results with different initiating agents. Thus, if world reserves of natural resources are doubled, their depletion and the consequent fall in industrial output will occur two decades later than in the standard world, but pollution will rise to an extent directly causing population and food production to decrease (p. 133). Indeed, pollution will cause population, food, and industrial output to fall precipitately even if natural nonrenewable resources are assumed to be unlimited. If this assumption is retained, and a high level of pollution control is also postulated, food output per capita and (with a time lag) industrial output will decline and make the system collapse. And so on.

To illustrate how growth in any one area appears inexorably to push growth in other areas, one might take the Green Revolution recently introduced in India and elsewhere. This "revolution" in agricultural technology comprises newly developed strains of wheat and rice, irrigation, and the heavy use of fertilizer. Grain yields per acre are multiplied. But expanding food supplies in India are apt to raise population growth by inducing a fall in mortality rates; the use of fertilizer, herbicides, and pesticides pollutes streams and, eventually, the ocean; the additional production of fertilizer raises industrial output which, in turn, adds to the depletion of mineral resources and to environmental pollution, as do the transportation of fertilizer, etc. Thus the feedback loops operate. And in the LTG model they require quantification.

The authors offer a stable equilibrium model that requires world population to be stabilized in 1975, industrial output stabilized in 1990, resource depletion cut to one-fourth of its 1970 value, and pollution generation per unit of industrial and agricultural output reduced likewise one-fourth of their 1970 levels. In this case the stoppage of growth would come about by deliberate human action. But such an equilibrated state of affairs would be impossible, the authors say, if these restrictive measures are delayed until the year 2000 (pp. 187-193).

The authors of LTG do not claim that their model permits "exact" predictions. They admit that it is imperfect, oversimplified, and unfinished (p. 26). But they do claim that it shows the behavioral tendencies of the variables represented in their system (pp. 130-131).

Critique

The LTG model consists essentially of a large set of mathematical equations expressing causal links which are fed into a computer. Projections into the future are simply the implications of the assumptions on which the equations rest. The value of extrapolation is determined completely by the validity of the assumptions. They drive the results mechanically. Their validity, in turn, depends on the adequacy of the causal model and, second, on the empirical data to which the model is applied. The adequacy of the causal model is, again, governed by two considerations. One is available knowledge of how the included variables interact—e.g., just how do changes in food supply per capita or in pollution affect the size of population over time? Or how do increases in agricultural and industrial output affect pollution? The other condition relates to the presence of all variable factors that significantly affect the interacting behavior of the other variables.

How does the LTG model measure up in these respects? With the information which the LTG authors have published so far, we are unable to tell how careful they have been in the use of statistical data, and in the art of curve fitting. It is generally known, however, that quantitative global data on things like industrial and agricultural production and on pollution are very crude, and also are presumably deficient in comparability over such time periods as from 1900 to the present. How true are the curves that are being projected?

The authors also have not yet released the technical analysis that led them to formulate their equations. All they say in the present publication is that they used the "best current knowledge" (p. 27) and chose the most "plausible" assumptions. However, unless they had access to superior private knowledge, and were independent of the knowledge in the public domain, the numbers they picked for feedback among their selected variables must reflect a very high and disturbing degree of guesswork and judgment. This is necessarily so since the present state of knowledge about these relationships is, generally speaking, very primitive. About the matters in question, when knowledge is primitive, it cannot be quantified. In the absence of the technical details which the authors settled on, we are unable to "test" their judgment against ours in terms of plausibility. Nevertheless, the low state of knowledge referred to makes the model inescapably *more or less* defective. Whether this defect, on top of the crudity of statistical materials, is critical in terms of grossly distorting the overall behavior of the LTG model, we simply cannot know.

However, even if we assume that *these* defects do not produce gross distortion, the results are additionally sensitive to the question of whether or not all important variables have been included in the model. The authors have deliberately (and wisely) excluded the intervention of "unique" but powerful events such as large scale nuclear war. But what about excluded variables which are unexceptional and yet known to affect significantly the behavior of the quantities on which the model is focused? Similar questions arise, of course, with other forecasts along similar lines.

Many economists[3] among the critics of the LTG model have castigated it for leaving prices and technology out of the causal model. They have asserted that the absence of these variables makes nonsense of the model. Kaysen, for example, observes that resources must be measured in economic, and not in physical, terms.

We also believe that this criticism touches on the central problem of the LTG model. It is not true, however, as some critics have alleged, that the LTG authors failed to consider prices and technology altogether. The book hints repeatedly at speculations about price changes and their effects as among the considerations on which the quantification of certain feedback loops were based—for instance, regarding the effect of diminishing raw materials supplies on industrial production (p. 68).

Furthermore, the authors do allow for certain crucial effects of price changes without making price an organic part of the model. Some economists have berated the authors for disregarding or underplaying the power of price changes to stimulate the discovery of additional supplies of nonrenewable resources or the recycling of such materials. Yet the authors demonstrate repeatedly that such effects cause only slight delays in the disequilibrating overall behavior of their model.

Thus, in the deviations from the standard world, they make such assumptions as a doubling of presently known reserves of nonrenewable resources, or of no limits to these resources at all; and yet disaster will strike, with pollution acting as the precipitating agent. Similarly, the book makes it clear that technological considerations were involved in the design and quantification of many feedback loops. Nevertheless, it is this impingement of changes in prices and technology and (to add one more important condition) of government regulation which is worth exploring further in order to evaluate the feasibility and worth of the type of forecasting represented by the LTG model.

Responses to Exponential Growth
On pp. 61ff., the authors of LTG give an interesting illustration concerning the limited supply of nonrenewable resources. They put the world's known resources of chromium at 775 million metric tons and infer that, with world consumption rising at 2.6 per cent a year, this resource would be depleted in 95 years. Assuming that reserves yet undiscovered could expand known reserves by a factor of five, chrome availability would be extended from 95 to 154 years. Assuming further that it became possible from now on to recycle 100 per cent of the chromium used, the volume of demand would come to exceed the volume of supply only in 235 years.

We need not concern ourselves with the particular numbers in this example of a material that is not among the scarcest. One thing we are told is obvious. The earth is finite, and the consumption of any finite matter, if not fully recyclable, will *eventually* lead to the exhaustion of its supply. Exponential growth of consumption only does it faster. This is the well known Malthusian paradigm. Nobody cares about what will happen eventually if the critical point may be thousands of years or more ahead; what scared people about the LTG model is its built-in exponential growth and the assertion that we are in the upper ranges of the exponential curves. Everybody knows that exponential growth is eventually impossible in a finite system. In the end, exponential growth proceeds at extreme speed and collapse occurs like an explosion. If we stay on the curves, we are told, collapse is not only certain but is less than 100 or 50 years away. Collapse now appears imminent!

But *will* we stay on the curves? This is the crucial question. Mankind does, after all, possess remarkable capabilities for problem solving. There are basically three distinct mechanisms for getting off the curves, or at least, to begin with, off their steeply ascending range: (1) the price mechanism, (2) the mechanism of technical innovation, and (3) the mechanism of public government.

To take the price mechanism first, it is well known that increasing scarcity generates rising prices and that these, in turn, tend to produce an increased volume of supply and a diminished volume of demand. Both modes represent corrective adjustments to increasing scarcity. Returning to the example of chromium, the LTG authors were evidently aware that rising chrome prices will lead to efforts at discovering more reserves and at recovering and recycling chromium already used. One response which, surprisingly, they did not mention is that a higher price of the material brought about by the costs of discovering and recycling may cause the demand for the material to decline. As a result, its consumption will then no longer grow exponentially or even linearly. We may get off that curve entirely.

There are, however, further and worrisome problems of which the authors of LTG may have been fully aware, and which may have caused them to dismiss this part of the adjustment process. Even if the amount of chromium used per unit of industrial output declines with rising prices, simultaneous increases in population and industrial output will swamp this effect inasmuch as these increases are likewise proceeding with exponential speed. Yet such swamping cannot be taken for granted. We have not had much experience with exponentially rising prices.

The other complicating problem is that a price-induced decline in the demand for chromium may happen *in part* because it has become cheaper to substitute for this material some other nonrenewable resource whose consumption rate rises acceleratingly as a result. We would then be getting off one exponential curve by getting onto the higher reaches of another until the problem of imminent collapse reappears. So let us assume that chromium stands for *all* nonrenewable resources. Now we can no longer get off one exponential curve by getting onto another. Let us assume, moreover, that all possible relief from technological advance has been exhausted, so that we can no longer postpone collapse by getting on a less steep portion of the exponential curve and start over again. In that event, why will rising prices not simply, though gradually, lead to switches of consumption toward a mix of products that minimizes the consumption of nonrenewable resources to a degree which is in or near equilibrium with a finite and perhaps very slowly diminishing supply? In that case, collapse will be hundreds or thousands of years away because mankind has gradually gotten off the exponential curve.

The posited rate of consumption of nonrenewable resources may or may not require the production of industrial goods to cease expanding or to decline in some measure. Whether or not this would be so would depend upon the ability of technology to permit the reduction of such materials in producing industrial goods by lowering material components or using more renewable or reusable materials. And if it happened, economic growth still need not come to a halt since consumption patterns might favor increasingly a mix of goods and services which minimizes the use of nonrenewable resources.

In Chapters 5 and 7 and in the Appendix we present empirical findings on the considerable price and income elasticities of economic sectors (communications). There is, however, the special problem of energy derived from fossil fuel—that is, from increasingly scarce nonrenewable resources. All other materials from such resources are taken from nature for purposes of production and then returned to it after more or less delay, some of it in forms permitting recovery and reuse, the rest in highly dispersed forms, as in pollution. In contrast, fossil fuel is converted into heat, all of which is eventually dissipated in the atmosphere and outer space, and irrecoverable. Here lurks a truly Malthusian problem! The production of most goods and services requires inanimate energy. Even if technology advanced to permit such production to become less energy-intensive, there are presumably severe limits to this adjustment if labor productivity is to be maintained at a high level.

However, this problem pertains solely to fossil fuel; it is not true of the (negligible) hydroelectric power. Moreover, it looks as if technology would permit methods of energy production that do not depend on fossil fuel. There is, specifically, nuclear energy derived from breeder reactors or from fusion processes. And there is the possibility of exploiting solar energy, of which an inexhaustible supply seems to be available. In conclusion, even in the case of energy, mankind is not condemned to stay on the exponential growth curve until disaster strikes.

It seems that the LTG feedback system works so crudely and dramatically (just as it is designed) because it disregards the free market price system, which is a very finely calibrated feedback mechanism. Fine calibration means that relatively small changes can touch off powerful equilibrating responses. This is so because the price system is a highly differentiated feedback system (much more complex than that in the LTG model), because it quickly aggregates a great many interdependent changes and reactions, because it produces usually very clear signals, and because man is highly attuned to these signals. (The LTG model may be more faithful in representing population growth and environmental decay where the price mechanism may not operate immediately.)

Technological advance is one—but only one—way in which the price mechanism generates adjustment to a situation of increasing scarcity. Yet while technological progress has some remarkable sensitivity to price stimuli (although usually leading to a slow response, say five to fifteen years), it is of course governed by other factors as well, such as autonomous advances in scientific knowledge, nonmarket support coming from public grants for R & D, and the entrepreneurial motivation that underlies innovation.

In Chapter 7 and the Appendix, the enormous—albeit medium to long term—impact of research and development on production functions of economic sectors is analyzed, and empirically demonstrated in the case of the U.S. communications sector. The results are surprising and important. In any event, technological innovation is not produced as dependably and quickly as are other responses on the demand and supply sides. Nor are they, like the other effects of price changes, in some sort of proportion to the size of the stimulus.

Thus, technological advance could be insufficient to correct a growing disequilibrium. But it could be also much more than sufficient, and this has been the general experience over the last 100 years or so. Nor is it a necessarily exhaustible response, as are other compensatory responses to rising prices. At any given state of the technological art, these other responses will gradually exhaust themselves. This would happen, for example, if agricultural technology were constant. Responses on the supply side would peter out once all arable land had been put into production and this technology had been applied everywhere.

But there is no such limit to the improvement of technology. (This is not to say that technology does not have, at any one time, limits of its own such as the state of scientific knowledge.) In any case, the technological contribution to mankind's ability to get off the steep end of exponential curves is less predictable than are these other corrective responses to changing scarcity. It is determined by a number of variable factors whose interrelationship is not well understood. In fact, there is an ad hoc factor about much technological progress; and this defies generalization which is a prerequisite of model building.

Government action—the other mechanism for adjustment—is, of course, the only mechanism where free markets do not exist. But even where they do prevail, governments intervene for various reasons and use the price mechanism to effect certain incentives and disincentives. However, in order to cope with problems of scarcity—including unpolluted air and water—governments can resort to a large battery of measures, such as taxation, rationing, regulations, trade policy, support of R & D, education, etc.

The government mechanism can either replace or supplement the price mechanism. Yet exclusive reliance on the one or other is apt to prove unsatisfactory on efficiency as well as social grounds. Thus it seems unacceptable to employ the price mechanism for controlling population growth. In the face of scarcity, prices ration by the purse and thus in a manner likely to conflict with other social objectives. This is one reason why free prices are usually suspended in time of war when extreme scarcities can emerge very suddenly, and all the adjustment must occur on the demand side for reasons of supply rigidity.

The problem of externalities is another major defect of sole reliance on the free price mechanism. For example, industrial pollution is a social cost of production which does not enter private cost or market prices. Or, from our point of view, getting on any exponential growth curve (or on its steep range) and thus posing the need for very rapid and extreme adaptation, could also be looked at as a negative externality. A depletion tax on nonrenewable resources might lengthen the time available for adjustment, and could finance relevant scientific and technological research.

However, reliance on government measures also has severe drawbacks. As the history of centrally controlled economies shows abundantly, it is impossible for a government bureaucracy to fix a system of prices as internally consistent, as finely calibrated, and as flexible over time as a system of free market prices normally operates. Price errors and inertia are common characteristics of state-run economies. In coping with increasing scarcities of great economic consequence, moreover, reliance on government has two other weighty defects. One relates to the fact that there still is for most commodities something resembling a global market, even if there are local modifications. Since our problem is a global one, the price mechanism is therefore congruent with the problem, at least in principle. The problem of adaptation would be compartmentalized in the case of reliance on the action of national governments. As a result, not only would some efficient national system suffer from the inefficiencies of others, there would also be the strong temptation to transfer the burdens of adaptation as much as possible on other societies. Though this would be a beggar-my-neighbor policy, making all societies *together* worse off, there could nevertheless appear to be at least temporary gains for some national systems. At best, there would be free riders.

The only alternative to this dilemma would be widespread acceptance that the problem is one of providing a global public good either by highly coordinated national action or by something approaching world government in the functional areas concerned. Unhappily, this alternative may not be feasible politically before the problem has reached severe crisis proportions. Naturally, coordinated government action is the only instrument concerning population growth and pollution, since these problems are completely outside the market system.

The other defect of sole reliance on government is that it would almost certainly act only with costly delay and hence prohibit a smooth process of adjustment. This probability arises from the fact that government action is necessarily political. Governments can act only to the extent that elites and publics are supportive. Now the actions in question clearly involve trade-offs between current and future benefits, of making sacrifices (as consumers, taxpayers, producers, etc.) before they are absolutely necessary. Given the usual time horizon of publics and even elites, this fact militates against the possibility of getting off the exponential curve gracefully—that is, before it becomes very steep. Finally, adaptation by means of public action typically lacks fine attunement and is also, of course, subject to the well known dance of stupidity.

The Necessarily Incomplete Model
We have gone into these details in order to indicate why, we assume, the authors of the LTG model did not include the crucial variables of adaptive

changes in prices, technology, and public policy. They are crucial because they constitute the means of adjustment to the problems posed by LTG. But the LTG authors might well have felt daunted. How could they—or we—predict, or design the model for predicting, changes in these variables even approximately on a national or global scale? The operational world involved is incredibly complex. This is obvious in political and bureaucratic processes. Just how would we formulate and quantify the feedback between sharply rising fuel prices and various possible government actions? Or the feedback from the action of one government to that of another?[4]

But let us take the relationships among increasing scarcities of nonrenewable resources, prices, and technological advance. The major problem is that history tells us very little about these relationships when prices mount explosively, as they presumably would, in the absence of government intervention, once we get on the steep incline of exponential curves. The fact is that historical trends have so far operated to preclude such empirical experience. Despite earlier Malthusian scares, and despite the specter of the *eventual* depletion of finite quantities of minerals and arable land, world raw materials and food prices as a whole have been falling over recent decades, rather than rising relative to other prices, and this has been associated with declining labor inputs in agriculture and mining. Corrective adjustments, in other words, have been working extremely well so far via the opening up or improvement of arable land, the discovery of new mineral deposits, the technology of working poor ores, recycling, and (to some extent) substitution of one material for another.

This raises, especially to many economists, the question of why the future should be different, at least for a long time to come. Take the matter of technological advance. Despite the record of the past, the LTG authors assume that technology will not improve fast enough to prevent disastrous collapse. They believe that the limits to growth have been pushed back in the past by a series of "spectacular technological advances" and that this good fortune has led to the "technological optimism" which is currently fashionable (p. 129).

The economist critics of the LTG model accuse its authors of technological *pessimism*. How can we tell who is right? It is, of course, easy to point to past technological breakthroughs that came as true surprises, and were hence unpredictable, and that changed scarcity situations drastically (although rarely leading to overabundance). There was a time when nobody thought of petroleum—let alone uranium—as a source of fuel, or could imagine the present productivity of arable land. And so it is not demonstrably absurd for optimists to expect the feasibility of expanding population and gross national products for a long, if indefinite, future.

But neither can the authors of LTG be demonstrated to be certainly wrong. Perhaps we have been living recently in a brief golden age, which in retrospect will look like a fool's paradise. Global population growth is continuing unabated, and so is world industrialization. On the other hand, the recent spurt in agricultural productivity has been bought at the price of increasing environmental pollution. Recent and future measures to check the deterioration of the natural environment may prove too late and insufficient to prevent a dramatic deterioration of the environment, and certainly of the quality of life. The sharply increasing consumption of nonrenewable resources will in some cases lead to depletion sooner rather than later. Will the new exotic technologies already under development, or other technologies not as yet dreamed of, come soon enough for practical application to prevent a world energy crisis?

In conclusion, equally expert participants in these controversies are operating far beyond firm, tested knowledge—i.e., precisely the kind of knowledge which is needed to mathematicize a growth model. If they all designed models of the LTG type, they would structure them differently and come to different results. And nobody could be sure which one or ones, if any, will prove right! The standard world of the LTG model, and its variations, must be regarded as *possible* futures; but no more. That makes it of no more than slight utility as a forecasting tool. It is of some utility, because we cannot confidently rule out that the future will resemble its forecasts. And even more, as Carl Kaysen[5] observed, it may prove useful because it may alarm us and quicken adaptive responses which, for the reasons indicated above (especially regarding government action) may come too tardily to permit reasonably smooth adjustments.

One further point is worth making, for it elucidates further the intrinsic difficulty of model construction about complex and moving realities. The LTG model is said to be dynamic, which is what Forrester called his prototype. But is it really, despite all the feedback loops incorporated in it? When the authors extrapolate their current trends appreciably into the future, they assume that the quantitative values for their feedback loops continue to be valid. But this is doubtful and apt to be quite misleading. This is so because trends of other phenomena not now regarded as significant enough in interacting with the key variables may come to affect the relationships of the latter significantly. Indeed, even factors not perceived to do so now may come to have such effect. There is therefore a considerable probability that the cross impact of these variables will not remain constant, and these changes will necessarily impinge on the behavior of the model. In other words, the LTG model *looks* dynamic, but it is so only in a limited way; in some respects it is actually static.

This defect is not, of course, one that can be removed, for we do not know what excluded variables will intervene significantly at what time to alter the interaction of the selected factors. This dilemma, however, does underline the excessively ambitious nature of the model, and of others which may imitate it in the future. When we go beyond what we know, neither sophistication of method nor the use of computers can compensate for this fundamental defect. We regard this as a most important conclusion.

Needless to emphasize, it would be foolhardy to construct models of the LTG type for forecasting political outcomes, as for instance the probability of a major war. In much of natural science (e.g., physics), there are *unchanging and measurable* relationships between phenomena (i.e., *quantities* of things). As we have seen, such constancy of numerical relationships does not exist in the social sciences. In economics, for example, such things as the marginal propensity to consume or to import, or the elasticity of demand for goods and services, change over short periods of time—in part because they are subject to human manipulation. But at least, when dealing with some of the variables in the LTG model, there are relevant statistical series, and there is a substantial amount of useful theory about problems of scarcity developed by economists.

If, nevertheless, this is too flimsy a basis to permit worthwhile forecasting models of the LTG type to be constructed, any such prospect is much more remote regarding political matters. How could we know which the indispensable variables are, and how they interact over historical time? And how could we express these interactive patterns in numbers? Finally, if we want to explain *particular* patterns or series of events in the political world, and especially in the world of high politics, we are apt to find their explanation to be remarkably ad hoc-ish, and what is general in them to be trivial. If this is so, how can it be otherwise when we want to predict particular series of events?

3. TIME SERIES ANALYSIS

Forming long time series is especially useful when one tries to forecast on the basis of past information. These are readings of events usually observed at regular intervals; they are, therefore, more than the mere enumeration of events, as for example when wars occurred at irregular intervals. Furthermore, the events must be amenable to some sort of quantification, however modest. It is natural that various predictors examined in this study rely heavily on time series.

There exists a vast amount of literature on the analysis of time series and the matter has become so complex that only a brief summary of the present state and how it affects our present inquiry can be given here. The literature has turned highly mathematical because of the extraordinary complexities which time series may show.[6] On the one hand, visual inspection may appear to reveal trends and cyclical regularities which upon closer analysis are nonexistent, or mere surface phenomena. On the other hand, series that seem to show nothing but random fluctuations are in fact the results of very definite big and small regularities intertwined in a complicated manner.

The potential fallacies in interpreting time series are best illustrated by series of stock market prices. There, analysts find many seeming regularities, such as major and minor cycles, which do not stand up under the scrutiny of such modern methods as spectral analysis. The result is that it has been shown conclusively that these supposed cycles are nonexistent, that prices follow a "random walk," sometimes embedded in various irregular long term trends.[7] In other words, they are totally irregular.

There is great suspicion that many activities are random to various degrees, and that many presumed and "apparent" regularities do not exist. Forecasting is, under such circumstances, definitely very restricted. At any rate, it is essential to arrive at an understanding of the mechanism which generates the numbers collected in time series.

An excellent illustration of immediate relevance for our purpose is offered by population figures. Population growth is well understood in terms of such variables as number of persons alive, by sex, age, life expectancy, childbearing age, marital status, and net reproduction rates. Although many refinements of concepts have been made over the last decades, most basic notions were well established in the 1930s. Yet it was precisely then that some of the most reputable researchers in the field predicted changes in the United States population that have since turned out to be totally wrong. It was later shown that their methods were faulty and that they were influenced by the pessimistic mood of the Great Depression.

Most projections depend on some subjective factor—as indeed all that is said in this report is dependent on the authors' individual outlook and experience, and will be appraised by readers who in turn have their own perspective. Even the wholly objective, quantitative, mathematical spectral analysis is a transformation of data that have to be *chosen* as inputs and *interpreted* as output. Subjectivity enters at both points. It may be the choice of the base from which measurements start, or the interval over which averages are struck, etc. Elsewhere (pp. 34ff.), the consequences of different choices were described showing the sometimes vast differences in results.

Population projections have an underlying structure that has become largely transparent. Projected future population figures rest on a very different, much firmer basis than any other *set* of figures produced by the writers examined here—and still there have been monstrous mistakes in projections. Even though we have learned much in the last 40 years, there is a possibility that these mistakes will be repeated. It is even more likely that mistakes will occur in other areas where we have had no similar experience.

In the literature examined for this study we find no awareness, or at least no explicit statements, of these far-reaching limitations. Of course, few time series are used, except by Fucks (see above). This is partly due to the difficulty of assembling relevant material in this form. Yet far more could have been done. This would have led to the construction of models, i.e., of interrelating of the data, which was done in the Forrester-Meadows model. The difficulties encountered in more such efforts would have shown clearly the limitations of the entire enterprise. They might even have shown that it is not possible to make logically consistent models. Logical consistency is the primary requirement for any successful effort in time series—as it is for any model construction whatsoever.

We should list the following pitfalls in time series analysis—other than the assumption of firm trends, expressible by suitable mathematical formulas.

1. In *aggregation series* there is usually a great change in composition, nowhere as important as in GNP. This applies to a country when there is a great deal of technological progress. For example, the 1935 GNP for the United States did not include any of the following products: electronics, TV, computers, nuclear reactors, or jet engines; and no skills and professions corresponding to this partial list of new products. From 1935 to the present is approximately the same length of time as from now until the year 2000, for which many projections are made. Some projections even go beyond that time. Once considered, this remark is indeed trivial; but it is also fundamental and therefore brought up here.

2. In *individual series*, where there may be little trouble of homogeneity (such as in certain raw materials), there still are grave questions. One example is the substitution of plastics for metals. In these cases the position of these materials *relative* to others has changed profoundly; i.e., the development of the series cannot be interpreted properly by study of the series alone. This means that one would have to fall back on a model which interrelates different activities, as will be described below. This, then, gives more reason for exercising extreme caution even when there is no apparent immediate objection.

4. THE "PROSPECTIVE" MOVEMENT: GASTON BERGER

The various efforts and techniques for studying the future we have examined so far are concerned with predictions of technical, economic, and political events. They move, therefore, practically in the same plane, though possibly in different directions. More or less in passing, we observed that the predictions made would themselves have an influence upon the world as expected. This would be the consequence of the conscious absorption of the expected states of our future into our plans, primarily into the plans of governments.

Different nations will make different projections for themselves, for others, and their interplay, thus resulting in projections for the world at large. Even if they had the same method—which they do not possess since this field is in a state of flux—there would be, even with the same data inputs, widely different interests. These in turn would set into motion policies for the future deemed by them necessary and useful. Out of this amalgam, quite different results will emerge than the individual forecasts predict. There is no escape from it: what we expect the future to be, becomes a vital input for our behavior. If we like what we expect, we want to hurry up its arrival and make sure that it happens. If we do not like our prospects, we want to modify the future as far as possible in order to mold it to our benefit. What is true for individuals is also true for nations. The individual seldom has decisive influence on his future, though plan he must. The complex interaction of many at any rate makes it certain that individual plans come true only rarely as projected.

Nations have more power over the future. Their influence will of course differ according to their size and structure as well as to their awareness of possible and probable future developments. We show elsewhere that there are tendencies so strong that individual nations are unable to counteract them singly without profoundly changing their life styles and aspirations. That, however, is seldom even considered and more rarely acceptable, since mostly it would mean upsetting political and ideological traditions. If that is the case, then underlying tendencies such as increasing raw material shortages and new political power distributions throughout the world will develop with increasing speed and momentum.

The political consequences are hard to assess. It would take a de Tocqueville or some prophet to outline the future. Many predictions are being made by many students of these matters; it is conceivable that one of them will be right. He will then be hailed as having had the right insight and understanding; yet it may have been merely a matter of chance, as so often happens. But perhaps de Tocqueville did have a rare insight when he wrote, regarding the Americans and the Russians: "Their starting point is different and their ways are not the same; nevertheless each nation seems to be destined one day to hold in its hand half of the world." There may be men of his stature and wisdom writing today but they are hard to identify.

The question is whether this type of qualitative prognosis can be deliberately developed; otherwise we will have to wait for men of such exceptional gifts to appear as accidents of nature—and, if they did appear, still run the risk of not listening to them.

This is, essentially, what the French "Prospective Movement" attempts to do. It was initiated after World War II by the philosopher Gaston Berger from numerous writings on the basis of which a loosely organized group formed itself. Among its most prominent members was Pierre Massé, then director of the various "plans" on the basis of which French economic policy was set.[8]

As an example we mention that in 1963 the French Prime Minister set up a committee "to study, in the light of future-bearing facts, all that might be useful to know now of the French nation in 1985, in order to throw light on the orientation of the Fifth Plan." This mission involved a projection onto the future to help orient decisions to be taken in the immediate future, 1965 (when the study was completed).[9] Other nations have not yet followed that example.

The essence of Prospective is to make clear that it is not enough to make projections by precedent, analogy and extrapolation which are only possible for a stable world. Living in a rapidly changing world we have, so the argument goes, to form *goals* for the future since they determine our actions. As a rule our goals are based on the knowledge of the present; but new goals are needed, involving projections. The new goals may indeed have to be completely new, and hence, may be extremely unpopular. For the fact is that tomorrow's problems do not exist today, yet they should be anticipated and acted upon now. Some of these problems arise from our present actions, some from chance. It is emphasized that the future is shaped by forces that now are submerged under more visible trends. It is difficult to observe and to assess them before they suddenly break to the surface. At that moment—if it is not already too late—it becomes very difficult to make the desired adjustments; it may even then be difficult to formulate proper goals and to get them accepted.

Prospective is thus primarily concerned with the intellectual and moral impact of the projected future and, thereby, in shaping this same future. This recursiveness is of the essence. Prospective attempts to concentrate our attention on something that must have been felt by anyone who has ever attempted to discern what the future is holding in store.

Prospective raises philosophical issues of great importance; it does not offer a hard and ready method to deal with the questions with which this study is concerned. For that reason we limit ourselves to this brief outline of the underlying thoughts due to Berger. One is tempted to apply to the Prospective Movement its own advice, viz. that the movement is itself one of those submerged forces which shape the future. This then would mean that our thinking about the future will have a greater influence on our present behavior than has been the case so far—whatever the techniques be by which the attempt is made to discover its shape and content. In this sense, Prospective is the frame within which the efforts of others, such as were discussed in the earlier sections, are contained.

CONCLUSIONS

The usefulness of even good forecasts depends, of course, on the normative needs of the consumer. Is a good forecast important to planning operations? A good forecast is one that will spare the consumer surprises of substantial impact for the success of his planning operations, or which will at least minimize such surprises regarding the objects of forecasting under consideration. But are there good forecasts in this sense? Unfortunately, we will know if a forecast is good in this respect only after the event.

The value of forecasts depends also on their credibility—that is, on the degree of confidence they inspire in the consumer. Since there are no clearcut criteria for evaluating the quality of forecasts in advance, credibility may, unfortunately, be inspired by factors other than their true (but unknown) quality. For instance, it may result from the reputation or persuasive powers of the forecaster, or from how closely the forecast coincides with what the consumer would like to do as a planner.

The credibility of forecasts should depend on such factors as the conjecturability of different subject matters. Although unique events like particular wars are unpredictable, parts of human behavior, strongly conditioned by attitudes deeply anchored in human personality, change only slowly and lend themselves to more prediction. Of course, many phenomena fall between these examples in terms of conjecturability and must be judged for credibility. As we mentioned earlier, the time element of forecasting is very important and can affect credibility. For most phenomena, short range forecasting is less hazardous than very long range forecasting. The relative rigorousness with which particular forecasting techniques were applied is another guide. Useful as they are, these guides do not take us far in evaluating the quality of forecasts.

Credibility will also rest in large part on the consumer's judgment about the judgment and imagination of the forecasters. Unfortunately, there are no dependable methods for evaluating these qualities in forecasters, or the judgment of consumers.

The economic and technological capability of nations and regions are only moderately conjecturable. Depending on the quality of inputs, forecasting these capabilities by means of trend extrapolation, with appropriate sets of alternative projections, should be useful for relatively short periods of time. Ten years would seem to be a reasonable limit. Similarly, the forecast of future technology should be of modest usefulness provided the time frame is not extended beyond fifteen or, at most twenty years. And even then the possibility that surprising events (e.g., political and military) will intervene disturbingly must never be ignored.

Thus, since there is an inverse relationship between the length of the forecasting period and the quality of the forecasts, the forecasting period should be kept to a minimum in planning operations. We cannot imagine that there are many important planning purposes of a specific character which call for a longer period than ten years, and we suspect that a shorter period is sufficient for most purposes. Since even these medium range forecasts can be upset by surprising developments, it is important that they be reviewed automatically every year, and immediately if an important upsetting event occurs. This is an adaptation to "dynamic programming."

In both areas the employment of available forecasting techniques, though helpful, should not be regarded as establishing the credibility of conjectures.[10] For forecasting the economic and technological capacity of nations and regions, trend extrapolation is certainly indispensable, but its application rests crucially on the choice of the base period, identification and evaluation of emergent trends, and consideration of alternative futures. All these choices are hazardous, and technical razzle-dazzle does not make them less so.

We again urge extreme caution in the use of forecasts of the overall technological capacity of states and regions. The quantitative indicators available measure reality in a very rough fashion at best. If value aggregates such as GNP are used as indicators, there are intractable technical difficulties in international and intertemporal comparison, especially for countries such as China. And, to repeat, political changes *must* be regarded as a source of disturbance radiating to economic matters as well. Finally, for reasons spelled out in the Introduction, it is hazardous to forecast military power by the technological or economic capacity of states, for very substantial international technological differences can be lessened if the inferior state is large in population and politically determined to allocate technological resources to the imitation and importation of foreign technology.

In considering future technology, some variation of the Delphi technique is of very modest value, but not indispensable. Delphi is of some interest because it provides an extensive range of expertise and some sort of feedback. These can be provided in other ways. Intuitive imagination of knowledgeable people is clearly most critical to the results.

In reviewing the Kahn-Wiener work, we questioned whether it is now more or less difficult to forecast the content of future technology than it was 30 or 40 years ago. Although forecasts made then were upset by highly surprising and very consequential inventions and innovations, perhaps the general quickening in the pace of change makes today's forecasting even more difficult. On the other hand, it is perhaps easier now than four or more decades ago because the processes of invention and innovation receive much more deliberate planning and ample funding than they used to. To advance technology systematically has become part of the new "knowledge industry."

It seems to us that both factors (and probably several others) affect the conjecturability of future technology. We offer a tentative hypothesis. The fact that so much scientific and technological advance has now become part of a systematic effort naturally permits us to do a better job forecasting the *immediate* implications and timing of those inventions we are pursuing *deliberately*. The supply of expertise for forecasting future technology has expanded and is continuing to expand. However, the fact that the pace of scientific and technological progress has accelerated may increase the probability of surprises, as there are more opportunities than ever for serendipity and synergism to turn out unexpected results. This means that intuitive judgment will remain as important as ever in penetrating the border area between the predictable and the unpredictable.

These intrinsic difficulties of evaluation suggest the desirability of soliciting two or more independent forecasts rather than one for any particular job on hand. To be sure, besides checking on the rigorousness with which techniques have been applied, there are no reliable criteria for comparing the quality of separate conjectures. But the more the conjectures differ, the more they remind the consumer of the hazard in using them. Furthermore, and more importantly, they permit him to organize feedback regarding the differences in conjecture.

Despite the inherently low credibility of conjecture in many subjects, one should not conclude that conjectures are worthless. The results of planning are likely to be worse if the planner makes his own implicit of explicit forecasts, for which his resources are apt to be inadequate, as he goes along. The planner could learn at least something from the forecasts of qualified people. At the very least, he should become more sensitive to the uncertainties looming in the future. He may also learn something about the nature of these uncertainties. And this is very important. As Bertrand de Jouvenel remarks, ". . . forecasting would be an absurd enterprise, were it not inevitable."[1,1]

Part III

Discussion

Chapter Five

Technological Capacity Prediction

POWER AND THE FUTURE TECHNOLOGICAL CAPACITY OF STATES AND REGIONS

Before we can properly conceptualize the problem of the future technological, political, and military potential of states and regions, several aspects of the problem need clarification.

Regional as compared to *national* technological capacity is relevant only where the capacities of several states in the same area are subject to military exploitation by a single center of decision making, regardless of whether the central authority rests on the dominance of one state or has confederal or federate character. This is in no way the case at the present time, but it could happen in the future. Thus there is some small chance at present that several West European states will coalesce politically (e.g., the members of the European Economic Community); this sort of merging could also happen elsewhere, even where present indications are largely or wholly lacking.

But since the development of regional combines, as defined, does not look promising now, and also since such a coalescing process takes considerable time to mature once it is initiated, our analysis and any attempts at conjecturing about future technological capacity must be undertaken primarily with reference to individual states—the state being the significant form of political, economic, and military organization. If the possibility of regional combinations emerges in the future, it then becomes useful to apply this larger framework *after* the future of national capabilities has been estimated.

There is also at the present time a strong tendency in the social sciences to perceive the imminent demise of the national state and to foresee its early replacement by international organizations, usually on the global level. These perceptions are usually touched off by the recognition of the increasing interdependence of societies, especially in economic and political matters, and of the growth of transnational relations between various groups which organize or engage themselves across national boundaries (e.g., labor unions, professional organizations, business firms, tourists, etc.).

Two other contemporary experiences are being noted in this connection: first, that national governments often find it difficult to control these transnational interactions, and second, that an increasing number of public tasks cannot be solved wholly or largely by national efforts, demanding international or supranational action for satisfactory performance. The noted facts are all truly observed. But to announce the impending death of the sovereign state is premature, to say the least.

To begin with, social interdependence has been growing even more *within* states than among them, and so has been, especially in democratic societies, the demand for *national* government action regarding an ever expanding range of problems. It is also clear that *nationalism* has only recently begun to penetrate to most extra-European areas. It is rampant in the less developed world, where organized societies are desperately trying to create politically integrated systems. This does not mean that certain public tasks do not require more international cooperation and coordination than has occurred in the past. Yet to speak of the sovereign state as a moribund entity, and of national boundaries as obsolete, is no more than a current fad.

Technological capacity is only one basis of a state's military potential, and the military impact of technological capacity can be fully appreciated only in relation to the other foundations of military power, especially economic capacity, administrative competence, and political commitment to military buildup. Briefly, *economic capacity* consists of a nation's productive resources, which are chiefly the labor force, capital goods, and land (natural resources).[1]

Technological capacity, which we want to single out for this study, is usually regarded as a part of a nation's economic capacity. At any one time, technological capacity exists in a body of knowledge diffused through the labor force. When a state mobilizes resources in order to produce and maintain military forces, it allocates a varying part of its productive resources to what we may call the military sector of society (in the United States in recent decades, the product of the resources so allocated has been estimated at varying from 6 to 10 percent of the GNP).

Administrative competence determines the efficiency with which the resources allocated to the military sector are employed toward producing usable military capabilities. Even though it is often crucially important, this determinant of military strength is frequently ignored. Obviously, if of two states allocating an equal combination of resources to the military sector, the government and military services of one make far better decisions on force structures, equipment, R & D, military strategy, and doctrine than the other, it ends up having correspondingly more military strength. The inputs were the same, but the output was not. Administrative incompetence, moreover, can lead to the production of a mix of forces and weapons which is unsuitable to meeting the particular conflicts in which a state becomes involved. Administrative skill is of central importance especially in the modern world in which military requirements and technological opportunities are subject to rapid change.

Political commitment or *will* determines the proportion of economic (and technological) capacity which is allocated to the military sector. To a considerable extent, the magnitude of allocation is a government response, conditioned by foreign policy goals, to stimuli received from the outside world. But two states possessing roughly the same foreign policy, and experiencing the same external stimulus, may respond differently in the amount of resources allotted to the military sector; and a difference involving a few percent of the GNP a year for five or ten years can obviously make a tremendous difference in the military strength generated.

But even if a state has sizable armed forces, there can be no military power without the will to employ them. In order never to lose sight of this crucial fact—that military forces do not necessarily equal military power—it is best to think of a state's armed forces, military potential, and reputation as putative power which, to become effective, must be actualized in international relationships of threat or war. There are many historical examples which demonstrate the importance of comparative national will, such as Germany's military performance in World War II, or the Israeli performance against the Arab states, or North Vietnam's against South Vietnam and the United States.

The importance of administrative skill and political will in the generation and use of military power raises the question of whether and how these conditions can be considered in forecasting enterprises. Regarding skill one would want to compare national outlays on defense with the value of national military outputs. But this approach is patently blocked by insuperable difficulties. Comparing national defense expenditures in real terms runs into the well known problem of converting amounts expressed in one currency into amounts expressed in another when national price structures exhibit great differences. But what makes this approach completely hopeless is that national defense outputs are heterogeneous in terms of force structures, weapons inventories, labor intensiveness, qualitative properties, and so on. And nobody so far has been able to suggest an alternative approach.

It is relatively easier to cope with the comparative measurement of political determination. The percentage of GNP allocated to the defense sector, and especially changes therein, can be regarded as rough indicators of the will to provide for defense. Figure 5-1 compares recent movements of this indicator for a number of states. There are two difficulties, however. First, this indicator must be used with caution. We have implied that it expressed the will of a society—which can change for many reasons—to be prepared militarily in the event, usually unforeseeable, that a serious crisis develops. But in order to use

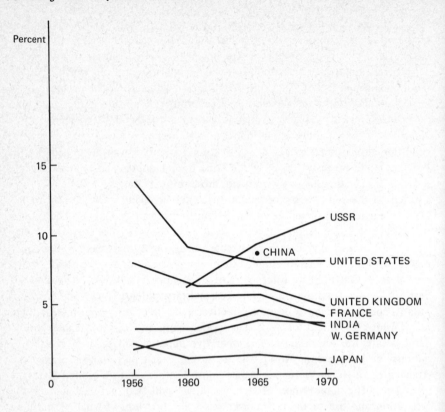

Sources: International Institute for Strategic Studies, *The Military Balance 1971-72*, London: International Institute for Strategic Studies, 1972, United Nations, *Statistical Yearbook*, New York: United Nations 1959 and 1965.
Gross Domestic Product is used for 1956.

Figure 5-1.   Defense Expenditures as a Percent of GNP

the indicator for this purpose, the movement of the data must be studied in a larger context. Four contextual factors are worth singling out.

First, trends in defense expenditures as a percentage of GNP must be checked against comparative movements in GNPs. Thus, on Figure 5-1, Japanese outlays appear declining because Japan's GNP increased so rapidly during the period. As we see in Table 5-1, Japanese defense outlays were actually also

Table 5-1. Defense Expenditure (in $ millions)

	1956	1960	1965	1970
United States	41,513	45,380	51,827	76,507
Soviet Union	29,600	27,000	37,000	53,900
Japan	278	421	848	1,640
France	2,975	3,881	5,125	5,982
West Germany	1,717	2,885	4,979	6,188
United Kingdom (Britain)	4,522	4,640	5,855	5,950

Source: International Institute for Strategic Studies, *The Military Balance 1971-72*, London: 1972 and United Nations, *Statistical Yearbooks*, 1956, 1960, 1965, 1970, New York: United Nations.

increasing, though less than her GNP. (On the other hand, we do not want to rely only on changes in absolute amounts since they may be affected by inflation.)

Second, the defense outlays of a state may level off because it has completed a major program of building military strength, while another state may be in a phase of catching up.

Third, a state's defense effort may decline, relative to that of comparable states, because it has retrenched its foreign policy objectives; for instance, it may have decided that certain allies no longer deserve or need a military commitment. Regarding this factor, it is important to ascertain exactly why the retrenchment of objectives occurred, and especially whether foreign policy retrenchment proceeded or followed a slackening in the defense effort.

Fourth, in interpreting changes in defense outlays, allowance must obviously be made for any critical military conflict in which the states concerned may be involved.

The second major difficulty with the indicator relates to the problems of all quantitative trend analysis. What time period should be selected for ascertaining a trend? Moreover, and much more problematic, on what basis can we assume that any recent trend will continue for long into the future? We are not dealing here with basic structures such as economic and demographic configurations, which usually change only slowly; rather we are dealing with public policy decisions which, as history demonstrates abundantly, *can* change very suddenly.

Of course, if the movements depicted in Figure 5-1 continued for very long, the military power of the Soviet Union would be bound to grow relative to that of the Western European states and the United States (unless the

Soviet government has extremely poor administrative competence compared with the governments of the other states). But we cannot assume that this recent configuration of trends will continue for long. In other words, the indicator of will, which we are examining, must first be checked by contextual analysis, and second, can at best form a basis of only relatively short term forecasts.

Technology affects military potential or strength directly *and* indirectly. Technological advance is directly applicable to military technology, as when a state gains the know-how to produce nuclear bombs. It is indirectly applicable by increasing the efficiency of the productive resources in the economy (and also possibly of the resources accounting for administrative competence).

In the modern world, technology has been more important than natural resources and capital investment in determining output per capita. (It should be noted, however, that the application of technology normally requires capital investment.) If China improved her agricultural technology appreciably, her military potential would tend to expand, since labor could be released from agriculture and employed in building highways, railroads, and factories. Alternatively, China could decrease agricultural imports and increase agricultural exports and thereby be enabled to import more capital equipment from abroad.

While natural resources have become generally overshadowed by technology as a constituent of military potential, they have not ceased to be significant, and this significance tends to rise as vital nonrenewable materials become globally scarce. As we demonstrate in Chapter 6 on the coming world energy squeeze, fuel is likely to become, at least for a few decades, a far more critical factor in military power than it has been historically. In the past, rich and powerful states usually possessed an assured supply of fuel, or had assured access to needed supplies. The new factor is that the rapidly increasing demand for petroleum will exhaust the world's known and probable reserves of this fuel before very long.

It should be noted, however, that this situation of scarcity will be terminated eventually by advancing technology which will supply energy from entirely new sources. Even though the indirect effect of a state's technological growth is indubitably important to its military potential, the focus of the present study requires special attention to the structure of technological capacity and its application in various states and regions.

Regarding capacity, it is instructive to note the history of successive key technologies. One hundred years ago, coal, iron, steel, and the railroads were the chief symbols of advancing technology and military power. They remained so, together with the coal-fired steamship, at the time of World War I. By World War II, the combustion engine in its various uses (automobiles, tanks, aircraft) was the salient symbol. Today nuclear energy and the other highly scientific technologies such as electronics and the laser are at the forefront of civilian and military technological progress. These changes do not mean that iron and steel, let alone the combustion engine, are no longer important bases of military strength. But they are taken for granted and are no longer the key technologies in industrial and military enterprise.

If one is interested in the technological capacity of states as a basis of modern military power, one no longer thinks of steel production alone as the key indicator. Instead, one looks for capacity in the aerospace and electronics industries. For detail, of course, one looks at steel among many other things. But leading symbols of technological capacity in the United States are no longer Pittsburgh and Detroit, but Route 128 around Boston and similar conglomerates on the West Coast.

Deliberately selective application makes for a very uneven technological capacity within many states. For instance, present Soviet technology applied in the consumer goods' industries, construction, agriculture, and even some capital goods industries (e.g., chemicals, computers) is distinctly inferior to that of the United States, Japan, and the highly industrialized West European countries; but on the whole, the Soviet Union is about equal to the United States in outer space and military technology.

To give another example, China has a highly underdeveloped economy by all general indices (e.g., GNP per capita, percentage of the labor force in the primary industries) but she was successful in developing a nuclear and even hydrogen bomb, and apparently has been doing so more quickly than France, which is economically and technologically far more advanced. There are some special historical circumstances (i.e., large scale Soviet aid in the 1950s) which contributed to this astonishing Chinese feat. But the point of both examples is that given the political will and capability, a state may allocate all or most of a very thin technological capacity to the military sector and achieve results far above its general technological and industrial performance—i.e., use the best of scarce scientists and engineers in military technology or, as in the case of China, in a particular area of military technology.

Given strong political commitment, the same selective application of the most efficient resources may take place with reference to administrative competence. The recent Soviet record of administering the general Soviet economy is not at all impressive. In fact, Soviet leaders are desperately casting about for appropriate reforms. We have no direct evidence, but it is conceivable—indeed plausible—that the Soviet government allocated a large share of its ablest administrators to decision making in the military sector; China may have acted on the same priority.

However, there is another reason why these countries achieve higher performance in the military sector than in the civilian sector of their national economies. The way most military economic sectors operate naturally fits a centrally administered economic system, while the achievements of the civilian sector seem to benefit from the decentralized form of decision making characteristic of most capitalist economies. These considerations, incidentally, suggest that the technological capacity of states may be uneven—e.g., appreciably larger—in certain military technologies, than in most fields of production, which may make comparisons of aggregate data misleading. They also show how important political commitment and administrative competence are intervening variables in bringing about such results.

It has been observed that compared with the Soviet Union, the United States has a tendency to *overdesign* military equipment. Overdesign occurs when fancier and more expensive components add only very little to comfort, safety, or other performance—or in more extreme cases, add nothing at all, or even turn out to be counterproductive because of more weight, increased manning requirements, or proneness to disrepair under rough field conditions—not to mention the steep increase in costs. To speak metaphorically, the richer state may use a jeep where two legs would do a better job. Thus some margin of a state's superiority in wealth and technology may be frittered away rather than invested in military superiority. Such overdesign reflects, of course, on administrative competence as well as on the working of pressure groups from industry. It is a waste of technological capacity.

If one is interested in the technological capacity of states from a military standpoint, it must be noted that military capabilities differ in technological content as well as in the level of technology required for their production. The observation has been made that there are three types of contemporary military conflict, symbolized by the submachine gun, the tank, and the ballistic missile. This distinction evidently aims at the differences between "sublimited" war, conventional war, and strategic nuclear war. This symbolization oversimplifies reality. Each kind of war can be fought with weapons of more or less technological sophistication. A technologically superior state may have not only better nuclear missiles but also better tanks and submachine guns than a technologically inferior state; it may therefore be able to use superior kinds of weapons for each type of war. For instance, it may use masses of helicopters in counterinsurgency operations in order to provide mobility in inaccessible terrain. Nevertheless, these three broad kinds of warfare differ appreciably in their technological demands. This means that a technologically inferior state may do well against a technologically superior opponent in a guerrilla type of conflict.

The tremendous differences among the technological capacity of nations may be markedly offset in practice because technologically inferior states can import technology, especially military technology, from technologically superior states. Military technology is presently being exported and imported on a very large scale. Imports primarily consist of purchases abroad of arms, and of licenses for local production. In the majority of cases, the technology of these imports far exceeds that of the importing country. At the present time the world is studded with arms in the possession of states which are unable to produce them. There is considerable evidence that a state importing sophisticated weapons (e.g., aircraft, tanks, missiles) has considerably less skill in using them in battle than do the states which developed and/or produced these weapons. The India-Pakistan war over Kashmir, and the Israeli-Arab war are good examples. Even though exporting countries frequently sell obsolete models abroad, imports of military equipment nevertheless clearly reduce the advantage which technologically superior powers enjoy. The military effectiveness of North Vietnamese troops against American forces in South Vietnam results in considerable part from their being lavishly equipped with Soviet arms.

Japan, Canada, West Germany, Britain, and several other highly industrialized countries in Europe import arms or produce them locally on foreign license partly because their technological capacity is lagging in particular areas, but also because their industrial and technological base is too narrow in terms of capacity to produce all the types of weapons they believe they require. Lack of sufficient scale in resources makes local development either uneconomical or unfeasible. These countries are compelled to be selective in the military systems they will develop themselves.

This point has enormous bearing on the evaluation and forecast of national technological capacity from a military point of view. It makes it clear that what is important is not only the level of technology but also the scale of the technological base; it makes it clear, furthermore, that technological capacity must be evaluated in relation to national *economic* capacity. However, since these countries are able to develop some highly sophisticated weapons themselves (and could do more of this if their political commitment permitted larger R & D expenditures), the nature of their selections—which depend on their administrative competence—may be crucial. The question of which choices they will make in future military technology is a matter of uncertainty beyond that of their future technological capacity in terms of level and scale.

Again, one should not exaggerate the importance of scale, since inferiority in scale may be compensated for (up to a point) by superiority in other conditions, such as superior will. Some small countries—especially Sweden and Israel—have produced an astonishing variety and excellence of military equipment. If the corresponding performances of Britain or France were in proportion to their superiority in population, they would be formidable arms producers indeed. A combination of political will and administrative skill can produce much military strength from a narrow economic base. Nevertheless, scale *is* important, as the present military superiority of the United States and the Soviet Union indicates.

To summarize the significance of the points made so far:

First, the significance of differences in the technological capacity of states can be diminished by the inferior state's (1) being especially adapted to the development of a particular military technology (structure), (2) having the political capacity to allocate an exceptionally large proportion of its technological capacity to the military sector (political commitment or will), (3) making highly efficient choices in weapons development (administrative competence), (4) importing military technology from technologically superior states, and (5) preferring modes of warfare in which general technological superiority has the least impact. Thus the development of national technological capacity must be evaluated in relation to economic capacity, administrative competence, and political commitment—all components of military potential which are difficult to forecast.

  Second, in attempting to forecast the technological capacity of states, a distinction must be made between technological level, technological structure, and technological scale. All of these are obviously affected by the stage of economic development achieved by states. Level and structure are also subject to government policy; and scale is also dependent on the size of the state in terms of population.

PROBLEMS IN PREDICTING THE LEVEL OF TECHNOLOGICAL CAPACITY

If one wishes to consider the future technological development of states, one should want to understand the conditions from which such development results. Unfortunately, knowledge in the social sciences about the *sources* of technological growth and achievement is at this stage rather flimsy. This is made clear by the speculations recently induced by European anxieties about the technological "gap" which has opened up between Europe and the United States. We will briefly examine these speculations for whatever light they shed on why some states are technologically superior to others.

  It is generally assumed that Western Europe is not inferior to the United States in the development of the sciences (although it probably lags in the social sciences, taken as a whole). The question is why the application of new knowledge, in the form of technological innovation, has been lagging in Europe in comparison with the United States. It should be noted, however, that America's superiority is not at all universal, and also that it seems to be declining at this time.[a] Western Europe leads the United States technologically in some fields (e.g., shipbuilding), and is roughly equal to it in automobile production and in several branches of chemistry and metallurgy. But the United States is still appreciably ahead overall, and its lead is especially strong in military technology and in the "new frontier" technologies (computers, other electronics, rockets, etc.). Five major hypotheses have been advanced for explaining the technology "gap."

---

[a]To a considerable extent, this recent decline is to be attributed to a decline in American government expenditures on R & D, while such outlays are rising in Western Europe, Japan, and the Soviet Union.

One thesis is that, on the whole, the American managerial class, public and private, is both more eager to innovate and more skillful in innovation. Innovation is an act essentially different from the production of new knowledge, including invention. The innovator is an entrepreneur who decides to apply new knowledge—whether a new technique, commodity, or service—once it is available. He invests, and risks, capital in the innovating act. Innovation requires risk taking and resourceful management, appropriate attitudes and skills. It has been widely observed that American innovators are more numerous (per 100,000 of population), await opportunities for innovation more eagerly, and are more disposed and free to create these opportunities by investing in R & D, than is generally the case in Europe. Moreover, Americans are perhaps, by and large, better trained (especially at some of the American business schools) in managing innovation (e.g., the study and promotion of markets) than European managers are.

According to a *second thesis,* technological innovation will tend to flourish in proportion to the funds spent on research and development, and to the rewards conferred on scientists, engineers, and managers. The "brain drain" is a response to higher salaries and better research facilities in the United States than in Europe. The critical factor in the flow of funds is the disposition of public authorities. Although R & D privately financed by business firms, foundations, and universities constitutes a large volume in the United States, a larger proportion has come from federal government. The supply of public funds is crucial, not just because of the large share of military R & D, but also because expected private returns on invention and innovation generally fall far short of social returns over the larger sections of the scientific and technological frontier. Under these conditions it does not pay private enterprise to invent or innovate, making public finance necessary if the social benefits are to be achieved. The recent decline in United States government funding of R & D is ominous for this reason.

Third, although demand for new knowledge and innovation is the strategic variable in pushing technological progress, the supply of inputs is another governing condition in the short run. The key resources are educated, trained, achievement oriented personnel, and a growing stock of basic scientific knowledge. Since training and basic research go hand in hand, the most critical item is the level of formal education and the number of trained scientists and engineers. The relevant statistics indicate that the United States is in these respects appreciably superior to all of Western Europe combined.

Fourth, American technological superiority over Europe is largely accounted for by the factor of scale. Many of the newly emerging technologies require a scale of application and a scale of effort, even in their recent stage, which goes beyond the resources that single European countries (not only the smaller ones) can afford. Yet affordable scale will grow where national income expands rapidly, as in Japan and perhaps before too long in China. The Western European countries could overcome their handicap of national scale if they were to manage to integrate their R & D efforts to a far greater extent than they have succeeded in doing thus far. Until now the European community has experienced great difficulties in tackling major technological innovations, as in the "Space Tug" (an additional stage in the United States development of the Space Shuttle). This is in part due to the fact that, in this kind of "community," there are several decision makers with separate interests that sometimes dominate the common goal. The Soviet Union has no such problems; neither has China. The latter country's potential appears especially enormous when one imagines the absolute number of scientists and engineers to reach the same proportion to the total population as it is in the United States at present.

Fifth, large and continuous changes in commercial, occupational, and educational patterns are an inevitable consequence of rapid scientific advance and technological innovation. Innovation will therefore tend to prosper in proportion to the disposition of the public (i.e., managers, workers, consumers, scientists and other professionals, politicians, and public administrators) to accept, if not welcome, change. This kind of social capability will prevail where there exists a deep consensus on the net value of innovation.

It seems plausible that all five hypotheses touch on the causes of the technological gap. Some are independent, and some are closely interrelated. Scale is heavily influenced by size of population and its general stage of economic development—that is, by the per capita size of the GNP. To that extent, the technological gap is simply a "size gap" or a "wealth gap." The social disposition to put up with the unsettling consequences of innovation is a prerequisite (although it may be assumed that the cultural adaptiveness involved is also a consequence of past innovation). The other factors flow primarily from the demand for new knowledge and innovation of their fruit. If this demand is diffuse and strong, talent turns to innovation, managers learn the skills of innovation, and funds will come forth for education, research, and development.

Most of the conditions to which natural technological growth is attributed cannot be directly appraised, much less predicted. This is not an unusual situation in the social sciences. One then looks for indicators which, first, are observable and, second, are closely associated with the phenomenon under study.

Two indicators suggest themselves: (1) national expenditures on R & D in general, and on military R & D in particular; and (2) data on higher education, especially the training of scientists and engineers. Unhappily, both indicators (or sets of indicators) raise problems of definition and sheer data availability. Comparisons of R & D expenditures raise the question of whether national figures are equally inclusive and the nearly intractable problem of differences of price ratios.

For example, if research personnel in some countries (e.g., the United States) earn salaries much larger than in others (e.g., the Soviet Union), are there compensatory differences in research productivity? We do not know. Just how is research productivity to be measured? Furthermore, availability of relevant data is especially restricted in the case of Communist countries. Information on education also raises the question of equivalence. Do numbers of graduate students in physics or engineering from different countries measure the same thing? Finally, there is the central problem of the efficiency with which research funds are allocated and with which scientists and engineers are employed.

In conclusion, there are no feasible indicators that could be used in an attempt to forecast the technological capacity of societies.

PROBLEMS OF PREDICTING SCALE AND STRUCTURE
OF TECHNOLOGICAL CAPACITY: THE UNITED STATES
TELECOMMUNICATIONS SECTOR

Predicting scale is relatively easy. One can simply choose aggregate GNP to indicate scale. A refinement would be to choose part of GNP contributed by manufacturing or service industries, or still more specific components.

On the other hand, the forecast of *structure* seems almost hopeless. Of course we can assume that economic development (as measured by increased GNP per capita) leads to well known structural shifts in national output and hence its productive capacity (i.e., from primary industries to secondary and tertiary industries). But forecasting the structure of national *technological* capacity looks impossible or next to impossible. Over the short term, structural predictions can be derived from the investment plan (and record) of governments and large private enterprises. Over the even shorter term, firmly extended expenditure patterns may also permit reasonably accurate forecasts. For example, persistently large and rising expenditures on the products of defense industries will shape industrial structure accordingly.

However, over any larger run of ten, fifteen, or more years, it becomes very hazardous to predict the factors of supply and demand that shape evolving technological structure. Of course, the forecasting problem in this area is far more difficult for national systems that are operating at the scientific and technological frontiers. Other societies are imitative. To what extent they will follow the leading states is a matter of time, resources and also, of course, of government policy which can accelerate or retard the process of adaptation.

In the following we will illustrate the potentials and problems in medium to long term forecasting, using the U.S. telecommunications sector as an example. The detailed approach in the construction and statistical estimation of dynamic simultaneous equation systems for individual economic sectors is described in Part IV, Suggestions on a Constructive Approach, and the Appendix. Here we use the results for illustrative purposes.

The model was formulated and its parameters estimated in March 1973 by Kan-Hua Young. The specification of the model and the estimation of the parameters are given in Appendix A.

The results presented here include a dynamic simulation of the sample period (1947-70) and several projections into the future (1970-90) designed to test the sensitivity of the projections to some of the relatively uncertain parameter values. Finally, the results of our dynamic simulations are compared with the result of a projection based on a simple extrapolation, which also incorporates a trend factor.

The U.S. telecommunications model evaluated here is a relatively simple thirteen-equation system of simultaneous first order difference equations. The following notation will be used for endogenous and exogenous variables throughout this study. (The sources of data are indicated in the parentheses):

Endogenous Variables

Q_1: Personal consumption expenditures for telephone and telegraph services in thousands of 1958 constant dollars (Tables 2.5 and 8.6 of "National Income and Product Account," July issue of each year, *Survey of Current Business*)[2]

Q_2: Business and government expenditures for telephone and telegraph services in thousands of 1958 constant dollars (Tables 1.21 and 1.22 of "National Income and Product Accounts," op. cit.)

P_1: Price index (1958 = 1.00) of telephone and telegraph services to individual consumers to be deflated by GNP deflator (Tables 8.3 and 8.6 of "National Income and Product Account," op. cit.)

P_2: Price index (1958 = 1.00) of telephone and telegraph services to business and government to be deflated by GNP deflator (Tables 1.22, 2.5, 1.21 and 8.6 of "National Income and Product Accounts," op. cit.)

Q: Total expenditures for telephone and telegraph services, i.e., the sum of Q_1 and Q_2

P: General price index (1958 = 1.00) of telephone and telegraph services, including services to individual consumers and to business and government. (Tables 1.21 and 1.22 of "National Income and Product Account," op. cit.)

R: Total revenue of telephone and telegraph services, in thousands of current dollars, i.e., the product of P and Q, or the sum of $P_1 Q_1$ and $P_2 Q_2$

K: Amount of accumulated capital in thousands of 1958 constant dollars (Table 9, p. 19 of Federal Communications Commission, *Statistics of Communications Common Carriers*, (Year ended December 31, 1970), Washington, D.C.: U.S. Government Printing Office, 1972, to be adjusted upward by ratio of total revenues to be consistent with National Income and Product Account and then deflated)

L: Number of employees in thousands of full time equivalent (Table 9, p. 21, ibid., or Table 6.4 of "National Income and Product Account," op. cit.)

C: Total cost of production of telephone and telegraph services in thousands of current dollars, including employee compensation, net interest, and capital consumption allowance (Table 1.22 of "National Income and Product Account," op. cit.)

Π: Gross profit, including indirect business tax and net profit in thousands of current dollars (ibid.)

I: Gross investment by the telephone and telegraph industry in thousands of 1958 constant dollars

M: New employment by the telephone and telegraph industry in thousands of full time equivalent employees

Exogenous Variables

N: Population of the nation (*Statistical Abstract of the United States: 1972*), Washington, D.C.: U.S. Government Printing Office, 1973.

Y: GNP in millions of 1958 constant dollars (Tables 1.1 and 1.2 of "National Income and Product Account," op. cit.)

P_y: GNP deflator (1958 = 1.00)

r: Price of capital stock computed by dividing the sum of net interest and capital consumption allowance by the amount of capital stock (Table 1.22 of "National Income and Product Account," op. cit.)

w: Wage rate of employee in the telephone and telegraph industry computed by dividing employee compensation by number of employees (ibid.)

D: Expenditures for research and development in communication and related industry (private and government) in thousands of 1958 constant dollars (Nos. 847 and 848, *Statistical Abstract of the United States*, op. cit.)

t: Rate of indirect business taxes on the gross profit earned

s: The rate of return to capital, which can be affected by the regulatory agency

The model specifications and parameter estimation are given in the Appendix. Among them the most important statistically estimated relationships are the demands for telecommunication services for residential and business uses, the production of telecommunication services, and the input requirements for capital and labor. A_{ij} are the estimated values of the parameters in the system of equations as specified in Chapter 7 and the Appendix. Based on those estimates we are using for this simulation the following values for A_{ij}:

Eq. (1)	$A_{10} = 0.0011$	$A_{11} = 0.7984$
	$A_{12} = -0.0039$	$A_{13} = 0.0023$
Eq. (2)	$A_{20} = -0.3371$	$A_{21} = 0.9970$
	$A_{22} = -0.0174$	$A_{23} = 0.0009$
Eq. (6)	$A_{60} = 1.1750$	$A_{61} = 0.9488$
	$A_{62} = 0.0459$	$A_{63} = 0.0459$
	$A_{64} = 0.0667$	$A_{65} = 0.0494$
Eq. (7)	$A_{70} = 5.8950$	$A_{71} = 0$
	$A_{72} = 0.6445$	$A_{73} = 0.2754$
Eq. (8)	$A_{80} = 0.6072$	$A_{81} = 0$
	$A_{82} = 0$	$A_{83} = 0.1157$

In addition, the values of depreciation rate and retirement rate for capital and labor in Equations (12) and (13) are assumed to be 0.05 and 0.025, respectively. These estimated values were used for basic simulations. To test the sensitivity of the simulation results to these estimates, the values of A_{10} and A_{20} were decreased and increased by half (or one) of their respective standard deviations (0.0027 and 1.0253), respectively, in two simulations for the future (1970-90).

Dynamic Simulation of Sample Period (1947-70)

Before the particular model was employed for projections into the future, we experimented with a dynamic simulation for the sample period (1947-70) using the observed values of 1947 endogenous and exogenous variables as well as the observed values of 1948-70 exogenous variables. The observed values of all exogenous variables for the sample period and the results of the simulation are presented in Tables 5-2 and 5-3 respectively. (Notice that in Table 5-3 the values for 1947 are observed values, since the simulation begins in 1948.) For comparison, the observed values of all endogenous variables for the same period are also provided in Table 5-4.

In general, the simulated results shown in Table 5-3 trace out the observed pattern shown in Table 5-4 reasonably well, except two price variables (Columns 3 and 4), probably because their precise solution values are difficult to obtain. Even for these two variables, their trends appear to be the same as the corresponding observed values.

Dynamic Simulations of Future
Telecommunication Industry (1970-90)

The simulation results for the sample period as shown in Table 5-3, though they are not entirely satisfactory, appear to indicate that the model as

Table 5-2. Actual Values for Exogenous Variables: Sample Period (1947-70)

	Popu-lation	GNP	GNP-Defl.	R	Wage	R&D	B-Tax	Interest Rates
1947	144.7	300	.75	0.03	2.82	.73	.33	0.01
1948	147.2	324	.80	0.03	3.02	.76	.40	0.02
1949	149.8	324	.79	0.03	3.18	.85	.40	0.02
1950	152.3	355	.80	0.03	3.36	.93	.43	0.02
1951	154.9	383	.88	0.04	3.56	.97	.50	0.03
1952	157.6	395	.88	0.03	3.80	1.05	.45	0.03
1953	160.2	413	.88	0.03	4.02	1.16	.46	0.03
1954	163.0	407	.90	0.03	4.21	1.27	.46	0.03
1955	165.0	438	.91	0.04	4.42	1.34	.44	0.04
1956	168.9	448	.94	0.04	4.56	1.68	.47	0.04
1957	172.0	452	.97	0.04	4.78	1.82	.48	0.04
1958	174.9	447	1.00	0.04	5.01	1.97	.46	0.04
1959	177.8	476	1.02	0.04	5.45	2.23	.45	0.05
1960	189.7	488	1.03	0.05	5.72	2.45	.47	0.05
1961	183.6	497	1.05	0.05	6.05	2.28	.47	0.05
1962	186.5	529	1.06	0.05	6.36	2.22	.43	0.06
1963	189.2	551	1.07	0.06	6.80	2.67	.43	0.06
1964	191.9	589	1.09	0.07	7.04	2.71	.44	0.06
1965	194.3	618	1.11	0.05	7.28	2.86	.34	0.08
1966	196.6	658	1.14	0.06	7.58	3.15	.31	0.08
1967	198.7	674	1.18	0.08	7.83	3.23	.35	0.08
1968	200.7	707	1.22	0.08	8.31	3.30	.36	0.08
1969	202.7	726	1.28	0.07	8.90	3.37	.38	0.08
1970	204.9	722	1.35	0.08	9.58	3.20	.40	0.06

Table 5-3. Solution Values for Endogenous Variables: Sample Period (1947-70)

Year	1 Q_1	2 Q_2	3 P_1	4 P_2	5 Q	6 P	7 R	8 K	9 L	10 C	11 II	12 I	13 M
1947	1.840	0.500	.750	2.440	2.340	1.110	2.300	14.440	0.640	2.300	.300	2.260	0.040
1948	2.060	0.566	.001	5.283	2.626	1.159	3.044	15.680	0.679	2.521	.523	1.962	0.055
1949	2.334	0.611	.455	3.596	2.945	1.103	3.247	16.729	0.688	2.690	.558	1.834	0.026
1950	2.598	0.695	.001	5.044	3.295	1.064	3.505	17.876	0.697	2.878	.627	1.083	0.026
1951	2.816	0.845	.783	2.641	3.661	1.208	4.422	18.103	0.706	3.276	1.146	2.121	0.026
1952	3.010	1.060	.001	4.180	4.070	1.093	4.448	20.514	0.714	3.330	1.119	2.366	0.026
1953	3.205	1.320	.922	1.404	4.524	1.057	4.780	21.900	0.723	3.564	1.217	2.412	0.027
1954	3.404	1.614	.001	3.222	5.018	1.010	5.067	23.215	0.732	3.777	1.290	2.410	0.027
1955	3.615	1.925	.896	1.459	5.541	1.086	6.015	24.617	0.740	4.256	1.758	2.503	0.027
1956	3.907	2.282	.001	2.860	6.189	1.035	6.409	25.894	0.750	4.455	1.954	2.508	0.028
1957	4.215	2.653	.808	1.303	6.868	.992	6.815	27.394	0.750	4.708	2.107	2.705	0.028
1958	4.570	3.035	.001	2.431	7.885	.943	7.169	29.120	0.768	5.012	2.157	3.095	0.028
1959	5.027	3.430	.485	1.751	8.456	.991	8.380	31.655	0.777	5.503	2.878	3.991	0.029
1960	5.503	3.861	.001	2.412	9.364	.998	9.347	33.586	0.787	6.178	3.169	3.515	0.029
1961	5.854	4.315	.578	1.537	10.168	.978	9.946	35.622	0.794	6.585	3.381	3.715	0.027
1962	6.248	4.808	.001	2.262	11.058	.990	10.945	37.648	0.802	6.982	3.983	3.805	0.028
1963	6.822	5.344	.348	1.797	12.168	.978	11.893	39.585	0.811	7.726	4.167	3.821	0.029
1964	7.311	5.928	.131	2.055	13.240	1.000	13.246	42.239	0.819	8.720	4.526	4.633	0.028
1965	7.813	6.575	.404	1.602	14.388	.944	13.579	44.161	0.827	8.226	5.353	4.034	0.028
1966	8.381	7.293	.172	1.880	15.674	.968	15.166	46.407	0.835	9.113	6.053	4.454	0.029
1967	8.892	8.064	.508	1.468	16.950	.958	16.207	48.425	0.842	9.502	6.705	4.338	0.029
1968	9.424	8.881	.215	1.642	18.305	.985	16.570	51.390	0.850	10.147	6.424	5.386	0.029
1969	9.973	9.744	.503	1.419	19.717	.948	18.690	55.180	0.857	11.570	7.120	6.360	0.029
1970	10.395	10.623	.391	1.468	21.618	.926	19.456	58.508	0.864	12.855	6.501	6.687	0.028

Table 5-4. Actual Values for Endogenous Variables: Sample Period (1947-70)

Year	1 Q_1	2 Q_2	3 P_1	4 P_2	5 Q	6 P	7 R	8 K	9 L	10 C	11 Π	12 I	13 M	14 N
1947	1.84	0.50	0.75	2.44	2.34	1.11	2.60	14.44	0.64	2.30	0.30	1.80	.213	144.70
1948	2.00	0.70	0.79	2.03	2.70	1.11	3.00	16.20	0.69	2.60	0.50	1.99	.242	147.21
1949	2.11	0.77	0.82	1.91	2.88	1.11	3.20	17.31	0.69	2.70	0.50	1.30	.207	149.77
1950	2.20	1.04	0.88	1.60	3.24	1.11	3.60	18.08	0.67	2.90	0.70	1.02	.187	152.27
1951	2.41	1.28	0.90	1.48	3.69	1.11	4.10	18.92	0.70	3.20	1.00	1.12	.231	154.88
1952	2.59	1.55	0.93	1.41	4.14	1.11	4.60	20.01	0.72	3.50	1.10	1.39	.230	157.55
1953	2.77	1.62	0.97	1.33	4.59	1.11	5.10	21.22	0.75	3.70	1.30	1.47	.246	160.18
1954	2.93	1.93	0.95	1.35	4.86	1.11	5.40	22.44	0.75	3.90	1.30	1.50	.225	163.03
1955	3.25	2.15	0.94	1.37	5.40	1.11	6.00	23.77	0.76	4.30	1.80	1.66	.235	165.93
1956	3.50	2.35	0.95	1.35	5.85	1.11	6.50	25.72	0.81	4.70	1.90	2.23	.278	168.90
1957	3.76	2.63	0.97	1.31	6.39	1.11	7.10	27.98	0.82	5.00	2.10	2.58	.253	171.98
1958	3.89	3.71	1.00	1.00	7.60	1.00	7.60	29.51	0.77	5.10	2.40	1.86	.196	174.88
1959	4.10	4.30	1.02	0.98	8.40	1.00	8.40	30.99	0.75	5.50	2.90	1.86	.211	177.83
1960	4.35	4.65	1.04	0.96	9.00	1.00	9.00	32.81	0.75	5.90	3.20	2.20	.225	180.67
1961	4.63	4.97	1.04	0.96	9.60	1.00	9.60	34.53	0.74	6.20	3.40	2.13	.215	183.69
1962	4.90	5.40	1.04	0.96	10.30	1.00	10.30	36.63	0.73	6.70	3.70	2.53	.212	186.54
1963	5.28	5.82	1.04	0.96	11.10	1.00	11.10	38.64	0.73	7.20	3.90	2.54	.219	189.24
1964	5.67	6.63	1.04	0.96	12.30	1.00	12.30	41.71	0.75	8.10	4.30	3.72	.239	191.89
1965	6.25	7.15	1.03	0.99	13.40	1.01	13.50	43.24	0.77	7.90	5.50	2.23	.245	194.30
1966	6.86	7.84	1.01	0.98	14.70	0.99	14.60	45.85	0.82	8.80	5.80	3.43	.281	196.56
1967	7.38	8.72	1.02	0.97	16.10	1.00	16.00	48.38	0.85	9.50	6.50	3.45	.276	198.71
1968	8.02	9.16	1.02	0.97	17.30	0.99	17.10	51.12	0.86	10.40	6.70	3.80	.265	200.71
1969	8.80	10.20	1.03	0.97	19.00	1.00	19.00	54.44	0.92	12.10	7.00	4.31	.318	202.68
1970	9.40	11.20	1.05	0.96	20.60	1.00	20.60	58.72	0.99	14.30	6.30	5.25	.346	204.88

Source: U.S. Department of Commerce, *Survey of Current Business*, Washington, D.C.: U.S. Government Printing Office, July issue, each year.

specified, together with the specific set of the estimated values of the parameters, can be used for preliminary projections of the U.S. telecommunications
industry. In order to use the model for projections, we must first determine the
values of exogenous variables[b] to be used. The following results of simulations
are based on the values of exogenous variables as presented in Table 5-5. These
particular sets of values are obtained by a simple projection procedure based on
the form of $X_t = a + \beta T + \gamma X_{t-1}$ with the parameters estimated by the least
squares procedure using 1947-70 data. There are, however, two exceptions:
(1) the tax rates were assumed to be fixed at the 1970 level, and (2) the
population from 1980 on is assumed to remain stable rather than decline, as
indicated by the simple projection.

The results of three alternative simulations for the period 1970 to
1990 are presented in Tables 5-6 through 5-8. These results are all presented in

**Table 5-5. Values Used for Exogenous Variables: Future Period
(1970-90)**

Year	1 N	2 Y	3 PY	4 SR	5 SW	6 D	7 ST	8 SS
1969	202.68	725.60	1.28	0.07	8.99	3.37	0.38	0.08
1970	204.88	722.10	1.35	0.08	9.58	3.20	0.46	0.06
1971	206.84	742.55	1.40	0.07	10.18	3.47	0.46	0.06
1972	208.67	763.09	1.46	0.07	10.85	3.67	0.46	0.07
1973	210.35	783.70	1.52	0.07	11.59	3.83	0.46	0.08
1974	211.86	804.36	1.59	0.07	12.41	3.97	0.46	0.08
1975	213.16	825.08	1.66	0.08	13.31	4.11	0.46	0.08
1976	214.24	845.83	1.75	0.08	14.32	4.24	0.46	0.09
1977	215.05	866.62	1.84	0.08	15.45	4.37	0.46	0.09
1978	215.57	887.45	1.94	0.08	16.70	4.50	0.46	0.09
1979	215.75	908.29	2.05	0.08	18.10	4.63	0.46	0.10
1980	215.75	929.16	2.18	0.09	19.62	4.76	0.46	0.10
1981	215.75	950.05	2.32	0.09	21.44	4.89	0.46	0.10
1982	215.75	970.95	2.47	0.09	23.43	5.02	0.46	0.10
1983	215.75	991.87	2.64	0.09	25.66	5.15	0.46	0.11
1984	215.75	1012.79	2.83	0.09	28.17	5.28	0.46	0.11
1985	215.75	1033.73	3.05	0.10	31.01	5.40	0.46	0.11
1986	215.75	1054.67	3.29	0.10	34.20	5.53	0.46	0.11
1987	215.75	1075.62	3.55	0.10	37.81	5.66	0.46	0.12
1988	215.75	1096.58	3.85	0.10	41.89	5.79	0.46	0.12
1989	215.75	1117.54	4.18	0.10	46.50	5.92	0.46	0.12
1990	215.75	1138.51	4.54	0.11	51.71	6.05	0.46	0.12

[b]Exogenous variables are variables not explained or determined within the
model; they are variables used as inputs in the model.

Table 5-6. Solution Values for Endogenous Variables: Simulation 1 Future Period (1970-1990)

Year	1 Q_1	2 Q_2	3 P_1	4 P_2	5 Q	6 P	7 R	8 K	9 L	10 C	11 II	12 I	13 M
1969	8.80	10.20	1.03	0.97	19.00	1.00	19.00	54.44	0.92	12.10	7.00	5.90	0.090
1970	9.13	11.08	0.38	1.39	20.22	0.95	19.30	57.88	0.86	12.86	6.43	6.17	0.029
1971	9.77	11.97	0.48	1.39	21.74	0.97	21.23	61.44	0.86	13.38	7.85	6.45	0.029
1972	10.42	12.96	0.36	1.54	23.33	1.00	23.38	65.26	0.87	14.32	9.06	6.89	0.029
1973	11.11	13.86	0.40	1.56	24.97	1.03	25.89	69.38	0.88	15.48	10.40	7.37	0.029
1974	11.82	14.85	0.30	1.69	26.87	1.06	28.39	73.82	0.88	16.77	11.62	7.91	0.029
1975	12.56	15.88	0.31	1.72	28.44	1.09	31.01	78.63	0.89	18.26	12.81	8.50	0.029
1976	13.33	16.93	0.22	1.85	30.27	1.12	33.91	83.84	0.90	19.78	14.13	9.14	0.029
1977	14.12	18.03	0.19	1.92	32.15	1.15	37.11	89.50	0.90	21.53	15.58	9.85	0.029
1978	14.94	19.15	0.11	2.04	34.10	1.19	40.67	45.66	0.91	23.48	17.18	10.63	0.029
1979	15.79	20.31	0.05	2.14	36.10	1.23	44.61	102.36	0.91	25.65	18.95	11.48	0.029
1980	16.65	21.50	0.00	2.23	38.16	1.27	48.68	109.45	0.92	28.01	20.67	12.21	0.029
1981	17.55	22.72	0.00	2.33	40.28	1.33	53.67	117.65	0.93	30.79	22.87	13.67	0.029
1982	18.46	23.98	0.00	2.43	42.44	1.39	58.99	126.37	0.93	33.95	25.04	14.59	0.029
1983	19.38	25.27	0.00	2.55	44.66	1.45	65.05	135.89	0.94	37.36	27.68	15.84	0.029
1984	20.33	26.59	0.00	2.68	46.92	1.53	71.80	146.30	0.94	41.19	30.61	17.20	0.029
1985	21.28	27.95	0.00	2.81	49.23	1.60	79.06	157.69	0.95	45.48	33.58	18.70	0.029
1986	22.25	29.33	0.00	2.96	51.59	1.69	87.49	170.17	0.95	50.30	37.18	20.35	0.029
1987	23.24	30.75	0.00	3.11	53.99	1.78	96.57	183.82	0.96	55.73	40.84	22.15	0.029
1988	24.23	32.20	0.00	3.30	56.43	1.89	107.10	198.76	0.96	61.83	45.27	24.13	0.029
1989	25.23	33.68	0.00	3.50	58.91	2.01	118.49	215.12	0.97	68.70	49.79	28.30	0.029
1990	26.24	35.19	0.00	3.72	61.43	2.14	131.67	233.04	0.97	76.43	55.24	28.67	0.029

Table 5-7. Solution Values for Endogenous Variables: Simulation 2 Future Period (1970-90)

Year	1 Q_1	2 Q_2	3 P_1	4 P_2	5 Q	6 P	7 R	8 K	9 L	10 C	11 Π	12 I	13 M
1969	8.80	10.20	1.03	0.97	19.00	1.00	19.00	54.44	0.92	12.10	7.00	5.90	0.090
1970	8.62	11.60	0.66	1.17	20.22	0.95	19.30	57.88	0.86	12.86	6.43	6.17	0.029
1971	8.73	13.01	0.69	1.17	21.74	0.97	21.23	61.44	0.86	13.38	7.85	6.45	0.029
1972	8.87	14.45	0.75	1.15	23.33	1.00	23.38	65.27	0.87	14.32	9.06	6.89	0.029
1973	9.03	15.93	0.78	1.18	24.97	1.05	25.89	69.38	0.88	15.49	10.40	7.37	0.029
1974	9.23	17.44	0.83	1.19	26.67	1.06	28.39	73.82	0.88	16.78	11.62	7.91	0.029
1975	9.45	18.99	0.86	1.20	28.44	1.08	31.01	78.63	0.89	18.26	12.81	8.50	0.029
1976	9.70	20.57	0.90	1.22	30.27	1.12	33.91	83.84	0.90	19.78	14.13	9.14	0.029
1977	9.97	22.18	0.94	1.25	32.15	1.15	37.11	89.50	0.91	21.53	15.58	9.85	0.029
1978	10.27	23.82	0.97	1.29	34.10	1.19	40.67	95.66	0.91	23.48	17.18	10.63	0.029
1979	10.60	25.50	1.00	1.33	36.10	1.23	44.61	102.36	0.92	25.65	18.95	11.48	0.029
1980	10.94	27.21	1.04	1.37	38.16	1.27	48.68	109.45	0.92	28.01	20.67	12.21	0.029
1981	11.32	28.95	1.07	1.44	40.28	1.33	53.67	117.65	0.93	30.79	22.87	13.87	0.029
1982	11.71	30.72	1.12	1.49	42.44	1.39	58.99	126.37	0.93	33.95	25.04	14.59	0.029
1983	12.12	32.53	1.15	1.57	44.66	1.45	65.05	135.89	0.94	37.36	27.68	15.84	0.029
1984	12.55	34.37	1.19	1.66	46.92	1.53	71.80	146.30	0.94	41.19	30.61	17.20	0.029
1985	13.00	36.23	1.23	1.74	49.23	1.60	79.06	157.69	0.95	45.48	33.58	18.70	0.029
1986	13.45	38.13	1.26	1.85	51.60	1.69	87.49	170.17	0.95	50.30	37.18	20.35	0.029
1987	13.92	40.06	1.29	1.96	53.99	1.79	96.58	183.82	0.96	55.73	40.84	22.15	0.029
1988	14.41	42.02	1.32	2.10	56.43	1.90	107.10	198.76	0.96	61.83	45.27	24.13	0.029
1989	14.90	44.01	1.35	2.24	58.91	2.01	118.49	215.12	0.97	68.70	49.79	26.30	0.029
1990	15.40	46.03	1.38	2.40	61.43	2.14	131.67	233.04	0.97	76.43	55.24	28.67	0.029

Table 5-8. Solution Values for Endogenous Variables: Simulation 3 Future Period (1970-1990)

Year	1 Q_1	2 Q_2	3 P_1	4 P_2	5 Q	6 P	7 R	8 K	9 L	10 C	11 II	12 I	13 M
1969	8.80	10.20	1.03	0.97	19.00	1.00	19.00	54.44	0.92	12.10	7.00	5.90	0.090
1970	8.10	12.11	0.98	0.94	20.22	0.95	19.30	57.88	0.86	12.86	6.43	6.17	0.029
1971	7.70	14.04	0.89	1.02	21.74	0.97	21.23	61.45	0.86	13.38	7.85	6.45	0.029
1972	7.32	16.01	1.16	0.93	23.33	1.00	23.38	65.27	0.87	14.32	9.06	6.89	0.029
1973	6.97	17.99	1.17	0.99	24.97	1.03	25.89	69.38	0.88	15.48	10.40	7.37	0.029
1974	6.85	20.02	1.35	0.97	26.68	1.06	28.39	73.82	0.89	16.77	11.62	7.91	0.029
1975	6.36	22.07	1.42	0.99	28.44	1.09	31.01	78.63	0.89	18.20	12.81	8.50	0.029
1976	6.10	24.16	1.57	1.00	30.27	1.12	33.91	83.84	0.90	19.78	14.13	9.14	0.029
1977	5.87	26.28	1.68	1.04	32.15	1.15	37.11	89.51	0.90	21.53	15.58	9.85	0.029
1978	5.67	28.43	1.81	1.07	34.10	1.19	40.67	95.66	0.91	23.48	17.18	10.63	0.029
1979	5.49	30.61	1.93	1.11	36.11	1.23	44.61	102.36	0.91	25.65	18.95	11.48	0.029
1980	5.33	32.83	2.08	1.14	38.16	1.27	48.68	109.45	0.92	28.01	20.67	12.21	0.029
1981	5.20	35.07	2.21	1.20	40.28	1.33	53.67	117.65	0.93	30.79	22.87	13.67	0.029
1982	5.10	37.34	2.36	1.25	42.45	1.39	58.99	126.37	0.93	33.95	25.04	14.59	0.029
1983	5.01	39.65	2.50	1.32	44.66	1.45	65.05	135.88	0.94	37.36	27.68	15.84	0.029
1984	4.94	41.98	2.65	1.40	46.92	1.53	71.80	146.30	0.94	41.19	30.61	17.20	0.029
1985	4.88	44.34	2.79	1.47	49.23	1.60	79.06	157.69	0.95	45.48	33.58	18.70	0.029
1986	4.85	46.74	2.94	1.56	51.60	1.69	87.49	170.17	0.95	50.30	37.18	20.35	0.029
1987	4.82	49.16	3.09	1.66	53.99	1.78	96.57	183.82	0.96	55.73	40.84	22.15	0.029
1988	4.81	51.61	3.25	1.77	56.43	1.89	107.10	198.78	0.96	61.83	45.27	24.13	0.029
1989	4.81	54.09	3.40	1.89	58.91	2.01	118.49	215.12	0.97	68.70	49.79	26.30	0.029
1990	4.82	56.60	3.55	2.02	61.43	2.14	131.67	233.04	0.97	76.43	55.24	28.67	0.029

Table 5-9. Extrapolated Values for Endogenous Variables, Future Period (1971-1990)

Year	1 Q_1	2 Q_2	3 P_1	4 P_2	5 Q	6 P	7 R	8 K	9 L	10 C	11 Π	12 I	13 M
1971	10.19	12.08	1.05	0.92	22.35	0.98	22.49	62.67	1.01	17.08	6.71	6.50	0.071
1972	11.07	13.00	1.05	0.90	24.24	0.97	24.59	66.98	1.04	20.92	7.10	6.56	0.065
1973	12.03	13.96	1.05	0.87	26.27	0.96	26.91	71.71	1.07	26.27	7.48	6.48	0.063
1974	13.09	14.96	1.06	0.85	28.46	0.95	29.48	76.89	1.10	33.76	7.84	6.56	0.064
1975	14.25	16.00	1.06	0.83	30.81	0.94	32.33	82.59	1.13	44.26	8.19	6.71	0.065
1976	15.52	17.08	1.06	0.81	33.34	0.93	35.50	88.86	1.16	59.07	8.53	6.89	0.067
1977	16.93	18.19	1.06	0.79	36.06	0.92	39.01	95.77	1.19	79.98	8.87	7.00	0.069
1978	18.46	19.35	1.07	0.77	38.99	0.92	42.92	103.40	1.22	109.57	9.21	7.29	0.071
1979	20.15	20.55	1.07	0.75	42.13	0.91	47.27	111.83	1.25	151.46	9.55	7.50	0.072
1980	22.01	21.79	1.07	0.73	45.51	0.90	52.11	121.17	1.29	210.82	9.88	7.71	0.074
1981	24.06	23.66	1.07	0.71	49.15	0.89	57.50	131.51	1.32	295.00	10.21	7.92	0.076
1982	26.31	24.38	1.08	0.70	53.05	0.89	63.50	142.99	1.35	414.39	10.54	8.13	0.078
1983	28.78	25.75	1.08	0.68	57.25	0.88	70.18	155.73	1.39	583.78	10.87	8.34	0.080
1984	31.50	27.15	1.08	0.67	61.76	0.88	77.68	169.88	1.43	824.16	11.20	8.56	0.082
1985	34.50	28.60	1.09	0.64	66.60	0.87	85.98	185.61	1.46	1165.34	11.52	8.77	0.084
1986	37.79	30.09	1.09	0.63	71.80	0.86	95.27	203.12	1.50	1649.80	11.85	8.98	0.085
1987	41.42	31.62	1.09	0.61	77.39	0.85	105.63	222.62	1.54	2337.02	12.19	9.19	0.087
1988	45.41	33.20	1.09	0.59	83.39	0.85	117.20	244.33	1.58	3312.87	12.51	9.40	0.089
1989	49.81	34.82	1.10	0.57	89.84	0.84	130.13	268.54	1.62	4698.21	12.83	9.61	0.091
1990	54.64	36.49	1.10	0.56	96.76	0.84	144.56	295.53	1.66	6664.91	13.16	9.82	0.093

order to indicate how sensitive the simulation results are to the estimated values of some of the parameters. The estimated values of the parameters as shown previously were used in obtaining the projection given in Table 5-6. The results of Tables 5-7 and 5-8 are obtained by changing the estimated values of A_{10} and A_{20} (i.e., intercepts of two demand equations). More precisely, the estimated values of A_{10} and A_{20} are decreased and increased by half of their respective standard derivations to −0.003 and 0.1756 respectively in the second simulation as shown in Table 5-7. Similarly, the estimated values of these two parameters are decreased and increased by one standard derivations to −0.0016 and 0.6882 respectively in the last simulation as shown in Table 5-8.

According to Table 5-6 the residential and business demands for telecommunication services will grow from $9 and $11 billions, respectively, in 1970 to $26 and $35 billions respectively in 1990 (approximately 5.4% and 5.9% annual growth rates). These projections taken together are probably too low but are consistent with the projected price level for telecommunications in general which increases steadily. The same general trend is projected for the price of business use of telecommunications but the opposite trend is projected for the price of residential use. It must be pointed out, however, these projected price patterns are probably the *most unreliable among all projected results*. These will be clear when we examine the alternative projections shown in Table 5-7 and 5-8. The general price of telecommunication service is projected to increase steadily, despite the fact that its past trend is fairly stable. This is largely because the past trends of residential and business uses closely resemble constant growth rate and constant absolute growth, respectively. The extrapolations of price levels are also quite different from the projections of our econometric model. The most unrealistic extrapolation among all these results is that of the cost of telecommunication services, which is shown to increase from $17 billions in 1971 to $6665 billions in 1990! The weakness of this approach is its failure to take account of the interrelationship among these variables. The most important difficulties—even in sector by sector medium and long term forecasting—are due to two important sets of factors.

1. Price and Income Elasticities

Based on the historical economic data of the United States from 1947-1970 we estimate in Chapter 7 the short run and long run price and income elasticities in the telecommunications sector for households to be

	Price Elasticities	Income Elasticities
Short Run	0.34	0.57
Long Run	1.51	2.56

These elasticities are calculated at the mean values of the observed prices and quantities during the sample period 1947-70. Leaving aside the statistical uncertainties in the exact magnitude of these estimates, they nevertheless importantly indicate the capability of socioeconomic systems—in this case the United States—to adapt to different demand-supply relationships, in this case in the rather important economic sector of communications. Thus, if in any one year of the projected time period (1970-1990) the price for telecommunications were to increase by 10 percent then this would be felt in that same year as a 3.4 percent reduction in the demand for telecommunications by households and, if the price increase were to persist, a 15 percent decrease in yearly demand for telecommunications in the long run—a quite dramatic adjustment. These ranges of price and income elasticities are also common to many other sectors of the economy. In addition to making forecasts of the scale and structure of technological capacity very uncertain (given the range and impact of price policy), the range of price elasticities found in empirical economic studies also are a major point of serious critique in the criticism of economically rather naïve LTG models reviewed in Chapter 4.

2. The R&D Impact on Production Functions

The historical data for the 1947-1970 period in the United States indicate an unusually—and to this degree unexpected—impact of R&D expenditures on the "production function" of telecommunications services, i.e., the quantitative inputs needed to produce a given level of service. Production function considerations include derived demands for capital and labor by the telecommunications industry.

The production function used in deriving the empirical findings for the U.S. telecommunications sector is:

$$ln Q_t = A (D_t - v) + \alpha \, ln K_t + \beta ln L_t \tag{5.1}$$

where

$$A (D_t - v) = \lambda + a \left[\delta \, ln P_t + (1 - \delta) \, \Sigma_1^{\infty} \, \theta (1 - \theta)^{v-1} ln P_{t-v} \right]$$

represents the level of technology which is assumed to be a function of capital and labor as well as all past research and development efforts given as P_{t-v}. (The notation used in (1) is consistent with the one given at the beginning of this section.)

In Chapter 7 as well as in the Appendix the empirical estimates are described in detail. The results and implications are best summarized by the marginal elasticities and the marginal returns of the production function variables.

	Short Run	Long Run
Marginal Elasticities		
(= average elasticities)		
Capital	0.0034	0.0667
Labor	0.0025	0.0494
R & D expenditure	0.0459	0.8965
Marginal Products		
(at means, billions of 1958 dollars)		
Capital (per billion of 1958 dollars)	0.0170	0.3325 (0.1870)*
Labor (per million employees)	0.0125	0.2463 (0.1375)*
R & D expenditure (per billion of		
1958 dollars)	0.2288	4.4694 (2.5168)*

*Discounted at 10% annually.

These results appear to be reasonable, though some of the estimates are not statistically significant. It must be pointed out that they are nevertheless unbiased estimates. The results above show that the returns to capital and labor in direct production of telecommunication services, with a given technology, are relatively low. On the other hand, *the return to R & D expenditure in the telecommunications industry seems to be very high.* Although according to our estimates, 1% increase in R & D expenditure for telecommunication technology will lead to only about 0.05% increase in output (with a given level of inputs), its ultimate effect will be approximately 0.90% which is quite substantial. In terms of marginal products, we find that a $1.00 increase of R & D expenditure (for communication and electronic equipment!) will bring about a $0.23 increase of output of telecommunication services in the short run, and eventually accumulate up to $4.47 (which, as is shown in the parentheses, is equivalent to $2.51 in present value, using a 10% discount rate). In comparison, the returns to increases in either capital (equipment) or labor are very low.

These results may be not unexpected, particularly for the communications sector. In other sectors of the economy—though hardly more important than the communications sector—the same impact of R&D on production functions for those sectors may not hold to the same extent. Each sector has to be studied separately first, before coming to a general conclusion. Nevertheless, these findings are a most powerful empirical evidence that stands against taking LTG "collapse" predictions at face value and that lend additional strong support to the critics of such predictions.[3]

Since research and development efforts and expenditures not only respond directly to the opportunities offered in the market, but also are importantly determined by government policy choices and deliberate R&D

funding decisions, the very recognition of a possible economic, technological, or other problem 10, 20, or 30 years hence leads to the possible alleviation of that problem through research and development fundings—if the problem is real and not imagined. Thus, the primary real issue seems to be *problem recognition*, rather than drastic policy decisions limiting the expansion of social economic systems.

Given the long lead time impact of some R&D expenditures, however, there will remain a short to medium term adaptation problem until technical innovation opens new economic and social options. One such sector— and possibly the only one—of the economy may be the energy sector.

Chapter Six

The Energy Variable

INTRODUCTION

In our discussion of various forecasting techniques and in the analysis presented in this chapter, we could not find any single material resource which decisively influences the economic and military power of any one nation or region, with one critical exception: *energy*.

The needs for energy can be forecast quite accurately; there exists a very close correlation between level of economic and social development of a society and its per capita energy consumption. Furthermore, although the composition of the different sources supplying energy changes substantially, the overall energy demand continues to increase exponentially, at rates between 4 and 10 percent (or more).

The single common source of most of today's energy supply, fossil fuels, is strictly limited. In Figure 6-1 the dramatic exploitation of fossil fuels to the present is shown and extended into the future. There is now no doubt that fossil fuels will be exhausted before very long. Yet very little, if anything, has been done about this ominous situation, either in regions still "richly" endowed with fossil fuels, or in regions short of these. What is the actual situation, and are there any implications for the outlook of nations and regions over the next decades, before other energy sources (fission and "breeding," fusion, solar) come to economic fruition?

THE DEMAND FOR ENERGY

The most dramatic development in history must be regarded as the development over the past 200 years of human society from an agricultural state to an industrial state. Hand in hand with this development has gone an exponential increase in the energy required to sustain economic growth. The per capita

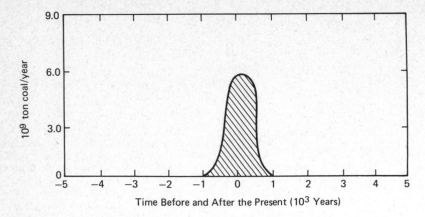

Source: Adapted from M.King Hubbert, "Energy Resources" in *Resources and Man*, Committee on Resources and Man, National Academy of Sciences, National Research Council, San Francisco: W.H. Freeman, 1969. See also: Harrison Brown, *The Challenge of Man's Future*, New York: Viking Press, 1954.

Figure 6-1. The Exploitation and Exhaustion of Fossil Fuels in Historical Perspective

energy requirements of different societies have been studied in some detail. In Figure 6-2, the daily energy consumed is shown in total and by sectors of demand (food, home and commerce, industry and agriculture, transportation).

Primitive man in a prehunting stage of development consumed roughly 0.3 kilograms of coal (or the equivalent) of energy. (At this stage it is mostly human energy.) *Hunting tribes* show an increase of energy consumption per capita to 0.7 kilograms: 0.4 kilograms go to providing food, 0.3 kilograms are expended in other uses. In a *primitive agricultural society*, the daily energy consumption per capita increases to 1.8 kilograms, about equally divided between the needs for agricultural production and transportation. In an *advanced agricultural society*, the total energy uses increase to 3.8 kilograms. In *industrial societies* (comparable to the technology of England at the end of the last century) this energy consumption is about 11.2 kilograms of coal, or its equivalent, while a *technological society* (the United States in 1970) consumes roughly 33.5 kilograms: 1.5 kilograms for food, 9.6 for home and commerce, 13.2 for industry and agriculture, and 9.2 for transportation. A rough approximation of the large energy consumption of 33.5 kilograms in a technological society therefore is 1/3 for transportation, 1/3 for industry and agricultural production activities and 1/3 for home and commercial activities.

Not only do the per capita energy requirements of advanced

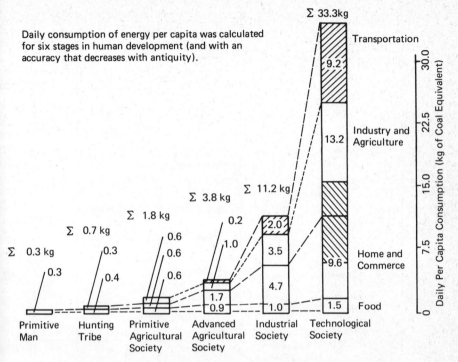

Daily consumption of energy per capita was calculated for six stages in human development (and with an accuracy that decreases with antiquity).

Figure 6-2. Energy Consumed per Day by Sectors of Demand

societies increase; an equally dramatic increase in total population figures occurred historically and added to requirements. It is only industrial and technological progress which made possible the vastly expanded subsistence base of modern states and nations. An agricultural society could in no way support, for example, a total population of 100 million people on the territory of Japan. Similarly, Western Europe, which is roughly half the size of China, could not support the equivalent of 400 million people, yet actually, in addition, produces a surplus of output for export. This dramatic expansion of the subsistence base was made possible by the technology used in the production of goods and services.

This coincidence of energy consumption per capita and the stage of development of a society suggests that energy consumption is a reliable index of the economic development of nations. Figures 6-3 and 6-4 show the relation between GNP, the per capita GNP, and the per capita energy consumptions of different countries. The GNP, total and per capita, is expressed in dollars; the energy consumption per capita is expressed in metric tons of coal equivalents. Figures 6-3 and 6-4 clearly indicate a high correlation between the Gross National Product and the energy consumed in a nation—either absolute or per capita.

The dispersion of the data in Figure 6-3 is much larger than that

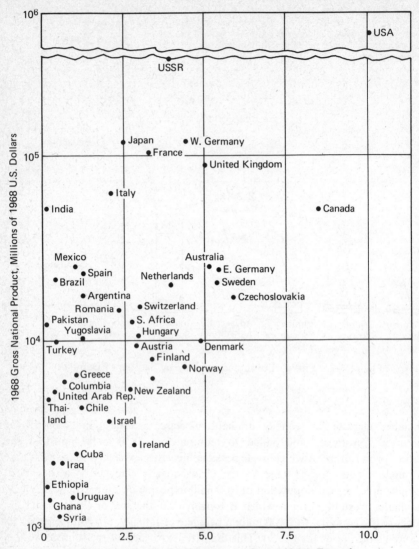

Figure 6-3. Gross National Product (Absolute) vs. Energy Consumption per Capita, 1968

Source: Adapted from Inter-Technology Corporation, *the U.S. Energy Problem*, Warrenton, Va., November 1971, p. 27.

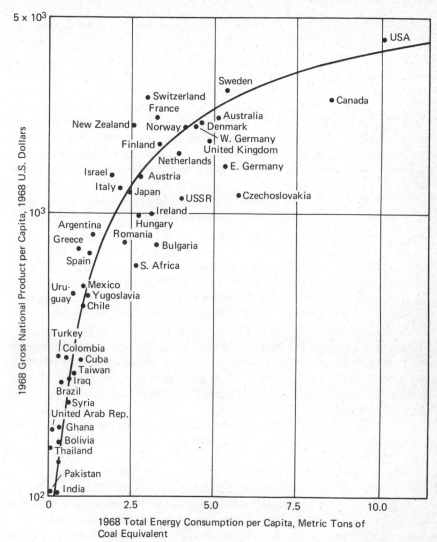

Figure 6-4. Gross National Product per Capita vs. Energy Consunption per Capita, 1968

Source: Adapted from Inter-Technology Corporation, *The U.S. Energy Problem*, Warrenton, Va., November 1971, p. 26.

shown in Figure 6-4. This is due to the choice of variables along the vertical axis: in Figure 6-3 the absolute value of GNP is plotted vs. per capita energy consumption. This omits one important explanatory variable, namely size of population. In Figure 6-4 per capita GNP and per capita energy consumption are shown and we observe the close correlation between these two.

Highest ranking with regard to the consumption of energy is the United States with the equivalent of 11.4 tons per capita of energy consumption per year. The energy produced in the United States was roughly equivalent to ten tons per capita in 1970. The remaining 1.4 of coal equivalent were imported from such countries as Canada, Venezuela, and the Near East (mostly petroleum).

The only other country with a similarly large energy consumption per capita is Canada, where we find a per capita energy of about 9 metric tons of coal equivalent per year. The production of energy in Canada is 9.6 metric tons of coal per capita, .6 tons being exported to the United States. The Soviet Union consumes about 4.4 metric tons of coal equivalent per capita and produces about 5 tons per capita—i.e., half the United States production. Again, the difference is exported. Most European countries rank in the same range of per capita energy consumption: West Germany (5.1 tons), Great Britain (5.4 tons), Czechoslovakia (6.3 tons), East Germany (5.9 tons), Belgium (5.9 tons), Sweden (6.3 tons) and the Netherlands (5.1 tons). The GNP figures, at least for the market economies, closely correlate with per capita energy consumption. The United States in this listing has a per capita GNP of $3,200 per year, Sweden $2,700, Germany $2,700, France $2,600, and the Netherlands $2,200 per capita per year.

Of course, the great difference in the per capita energy consumption of North America (about 10 tons) and other developed countries (about 4 to 5 tons) may not only be an expression of degrees of economic development. Rather, in this instance, it may also measure some degree of waste in the consumption patterns of the United States and Canada, induced in part by the historical abundance of energy resources and the direct and indirect subsidization of their production. Thus, in the case of North America a "cushion" of energy use adaptation may be available, possibly in the neighborhood of 30 to 40 percent of the actual energy consumed.

Overall the energy consumption per capita seems to be a relatively good indicator of the stage of development of the society as well as of the economy. Also, the conclusion is inescapable that energy consumption and energy sources importantly influence the power of nations and regions.

Moreover, due to the distortions inherent in comparisons of GNP, energy consumption per capita is a much more "measurable" index of the material base of power. Yet, even here we find serious difficulties (1) in converting production or consumption of coal in different countries to equivalent metric tons of coal, since the energy content and the quality of coal differ widely; and (2) in converting different energy sources, their production, and consumption in a country to equivalent metric tons of coal.

In Table 6-1 a comprehensive set of scales for transformation of different energy units is shown. Also listed in Table 6-1 are some of the major conversion numbers used to arrive at "equivalent metric tons of coal."

There is no other quantitative index of material production with any

Table 6-1. Conversion Scale for Major Energy Measurement Units

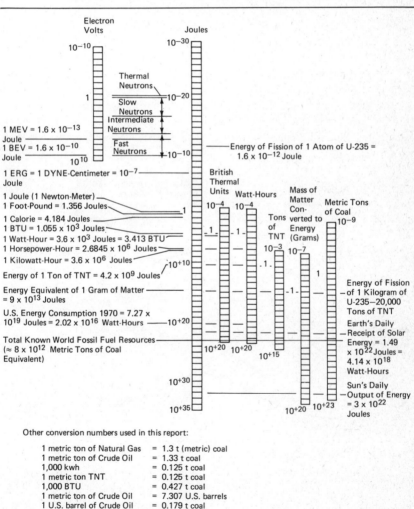

Other conversion numbers used in this report:

1 metric ton of Natural Gas	= 1.3 t (metric) coal
1 metric ton of Crude Oil	= 1.33 t coal
1,000 kwh	= 0.125 t coal
1 metric ton TNT	= 0.125 t coal
1,000 BTU	= 0.427 t coal
1 metric ton of Crude Oil	= 7.307 U.S. barrels
1 U.S. barrel of Crude Oil	= 0.179 t coal

such high correlation with per capita GNP. Some of the very developed countries do not have, for example, a large steel industry, one other variable that most immediately comes to mind.

Total agricultural production might be negatively correlated, if at all, with the GNP per capita and the state of development of an economy. Figure 6-5 shows a very generalized model on the development of economies with regard to the agricultural, industrial and services sectors. Along the horizontal scale one can measure the degree of development of a developing economy in terms of the shares of GNP contributed by the agricultural, industrial, and service sectors. In the United States today the total agricultural and forestry sectors do not make up more than 5% of the GNP. Similarly, the labor force allocated to United States agriculture and forestry does not amount to more than 3% of the total male labor force and to less than 5% of the total female labor force.

Thus, while in an agricultural economy the total output per capita of agricultural products (wheat, corn, etc.) might be a measure of the standard of living in that economy, it is no longer the case for developed countries. A similar *relative* downward trend is noticeable today with regard to the output of industrial goods. In the United States, the services sector already exceeds the industrial production sector. Other countries, such as Sweden, Austria, West

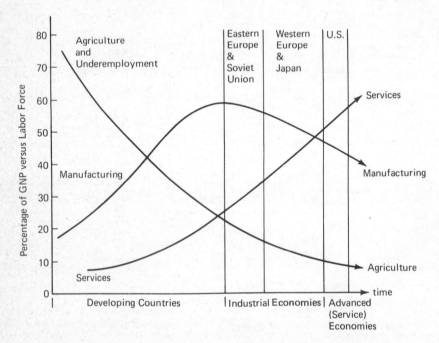

Figure 6-5. The Effects of Technological Change on the "Sources" of Gross National Product

Germany, the Netherlands, show similar trends. Thus, most quantitative material indices (such as total industrial production, steel, fertilizer, and cement production) are not likely to show consistently a high correlation with the per capita GNP of different countries.

The single fact about energy consumption is that, irrespective of whether agricultural production, industrial production, or services are emphasized within an economic system, all these require substantial amounts of energy. The more an economy changes from an agricultural to an industrial and to a services economy, the higher are per capita requirements of energy *in all three sectors*. Figure 6-2 gives the corresponding figures for different stages of development of societies and the associated per capita energy production per day.

This raises the next question. What has been the increase in worldwide demand for energy, and what is the distribution of energy resources? The major sources of energy, worldwide, are coal and lignite, petroleum, and natural gas. Figure 6-6 shows the total growth in production of coal-lignite, petroleum, and the combined production of lignite and crude oil.[1]

Coal has been mined for over 800 years. Yet of the *cumulative* coal produced in the world, over half was produced in the past 31 years. Over one-half of the total world's cumulative production of petroleum was produced in the past twelve years, from 1956 to 1968. Today (in 1972) about 30% of the total world energy produced is produced by the United States.

The fact that the United States uses today 30% of the total energy produced in the world indicates that other countries will try to develop similar patterns of energy use, which in turn will lead to a further sharp increase in the demand for energy and potentially impinge on the national interests of the United States.

World production of coal as shown in Figure 6-6 expanded between 1860 and 1913 on the average at a rate of 4.4% per year, implying a doubling of coal production every sixteen years. Up to World War I, coal, of course, was *the* major resource of industrial nations. Countries which did possess coal are the states where industrial and military power developed the most (Great Britain, Germany, and, to a lesser extent, the United States and the Soviet Union).

In the period between the two World Wars, coal production slowed to 0.75% per year, with a doubling rate therefore of about 93 years. This was due to two factors: (1) the rapid introduction of crude oil as a replacement for coal; and (2) a worldwide ecoomic depression in the 1930s, which indirectly shows up in a much decreased expansion of energy production overall (and confirming the high correlation between level of (economic) activity (GNP) and energy consumption).

After World War II the coal production rate again expanded to an annual rate of 3.6%, a doubling period of twenty years. These figures do not include coal production in China where production has expanded greatly during the same time.

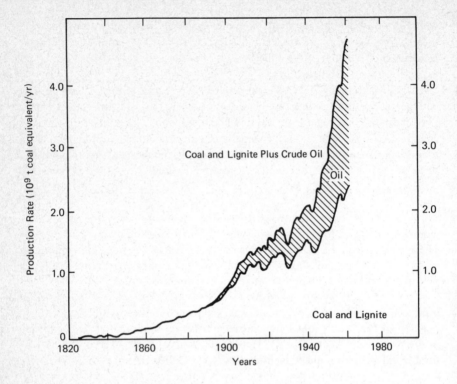

Source: M. King Hubbert, "Energy Resources," *op. cit*., p. 163.

A thorough statistical-quantitative review of the world energy situation is contained in Joel Darmstadter, Perry D. Teitelbaub, and Jaroslav D. Polach, *Energy in the World Economy*, Resources for the Future, Baltimore and London: The Johns Hopkins Press, 1971.

For further reference see also National Petroleum Council, *U.S. Energy Outlook*, a report of the National Petroleum Council's Committee on the U.S. energy outlook, Washington, D.C., December 1972.

Figure 6-6. World Production of Thermal Energy From Coal and Lignite Plus Crude Oil

The world production of *crude oil*, a major energy source since the early decades of this century, has expanded from 1890 to the present at a nearly constant worldwide rate of 6.9%, with a doubling period therefore of 10.4 years.

Before 1900 the major supply of total worldwide energy was

centered in Germany and Great Britain, and, to a lesser extent, in the United States; in the period between the two World Wars a shift of total world energy output occurred in favor of the United States. After World War II close to half of total world energy was produced in the United States. Concurrent with this shift was the ascendance of United States power.

Between 1860 and 1907 the United States production of *coal and lignite* expanded at an annual rate of 6.6% per year with a doubling period of eleven years. This rate was nearly 50% higher than the worldwide expansion of energy production during the same time period. From 1910 to the present the United States coal production has continued at about the same total production rate of about 500 million metric tons per year (see Figure 6-7).

The addition to the United States energy supply came from crude oil production and later on from natural gas. United States crude oil production

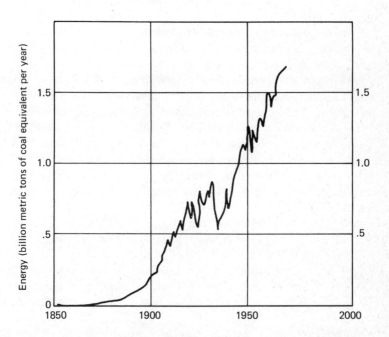

Source: M. King Hubbert, "Energy Resources," op. cit., p. 165.

Figure 6-7. U.S. Production of Energy from Coal, from Petroleum and related sources, from Water Power and from Nuclear Reactors is charted for 120 Years. The Petroleum Increment Includes Natural Gas and associated Liquids. The Dip at Center reflects Impact of Depression.

from 1875 to 1929 increased at an annual rate of 8.3%, thereby doubling every 8.7 years. Since 1929 the production of crude oil has leveled off. Production of *natural gas* from 1905 to the present has expanded at a constant rate of 6.6% per year with a doubling period of about 11 years.

In the *industrial development phase* of the United States between 1850 and 1907, energy used in the United States expanded at an annual rate of 6.9% per year with a doubling of energy requirement every 10.4 years. The development phase of the United States therefore occurred over a 60-year period from 1850 to 1910. By 1910 the United States had achieved roughly an industrial position comparable with those of Germany and Great Britain. Since 1907 the annual rate of energy use per year has expanded at about 1.7% per year with a doubling period of 41 years. However, in the last decade, energy consumption in the United States took a sharp upward turn, averaging 5% in the past five years, during a time of relative economic stagnation.

With these developments in the United States and parallel developments in other nations, what is the situation in energy resources?

Energy Resources: Size and Distribution

In the following, we will show a few summary charts that reflect the resources situation.

In Figure 6-8 world petroleum resources are listed (in equivalent metric tons of coal) with the exception of China. The Western Hemisphere overall has about 100 billion tons of "coal equivalent" oil resources (see Table 6-1 for conversion numbers). Of these, 13 billion are in Canada, 46 billion in the United States, and the rest in Latin America, mainly Venezuela. With projected annual United States energy consumption approaching five billion metric tons of coal equivalent by 1990, the total reserves of the Western Hemisphere would amount to about twenty times the 1990 energy consumption of the United States alone.

We see from Figure 6-8 that the Soviet Union and China are estimated to have about 68 billion equivalent coal tons in oil resources, while the Far East is projected at 27 billion coal tons of oil resources. The energy *needs* of any of these areas easily equal the projected resources in this time frame (1970-2000). The only *net* surplus areas, when compared with actual energy consumption patterns of today are the Middle East (81 billion tons) and Africa (34 billion tons).

Figure 6-9 shows the total estimated world resources of coal and lignite and their distribution. Figure 6-9 also shows the rough relation of the total oil resources to coal and lignite resources. *Total known world petroleum resources are insignificant when compared to coal and lignite resources.* The total estimate of petroleum resources are plotted on the left side of Figure 6-9. Roughly, coal and lignite resources amount to *40 times* the total world petroleum resources.

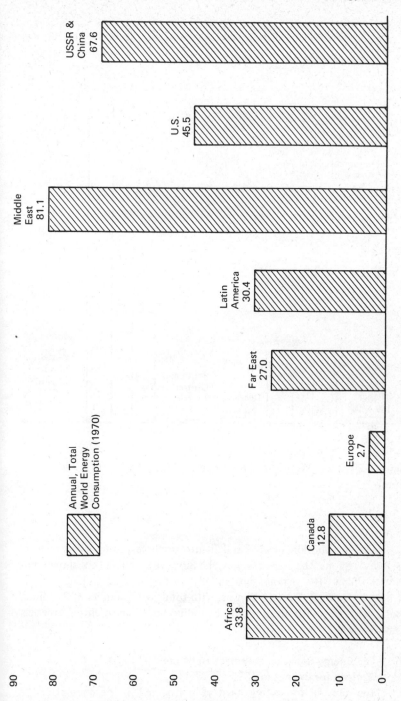

Figure 6-8. Total World Petroleum Resources (1970)
(2,090 Billion Barrels or 300 Billion Metric Tons of Coal Equivalent)

Metric Tons of Coal Equivalent (in Billions)

Annual, Total World Energy Consumption (1970)

USSR & China 67.6

U.S. 45.5

Middle East 81.1

Latin America 30.4

Far East 27.0

Europe 2.7

Canada 12.8

Africa 33.8

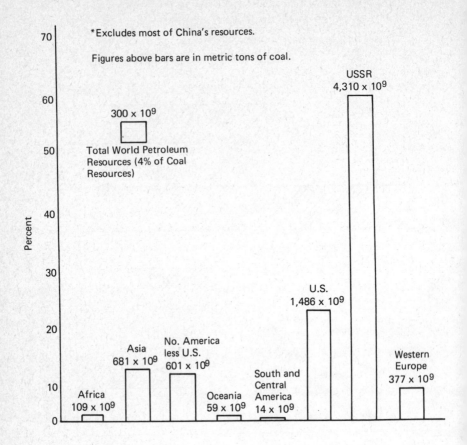

Figure 6-9. Total World Coal Resources (1970) 7,637 x 10^9 Metric Tons*

The distribution of coal and lignite resources, however, is concentrated in a few regions: the United States, the Soviet Union and (not shown, but well known) China. The regions substantially lacking in coal and lignite are: Japan, with no resources; Western Europe, with total coal resources of 37 billion metric tons; and all of the third world, including South and Central America, Africa, and Oceania.

The Energy Squeeze: A Projection of the Demand for Energy to 1990

The demand for energy must be considered in the context of the overall economic and technological growth and especially the propensity of many economic systems to advance to the levels of consumption already achieved elsewhere (usually by the United States).

The technology of a country can be described by input-output tables. For the major countries such input-output tables are readily available—although often not at the desired level of aggregation or classification. The single most important exception is China—for which hardly any economic information is available. For China we therefore approximated results by simple extrapolation of existing trends over the next decades.

Table 6-2 shows the available figures for China (1965-66) and the corresponding figures for five other major areas. The Gross National Products of the six regions were computed on the basis of *Purchasing Power Equivalent* (PPE) rates. These we obtained on the basis of different sources listed in footnote 2 of Table 6-2. The PPE rates represent the most realistic exchange figures for the purposes of our study, i.e., comparison of the economic production of various nations, allowing for differences in relative prices in major industrial sectors, taxation, and social services offered.

Table 6-2 lists the population figures for these regions and major quantitative data for energy and basic materials. We included the production of electricity, crude oil, and coal in the energy sector, and also give the aggregate total production and consumption of energy (including natural gas and nuclear energy) in equivalent metric tons of coal. As basic materials steel, cement, and fertilizer output were used, reflecting 1960s technology.

We then allowed for different rates of economic growth in the next 24 years in the various sectors. The rates used are given in Table 6-3. The justification of each of these rates would require more analysis than is possible here. For China we list in Table 6-3 alternative industrial growth rates of 15 and 10%, which are admittedly optimistic. The long run rate of growth for the United States has been a little less than 5%. Under good economic management, the United States economy should be able to sustain a rate close to 5% for quite some time (as in the 1960s), which was the actual growth rate of aggregate United States energy consumption from 1966 to 1970. The Soviet Union averaged 7 percent. Given the great backlog in the Soviet consumer sector, and technology related to it, plus the presently unlimited material resource endowment, a 7 percent rate for the Soviet Union is quite realistic. In the 1960s Japan supposedly averaged annual growth rates of 14 to 15 percent but we expect her rate to be lower than that in the next decades, both because of her very poor energy and raw material endowment and the closing of the technological and economic gap that existed between Japan and the United States. Thus, for Japan and the European Economic Community (EEC—six countries) we postulate rates of growth at 7 percent, though this may be a somewhat optimistic estimate for the EEC.

A separate analysis was made for the energy sector of China, because the projections of coal production were clearly incompatible with present resources, technology, production and distribution systems. The postulated

Table 6-2. Economic Indicators of Six Major Regions in 1965-66[1]

Country	PPE[2] rate 1966	GNP 1966 in PPE 10⁹ $	Population 1966 10⁶	Quantitative Indices 1965 (metric system) ENERGY — Electricity 10⁹ kwh	Crude Oil 10⁶ t	Coal 10⁶ t	Total Energy[3] 10⁶ t coal equivalent Production	Consumption	BASE MATERIALS Steel 10⁶ t	Cement 10⁶ t	Fertilizers 10⁶ t	Military Budgets[4] 1966 PPE 10⁹ $
United States	1.00	747.6	197	1,221	99	475	1,633	1,791	121	65	50	63.3
Soviet Union	1.20	428.4	233	507	57	378	925	829	91	72	31	56.4
China	1.40	100.0[5]	750	50	10	250	272	272	12	10	6	9.1
European Economic Community	1.16	371.9	184	402	15	217	311	576	86	87	n.a.	15.3
Japan	2.05	199.4	99	180	1	51	62	175	40	33	15	1.9
India	1.27	46.8	502	29	2	64	74	84	6	10	2	1.9

[1] Sources: United Nations, *Statistical Yearbook*, 1968; B. Richman, *Industrial Society in Communist China*, Random House, New York, 1969; Chu-Yuan Cheng, "The Cultural Revolution and China's Economy," *Current History*, September 1967, pp. 148-17; N.P. Federenko, "Planning of Production and Consumption in the USSR," *Technological Forecasting*, Vol. 1, No. 1, June 1969, pp. 87-96.

[2] Purchasing Power Equivalent (PPE) rates were calculated by us on the basis of the following sources: Gilbert and Kravis, *Comparative National Products and Price Levels, A Study of Western Europe and the United States*, OECD, Paris, 1958; Beckerman and Bacon's article in *The Economic Journal*, September 1966; S. Cohn, "Soviet Growth Retardation: Trends in Resource Availability and Efficiency," *New Directions in the Soviet Economy*, Part II-A, Washington, U.S. Government Printing Office, 1966; International Bank for Reconstruction and Development, *World Bank Atlas of Per Capita Product and Population*, 1966; B. Richman, *Industrial Society in Communist China*, *op. cit.*

[3] Based on the conversion numbers shown in Table 8.

[4] U.S. Arms Control and Disarmament Agency, *World Military Expenditures, 1966-67*, Washington, D.C., U.S. Government Printing Office, 1968.

[5] 1966-1968 average, subjective estimate by outside sources.

energy consumption growth rates projected in Table 6-3 rest on several considerations. From historical experience (the United States for example) a developing country like China could expect annual expansion rates of the use of energy between 7 and 10 percent. These rates can be sustained over a very substantial period of time.

Western Europe and Japan (which are in an adaptation phase to United States standards) can be reasonably expected to increase annual energy consumption at rates between 5 and 7 percent annually. The United States can be expected to drop to annual energy requirement increases of between 3 and 4 percent. In this respect, the average for the United States since 1910 is slightly misleading. There were two major World Wars which retarded the overall worldwide industrial and economic development very substantially, and therefore the total energy needs and requirements that can be expected in the next two to three decades will be higher, with the expectation, of course, that no major world conflicts will occur in this time period. Therefore, for developed countries, we could postulate that the per capita energy growth might occur at a rate of 2 percent. This implies that whatever population growth occurs will add to the annual per capita increase in energy consumption. Thus, for the United States, the long term energy growth rate should be between 3 and 4 percent which equals the long term economic growth rate for the United States economy for the past 100 years.

The above extrapolations are confirmed when looking at per capita energy consumption trends. In Tables 6-4 and 6-5 we assembled the basic statistics of the earlier tables in slightly different form: population figures, energy production figures, consumption figures, per capita consumption figures, as well as the actual deficit between the production and consumption, are shown by countries and regions. According to Table 6-4 the United States did use the equivalent of two billion tons of coal in 1970. The annual energy consumption in the United States is 11.1 metric tons of coal equivalent for every person.

The next highest ranking country with regard to the total energy produced was the Soviet Union with a consumption of energy of about 1.1 billion tons. Both the United States and the Soviet Union have total energy reserves sufficient to supply foreseeable energy needs, although the United States imports about 10 percent of the total energy requirements, equaling the absolute energy imports of Japan. This import is explained by economic considerations—Mideast petroleum production costs are one-tenth of some United States productions costs—and the relative scarcity of some particular fossil fuels such as natural gas.

Japan, with a population of about 104 million in 1970, produced an equivalent of 55 million tons of energy and consumed 332 million metric tons of coal equivalent. Thus, *Japan is producing only one-sixth of its total energy consumption domestically* and has a negligible chance of improving that ratio especially given the expected increase in demand for energy per capita. A similar

Table 6-3.   Projections of Six Major Regions to 1990 Based on Table 9 and Growth Trends of 1950-68

Country	Annual Growth Rate[1] Percent	GNP in PPE 10^9 \$	ENERGY					BASE MATERIALS		
			Electricity 10^9 kwh	Crude Oil 10^6 t	Coal[2] 10^6 t	Total Energy[3]		Steel 10^6 t	Cement 10^6 t	Fertilizers 10^6 t
						10^6 t Production	Coal Equiv. Consumption			
United States	5	2,500	3,900	320	1,500[2]	5,270[6]	5,780[6]	390	210	160
Soviet Union	7	2,300	2,600	290	1,900[2]	4,690	4,200	460	370	160
China	15 [10]	2,200[4] [1,000]	4,000[4] [500]	800[4] [98]	810[4] [2,400]	2,340[4] [2,680]	2,340[4] [2,680]	400 [140]	290 [98]	170 [60]
European Economic Community	7	2,000	2,000	76	1,100[2]	1,580[5]	2,900[5]	440	450	n.a.
Japan	7	1,100	900	5	260	310	890[5]	200	170	80
India	10	505	300	20	630	730	830	30	100	20

[1] Based on performance over the past 20 years, the long term U.S. growth rate actually is between 3 and 4 percent; that of the Soviet Union may slow down, though the resource endowment and the needs of the consumer sector allow the Soviet Union still substantial expansion (to reach U.S. standards of 1969); China's actual rate in 1966 was around 20 percent.* For the next decades both resource endowment and needs allow China nearly unlimited growth; the real bottenecks in China are human and organizational capital. The E.E.C.'s expansion rate is close to its recent performance, not its long term, somewhat lower rate; Japan's rate is considerably below the 14 to 15 percent of growth in recent years. However, as the table shows, even at a 6 percent rate, Japan will develop *serious* gaps in energy needs and base material needs. India's 10 percent rate is based more on the foreseeable needs of expansion than the actual performance of India in the past 20 years. If successful economic reorganization takes place in the next years, India may actually show much higher growth rates; however, India's resource endowment in all fields (agriculture, energy, base materials) is much lower than that of the other regions considered, except for Japan.

[2] Coal production will not expand at the indicated rates; however, other energy sources (nuclear fission [breeders], magnetohydrodynamic, fuel cells, solar) will be substituted.

[*] Indications are that the 1969-71 annual growth rates *averaged* between 10 and 12 percent annually. However, growth rates of some key sectors (petroleum, machinery, etc.) were substantially higher.

[3] Includes natural gas production.

[4] The energy sector for China, at a 15 percent rate of annual growth, gave 4,800 million tons of coal equivalent for 1990. However, China's energy sector in 1966 was still based on coal, which sector expanded only at a much reduced rate. China did achieve a coal production of about 500 million tons in 1959, but could not put these to economic use. Also, we anticipate that China's production will not expand much beyond this figure as more economic energy resources are available to China. Therefore, we estimated its probable expansion in the energy sector with a 5 percent rate for coal (806 x 10^6 tons in 1990) and a 20 percent rate for petroleum, hydroelectric and other sources (1,530 x 10^6 tons in 1990). This gives us 2,340 for 1990 overall, or about a 10 percent annual growth of this sector. This is also reflected in the GNP projection of $2,200 x 10^9 which otherwise, at 15 percent, would have been $2,900 x 10^9.

[5] In both the E.E.C. and Japan a serious energy base gap exists today and will increasingly be felt in the next decades. Both regions will have to invest and develop intensively new energy source fields (nuclear fission breeders, fusion, solar) to achieve the projected 1990 requirements.

[6] The actual consumption figure for the United States was about 2,300 million and in 1970 reflecting exactly an annual growth rate of the demand for energy of 5 percent, and this in a period of *relative* economic stagnation.

Table 6-4. Energy Production/Consumption by Country

Country	Population in Millions	Total (in 10⁶ metric tons) Per Capita (in metric tons per year) 1970			Actual Deficit Prod.–Cons.	Potential Consumption at 1970 U.S. Rate Per Capita	
		Production	Consumption	Consumption per Capita		Potential Total	GAP (Actual–U.S. Level)
United States	205	2,054	2,282 33%	11.1	-228	n.a.	n.a.
Soviet Union	243	1,213	1,079 16	4.4	+	2,697	-1,618
Japan	104	55	332 5	3.2	-277	1,154	-822
Germany (W)	60	175	315 5	5.1	-140	666	-351
France	51	59	193 3	3.8	-134	566	-373
Italy	54	26	144 2	2.7	-118	599	-455
Netherlands	13	49	66 1	5.1	-17	144	-78
Belg.–Lux.	9.7	12	59 1	5.9	-47	77	-18
G. Britain	56	164	299 4	5.4	-135	622	-323
Sweden	8.0	5	51 1	6.3	-46	89	-38
Austria	7.4	11	25	3.4	-14	82	-57
Switzerland	6.3	4	21	3.4	-17	70	-49
Norway	3.9	8	19	4.8	-11	43	-24
Denmark	4.9	0	29	5.9	-29	54	-25
Portugal	9.6	1	7	.7	-6	106	-99
China	760	420	426 6	.5	+	8,436	-8,010
India	550	87	103	.2	-16	6,105	-6,002
World (incl. others)	3707	7,000	6,843 100	1.9	+	41,148	-34,305

Table 6-5. Energy Production/Consumption by Major Regions

Region	Energy — Total (in 10⁶ metric tons of coal equivalents) Per Capita (in metric tons of coal equivalents) 1970					"Potential - 1970" Consumption at U.S. Rate 1970		
	Population	Production	Consumption	Per Capita Consumption	Actual Deficit Prod.–Cons.	Potential	GAP Actual-Potential Consumption	% Actual
United States	205	2,054	2,282	11.1	-228	n.a.	n.a.	40
Soviet Union	243	1,213	1,079	4.4	+	2,697	-1,618	37
EEC (6)	188	321	777	4.1	-456	2,087	-1,310	39
EEC (9)	284	514	1,228	4.3	-714	3,152	-1,924	29
Japan	104	55	332	3.2	-277	1,154	- 882	29
China	760	420	426	.5	+	8,436	-8,010	5
World	3,707	7,000	6,843	1.8	+	41,148	-34,305	6
World - 4 Regions	2,871	3,164	1,922	.7	+	31,868	-29,946	6

n.a. = not applicable

situation holds for Western European countries: West Germany, with a total energy consumption of 315 million metric tons, produced only 60% (175 million metric tons); France, with a domestic consumption of 193 million metric tons, produced less than 1/3; Italy, with a total of 144 million metric tons of energy consumed, produced only 30 million tons or roughly 15% of its needs; and Great Britain had a domestic energy consumption of 299 million tons and a production of only 164 million metric tons.

Overall, the European Economic Community (six countries) had a total energy import requirement in 1970 of 456 million metric tons of coal equivalent, while the EEC and EFTA jointly imported the equivalent of 714 million metric tons. *Together the energy imports of thirteen Western European countries and Japan amounted roughly to the total energy consumed in the Soviet Union.* Yet most of these countries had only about *half* the per capita energy consumption of the United States. The Soviet Union had a per capita energy consumption of 4.4 metric tons per year or about 40 percent of that of the United States. Industrial states such as West Germany and Great Britain, the Netherlands, Belgium, and Luxembourg had an annual per capita consumption of roughly half that of the United States. China had a per capita energy energy consumption of approximately 0.5 metric tons (10 percent of Western European countries or 5 percent of the United States). Finally, all of Western Europe had a per capita consumption of about 4.3 metric tons while the *worldwide* average consumption was roughly two metric tons of coal per capita.

When all of these data are combined into one overview representation, we find a rather surprising insight into the actual power relation of the major regions of the world and their relative positions. In Figure 6-10 the consumption, production and "energy gap" figures (arrows) are shown for all major countries and regions. The horizontal axis measures the population size (in logarithms) and the vertical axis measures total energy production and consumption in millions of metric tons of coal equivalent (1970 data). Arrows connect consumption figures to production figures of individual countries. Thus a downward pointing arrow indicates an energy gap (consumption exceeds production) and an upward pointing arrow indicates an energy "surplus" (production exceeds consumption for that country). The length of the arrow indicates the relative size of the gap.

We also define four measures of achievement (power) levels:

1. An *absolute "Great Power" achievement level*, which we define as the minimum of the absolute energy consumption levels reached in either the United States or Soviet Union. This definition is based on the assumption that in order to maintain technical-economic-military-political activity levels typical of "great power" nations, minimum absolute energy consumption levels have to be reached.

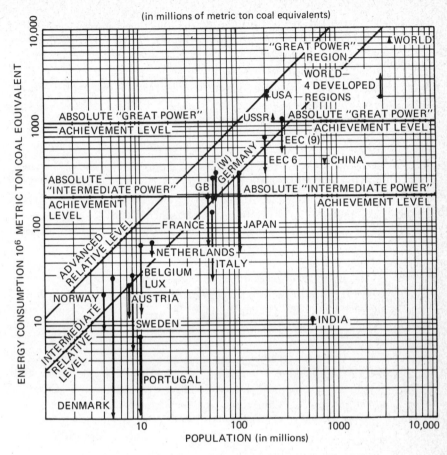

Figure 6-10. Energy Consumption, Production and Dependency by Major World Regions

2. An *absolute "intermediate power" achievement level*, which we define as the minimum of the absolute energy consumption levels reached in any of these countries: Japan, Germany (W), Great Britain or France. The reasoning underlying this assumption is similar to the one given in (1). The two horizontal lines in Figure 6-10 indicate these two absolute achievement levels.

3. An *advanced relative achievement level*, defined as the maximum per capita energy consumption level of either the United States or Soviet Union.

4. An *intermediate relative achievement level*, defined as the minimum per capita energy consumption level in any of these countries: Japan, Germany (W), Great Britain, or France.

The upward sloping lines (from lower left to upper right) in Figure 6-10 indicate these two relative measures.

Using these definitions some important conclusions and insights can be drawn from Figure 6-10.

1. With regard to "great power" status among the major world regions, the European Economic Community of nine ranks well within the absolute and relative achievement levels, as defined above, in terms of energy consumption patterns in population, in total energy and per capita energy consumed. Only the United States and the Soviet Union rank within the same area.

2. Japan well exceeds the absolute "intermediate power" energy consumption level, but in per capita energy consumption Japan ranks the lowest when compared to the EEC(9), the EEC(6), or individually to Germany (W), Great Britain, or France.

3. China lies well above the absolute "intermediate power" level in consumption and production, but falls well short of energy consumption levels defined as absolute "great power" levels or relative intermediate levels. Given the large population size of China, and its substantially different social and economic approach toward the solution of its problems, the relative (per capita) levels may be a less meaningful measurement in the case of China. Nevertheless, the absolute gap remains quite large.

4. Of the five major regions, three regions—the United States, the Soviet Union, and China—are relatively self-sufficient. In the Soviet Union and China energy production exceeds consumption, and in the United States the drop of consumption levels to domestic production levels would leave the United States still substantially above any other country in absolute and relative energy availability.

5. Of the other two major regions, the EEC(9) drops *substantially below* the absolute "great power" level and even the *relative* intermediate achievement levels in terms of production of energy resources. If Europe was cut off from outside energy imports—for military, political, economic reasons— Europe could not maintain relative economic-technical production and activity levels associated even with intermediate powers. The absolute energy production levels, however, would suffice to maintain Europe at the level of about China.

6. Japan's consumption levels exceed or reach both relative and absolute intermediate levels. But (similar to the EEC(9)) Japan, when cut off from outside energy supplies, would reduce its energy supply levels such that Japan would be relegated to a status *considerably below any intermediate* power levels.

7. There are no short term or intermediate technological, economic or other developments in sight that will or can change the de facto dependencies of either Europe or Japan on outside sources whatever their economic or other development achievement levels will be in the next two decades.

8. The "rest of the world"—underdeveloped as it is—subsidizes very substantially the energy consumption achievement levels of three of the most developed regions (Japan, Europe, and to a lesser degree the United States).

9. Individual countries within Europe, with the exception of Germany (W), Great Britain, and Benelux, are even worse off than Japan in their energy dependency.

10. With the change in United States energy policy from one aimed at self-sufficiency to one of active imports, the situation of Europe and Japan becomes serious even with the open access to outside energy sources: while to the United States the access to these same sources means merely an (important) improvement in its efficiency of the energy sector, to Japan and Europe the entry of the United States means a threat to their relatively fixed outside supplies in an already precarious situation.

11. The United States advanced energy consumption achievement level does incorporate a substantial amount of wasteful use of energy resources, rather than technical and economic achievement levels so much in excess of those of Europe and Japan.

The differences in the *per capita* consumption levels may, therefore, reflect not only different degrees of economic development, but be explained in part at least by outright waste of energy resources. Of course, the mere fact that one can indulge in waste may reflect advanced levels of affluence and wealth. Thus, in the case of the United States, and Canada, it may be possible to produce and sustain the same levels of economic activities with a more economic use of energy resources. This can be induced through either a new price policy in the production and distribution of energy resources, or tax policies and incentives, or—worst of all—direct regulation and allocation. Such a new approach might reduce the difference in per capita consumption patterns (ten tons vs. four to five tons) and also lead to external benefits in reducing environmental damages of energy production, distribution. and final use.

There is ample room for adaptation among different energy resources in final demand patterns, and in conversion and distribution systems; e.g., restriction of waste within the present pattern of energy production and consumption). Figure 6-11 shows the actual situation for the United States, in 1970, in the use of energy resources, their transformation to final demand, useful work, and waste. From Figure 6-11 we see that about 50 percent of the total energy resources consumed in the United States in 1970 were, ultimately, wasted. Of the total energy consumed in the United States (about 65 X 10^{15} BTUs), about 32 X 10^{15} BTUs were wasted (or about 1.1 billion tons of coal equivalent).[a]

However, in order to gain a better insight into useful versus waste energy in the United States, one has to look at the particular transformation process, first in a very aggregate sense within the United States. In Figure 6-11 we see the rough breakdown of energy resources supplied for the United States' energy consumption: natural gas and natural gas liquids, petroleum and coal, hydroelectric power, and nuclear power. The two major sources of United States energy supply—natural gas and petroleum—are the resources we identified earlier as particularly scarce over the next ten to twenty years, even within the United States. Nuclear power and hydroelectric power make up only minor amounts within the overall supply of energy resources to the U.S.

Any one of these fossil, hydroelectric and nuclear energy resources are then put to two possible uses: the production of electricity and fuel for direct consumption. Roughly 25 percent of all the energy resources produced in the United States go into the production of *electricity*. From Figure 6-11 we see that, of the total electricity produced, a very large amount—that is, 70%—is energy lost in the process of generation and transmission of electricity. Only about 30 percent of the electricity is finally used in households and by commercial as well as industrial users. There seems to be a major opportunity, particularly in the United States, in research and development as well as price policy for energy resources, either to restrict the consumption and production of electricity substantially, or (much more likely and desirable) to increase the efficiency of electricity generation, transmission, and use.

For example, doubling the overall price of energy, or of electricity alone, would lead to completely different outcomes of benefit-cost analyses when analyzing research and development projects of electricity generation, electricity transmission, and final uses of electricity. New technology, although more costly and expensive, at today's prices and costs would be justified with the new price system. Similarly, with the introduction of an energy waste *penalty* function, a similar effect could be induced. Given the "waste" pattern of United States energy use today, there seems to be a particular opportunity for such economic analyses and the introduction of "political prices."

---

[a]One has just to think of the physical effort needed to mine the equivalent of 1 billion tons of coal only to then "dump" this production on a "waste pile." The ecological costs of the waste of energy have to be added to this.

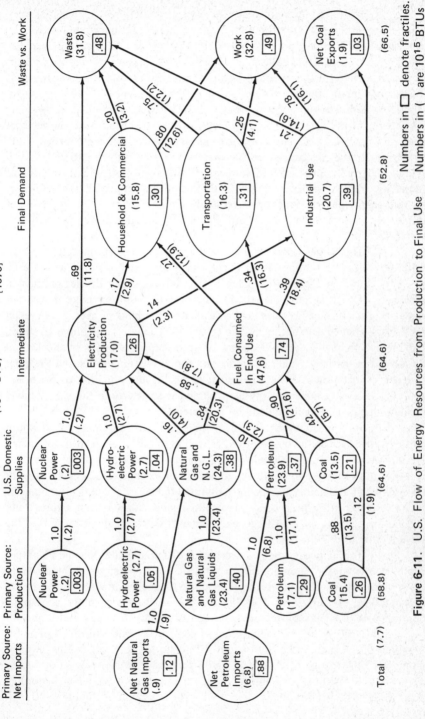

Figure 6-11. U.S. Flow of Energy Resources from Production to Final Use

More than two-thirds of the total energy resources produced now go to the production of fuel for end uses. Of these, the demands for fuel by household and commercial users, for transportation, and for industrial users are about equally large. Household and commercial users as well as industrial users incur a relatively small amount of waste: the former waste about 20 percent of their energy inputs, the latter about 25 percent of the inputs.

For the third major user of fuel—the transportation sector—(about 30 percent of the total energy consumed in the United States), we notice that nearly *75 percent of the energy inputs used for transportation are wasted*. Only 25 percent of the energy used for transportation is transformed into useful work energy under a hypothetical 100 percent efficient—zero loss—transformation of the energy inputs. Again, it seems to us that through an improved price policy or a waste energy penalty function, a very substantial transformation in the use of means of transportation can be brought about toward more energy efficient systems.

The large variance of the net energy propulsion efficiency of different means of transportation (road, rail, water, and air) even within each mode, is shown in Figure 6-12. Each horizontal bar shows the net propulsion efficiency of each system, measured in number of passenger miles moved per gallon of fuel. The efficiencies are calculated on the basis of average figures in present experience, and not maximum capacities. The inset in Figure 6-12 shows the average frequency and efficiency of transportation modes in the United States. Given the large choice of modes and systems within modes, and the great variance of net propulsion efficiency, it highlights the potential of price and taxation policies to adjust energy demand and use patterns in the U.S., a mode highly preferable to regulation and quota systems.

In countries such as China, India, the African countries, or South America, the per capita consumption, as well as the absolute quantity of energy consumed are still dramatically low; the problem there is not one of waste and conservation of energy by more economic use of existing resources, but one of mere physical availability for the most essential industrial and agricultural needs. Hand in hand with these low per capita energy consumption figures (and production figures), of course, go exceedingly low standards of living (see the Introduction to this chapter).

The implications of a worldwide "United States standard" of per capita energy consumption are shown in the last two columns of Tables 6-4 and 6-5. Were any of the other major regions to achieve the same per capita consumption of energy as the United States, it would imply an annual consumption of energy by the Soviet Union of about 2.7 billion metric tons of coal, of the EEC of about 2 billion tons of coal, of the EEC and EFTA of about 3 billion tons of coal, by Japan of about 1.2 billion tons of coal, and by China of about 8.4 billion tons of coal. *The figure for China alone*—with an estimated population in 1970 of 760 million people—would imply a total energy production by China that is in excess of the total world energy production in 1970.

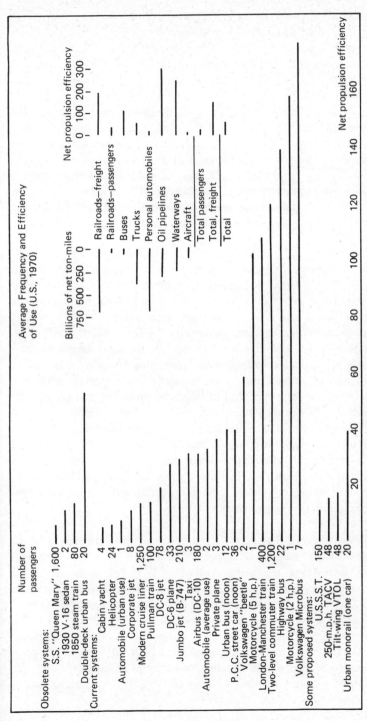

Source: Rice, Richard A., "System Energy and Future Transportation," in *Energy Technology to the Year 2000*, a special symposium published by Technology Review, January, 1972.

Figure 6-12. Net Energy Propulsion Efficiency of Transporation Systems

The deficits in potential development with the great energy deficits in Western Europe and Japan already existing, identical per capita production figures for Western Europe as those already achieved in the United States imply that the EEC and Western Europe would have to import the equivalent of about two billion metric tons of coal per year *in addition to* the energy already imported by them of about 700 million tons. This means, roughly, that Western Europe would have to import annually a total of energy exceeding the total energy consumed in the United States in 1970. Clearly, these anticipated energy requirements cannot be met by fossil fuels. Human inventiveness, particularly when stimulated by economic incentives, will find answers and long term solutions to the energy requirements of industrial and postindustrial societies. This optimism would be unwarranted if not supported by known potentials in the physical sciences. Yet there are ample technological options available for research and development that seem to justify our "long run" optimism. Among these are:

Nuclear Waste Disposal.   A medium term solution to the energy problem may be nuclear fission energy, including breeder technology. The single most important adverse effect of this energy option today is the need to dispose of the radioactive waste materials, particularly some actinides. Yet the advent of new space transportation capabilities, particularly the Space Shuttle System, do open the possibility of a safe long term disposal of the most dangerous, long lived radioactive wastes under acceptable and controlled operating risks, and at acceptable costs to the users. This option is particularly important when one considers the world wide waste control and disposal problems, and not just the United States.[2] For the United States alone, and taking low projections of waste disposal needs, eight Space Shuttle flights would be needed in 1985; in subsequent years this flight level would steadily increase to reach about 50 flights by the year 2000. This option needs careful technical and economic analysis, but the data available to us indicate, for the first time, a solution that in our opinion will considerably accelerate the introduction and economic development of this medium term energy option.

Fusion Energy.   The potential and the many different approaches to developing this energy source under controlled conditions are well known. Several broad approaches are being reached today: Tokamaks, Stabilized Mirrors, Theta Pinch-Scylla IV, and others.[3] Particular attention is being given to laser-initiated fusion and the extension of the range of the Tokamak technology—with noticeable new results in recent months.[4]

The energy attainable by fusion of all the deuterium in a cubic meter of sea water (roughly one metric ton of water) is 12×10^{12} joules. To get a quantitative understanding of this number, this energy content (just of the deuterium) corresponds to the chemical energy content of 33,000 metric tons of coal. The ease of separation of deuterium from plain sea water has to be compared to the physical as well as human, social, and environmental effort of mining 33,000 tons of coal. Equivalently, the total U.S. energy production in 1970 amounted to about two billion metric tons of coal equivalent.The same energy content is contained in about 60,000 tons of sea water (about 60m x 10m x 10m!).

Similarly, the total world energy production in 1970 of about seven billion of metric tons of coal is contained in equivalent form in the deuterium of 200,000 tons of plain sea water (about 200m x 10m x 10m). Of course, these simple physical numbers are misleading. However, in the very long run outlook for nations and the development of mankind, certainly the advent of fusion power in one form or another promises a practically unlimited expansion of energy resources which, in addition, would be ecologically clean, with the exception of heating effects.

Solar Energy. The second potentially "unlimited" source is solar energy. The earth's daily receipt (at the surface) of solar energy corresponds to about 1.49×10^{22} joules, which again is more than 100 times the yearly energy consumption of the U.S. in 1970 (two billion metric tons of coal equivalent). Thus the daily input of energy received by the earth from the sun corresponds to about 200 to 300 billion metric tons of coal.

The most immediate way of capturing and utilizing solar energy will be through *biochemical* utilization options. Other ground based systems are also being explored, yet the zones of abundance of unused solar energy on the ground (deserts, oceans) do not coincide with the regions of energy demand. Of course, in near earth space, the solar energy is equally existent and can be captured by space based systems. Technically, this is being achieved today on a very small scale in solar electric propulsion systems as well as solar electric power systems supplying spacecrafts. On a much larger scale, these energies can be possibly tapped and transmitted through a variety of techniques. A space based solar power station design has first been proposed by Peter Glaser.[5] Whether such a station is technically and economically feasible today is an entirely different question. In the long run, with further developments of technology, the existing solar energy will be captured in space and transmitted to earth.

With some very courageous projections of technology, Peter Glaser proposes a 3,000 to 15,000 megawatt power satellite station with a solar collector in space of 12 km x 5 km and a microwave transmission system over 22,000 miles to a receiving antenna system with a ten to twenty km diameter on earth. Whatever the exact numbers and the efficiencies involved—particularly of solar cells as used by Glaser—as well as the feasibility to deploy solar collecting stations of that size in space, the numbers themselves are fascinating. The 10^7 kilowatt space energy station with a 5×10^6 kilowatt output at the ground is roughly equivalent to the average range of interest of potential power levels.

Space based energy processes would allow to overcome even the heating effects of the environment of any excessive earth based energy use.

Without discussing in detail the feasibility (technical or economic) of any one of these two sources of energy, it is clear that over a very finite period of time the technology will be available and ready to use the fusion energy resources of the earth as well as those of the sun—two independent, unlimited, and ecologically clean sources of energy for mankind. However, it is clear that such developments cannot take place within the next 30 years or so, given present technology. Thus enormous differences among countries will remain. Even if new technology becomes available there would be tremendous demand for capital and great time delays in introducing new techniques at the required rates.

World Energy Squeeze: International Economic, Political, and Military Implications

The foregoing forecast of a world energy squeeze will certainly have important international *economic* repercussion. The consequences of a severe international energy shortage will affect in various ways the less developed countries. It will be a disadvantage to the net importers while benefiting the net exporters of fuel. Here, however, the focus is on the likely consequences for those nations which are, actually or potentially, the world's political, economic, and military powers.

Our analysis will necessarily be speculative. Although a world energy crisis is sure to come over the next several decades, its precise magnitude and configuration is uncertain, since these depend on the nature and speed of the adjustments undertaken by the fuel importing and exporting countries. But the impact of, and the national responses to, the emerging crisis are much more uncertain since the major actors can choose their responses from a range of interdependent options.

Impact on the International Distribution of Income and Wealth. There should be some *appreciable shifts* in the international distribution of income and wealth even if we assume, as a first approach, that the impending energy shortage will take its immediate effect through the medium of a free international market system of the type envisaged by the General Agreement on Tariffs and Trade (GATT). In any free market, producers of fuel would obviously gain relative to the consumers. Given a demand which is highly price inelastic, and a supply which is much less so, the terms of trade would shift strongly in favor of the oil exporting countries and against the oil importing ones.[b]

---

[b]Our analysis will concentrate on oil, although as oil becomes scarcer and oil prices rise, there would also be an increasing shift of demand to coal, with—at least for some countries such as Japan—roughly similar effects.

However, as long as oil continues to flow in response to demand, this shift in the terms of trade should be bearable, though very uncomfortable to the rich importing countries. If we assume that the increasing price of oil, and increasing imports of oil, lead to an eventual doubling of their *total* import bill, the effect on income would depend on the size of imports relative to GNP. This is only *around 5 percent* in the United States. The impact would be correspondingly larger where imports range to 15 percent of GNP or more, as is the case in Japan and several Western European nations.

Incidentally, the burden of larger and more expensive oil imports to the United States might be well offset, more or less, by the effects of the sharply increasing world demand for food. This demand is rising not only as a result of continuing population growth but also because expanding demands for better food in countries experiencing continuous economic development. The American capacity to produce additional food and fodder is much larger than present output rates indicate; and this country could come to reap great export and income gains from this other bonanza which, not inconceivably, might entail consequences comparable with those resulting from the energy squeeze. Regarding the international distribution of these effects, it should be noted that of all the main power centers only the United States would benefit. Western Europe and Japan will continue to be regular importers of food and fodder, and China and the Soviet Union are apt to be heavy importers whenever weather conditions diminish local crops.

Since the increase in the costs of fuel imports would be consummated over a considerable period of time, neither the wealth nor the further economic growth of the affluent world would be seriously affected. The opposite effect in the oil exporting countries would be much more dramatic since nearly all of them are countries of small population. Any 10 percent rise in the import bill of the United States, the EEC (including Britain), and Japan alone would expand the income of the OPEC countries dramatically and with unforeseeable consequences of internal and external political relations.

However, the way in which the energy squeeze will work itself out internationally will almost certainly not be left to the operation of free market forces. The oil exporting countries can obviously do better if they set up a monopoly for the purpose of reaping monopolist profit. The establishment and behavior of the Organization of Oil Exporting Countries (OPEC) makes it clear that this is what the major exporting countries intend to do. The achievement of monopolist prices will, of course, make the burden on the importing countries correspondingly more painful, and may also accelerate the speed with which the pain is inflicted. Having the importing countries literally "over a barrel," OPEC could attempt to squeeze the rich importers mercilessly, and an extraordinary international shift of wealth could ensue if this attempt succeeded.

Such an attempt, however, presupposes that the monopolists would stay united, and it would certainly meet increasing resistance on the part of the big importing states. Such extortion would speed up the search for alternative new fuels in other parts of the world, and cause a shift from scarcer to relatively more abundant forms of energy. But what about resistance by means of economic counter pressures, and by means of military threats? Exactly because energy is such an extremely vital need of the importing countries, these countries would have no effective leverage on the basis of *economic* power. There is surely nothing that the rich oil exporting countries could not buy somewhere, or anything they would need to import as urgently as the rich industrial countries require fuel. In fact this lopsided dependence amounts to a vast shift of national *economic* power to the oil exporting states. Nor, in view of their past experience with Western powers, would they be especially susceptible to moral and political argument.

On the other hand, the main oil exporting countries would be vulnerable to the *military* power of the large industrial states. If only because of their small population base, the former countries' new wealth would not generate military strength comparable with that of the latter. Therefore, if the oil importing powers were united in their will to use military threats in order to curb the monopolist practices of the exporting states, these latter would have to be reasonable. However, the prospects of the importing states marshalling the will to be tough and to act in unison seem very remote. And even if some of them would be disposed to resort to force, it is most probable that some other military powers would back the exporting countries; especially the Soviet Union and, perhaps, China—themselves not vitally dependent on oil imports—might well see it in their interest to oppose the big capitalist states. Only if the importing countries became very desperate would they be likely to have recourse to force. To that extent, there would be a threshold of monopolist extortion which the exporting countries would find risky to cross.

Consequences for the International Distribution of Power and Influence. We have already concluded that if a severe world energy squeeze unfolds, as is virtually certain, the countries depending on fuel imports will lose international economic bargaining power vis-à-vis the fuel exporting states, and that this will be commercially very costly. We have also concluded that this development will *not* be accompanied by a corresponding shift in the bases of military strength as long as international oil flows are not interrupted—that is to say, as long as whoever has the financial wherewithal is dependably able to buy. It is precisely the possibility of such interruption, and the threat to interrupt, which poses another serious question about the future world power structure.

Two kinds of vulnerability can be readily distinguished: one concerned with dependability of supply as far as oil exporting countries are concerned, and the other involving dependability of supply lines, which, as pointed out in the foregoing, various countries might attempt to interrupt or, for purposes of blackmail, threaten to interrupt.

The Soviet Union will be essentially self-sufficient in petroleum if it makes the heavy investments needed to transport oil and gas from distant Siberian fields. The Chinese situation is less well known and less conjecturable. However, even if her at-present extremely low energy consumption per capita rises more or less continuously in the future, it is reasonable to assume that China will be largely self-sufficient, if only because her government is apt to pursue courses of action to maintain independence in so vital a matter. The West European powers, however, will, even by 1980, depend mostly on the Middle East and North Africa for about 85 percent of their oil supplies, and Japan's dependence on the outside world will be virtually absolute. Regarding oil, the United States will be in an intermediate position, requiring probably more than half its supplies from abroad by 1980, and perhaps as much as one-third from North Africa and the Middle East. Hence, not only will the United States be unable to supply Western Europe or Japan in an emergency, but this country will itself be vulnerable to the threat of interruption.

Neither Japan nor the West European countries maintain much more than a month's oil supply at home; and to augment this reserve substantially would be expensive. In an emergency, they could obviously ration fuel use for a time, and limp along. This is particularly true of the United States, where energy use is extremely wasteful. There is thus here a large hidden reserve that is difficult to assess statistically at present.[c] But it is also obvious that these economies would eventually grind to a paralyzing halt, or something close to it, if outside supplies were cut off for long. Their vulnerability, from this point of view, will be extreme.

We have argued above that this dependence is subject to commercial exploitation even though, beyond a high threshold, extortionate demands might provoke these countries to seek relief through military threats. But what if this vulnerability is exploited for political and power purposes?

Except for pressures on behalf of Arab objectives against Israel, and perhaps on behalf of suppressed black populations in South Africa and in the Portuguese colonies, this danger may not come to be very large, since the main exporting countries would have to act in unison. The danger might become larger if a great power such as the Soviet Union organized and led the oil exporting countries for such purposes of political pressuring. Still, although such probabilities look low at this time, even a small subjective probability of such ominous contingencies is worrisome when vulnerability is so great. If a political demand, backed by a threat to cut oil supplies, involved matters of great importance, the threatened countries could, of course, resort to military counter threats, provided they possessed the military means to make such threats effective over considerable distances.

---

[c]An effort ought to be made to determine *well in advance* of a critical moment what measures could be taken to reduce the present phenomenal waste in various degrees and to consider the cost of such interferences with present day usage.

Indeed, if a rising world energy squeeze leads to early indications that blackmail is a likely consequence, Japan and the West European powers may feel a strong incentive to provide themselves with the military means to operate overseas in sufficient strength. Whether they will react to this incentive, or do so sufficiently, is impossible to say at this time, especially since these importing countries have an alternative whose short run costs may seem comparatively less discouraging. Aware of their weakness, they may adopt foreign policies designed to accomodate and placate the oil exporting countries consistently. That is to say, they would pursue policies which they ordinarily would not adopt were it not for their vulnerability. In effect, their autonomy to make foreign policy would be reduced, and their international power and influence would be decreased sharply from what it is at present.

The United States, though less vulnerable than Japan and Western Europe, will nevertheless not escape some of the very same consequences ·of weakness unless it adopts suitable precautions very soon. If it does not act promptly to prevent a vulnerable dependence on foreign energy supplies, the United States will find its international power and influence markedly enfeebled.

Conjecture and the Problem of Public Policy.   The issues we have opened up in the foregoing raise a serious question about the utility of conjecture in terms of its use in guiding public action. On the matter of world energy we are in an area in which forecasting is fairly safe. We cannot be sure about precise magnitudes, dates, and configurations, but unless a miracle occurs, the world's capitalist states will be increasingly dependent on foreign sources of energy, and energy is at the very heart of industrial life. *There is no substitute for it.* And while international economic interdependence is useful when not exploited for malevolent purposes, the absence of such purpose cannot be guaranteed. But conjecture seems to have had no or little effect on public policy. This is perhaps understandable in the case of Japan and Western Europe, for they have no obviously satisfactory remedies. It is much less understandable in the case of the United States, which does possess interesting options.

What could the United States do to avoid or minimize a precarious dependence that could involve the most serious risks to American welfare and security, and to reduce such risks to other energy importing countries, especially the Western European nations and Japan?

The question is one of a transition period stretching a few decades into the future, for it is generally assumed that the new energy technologies should be practically available before very long. One remedy is, of course, to use energy less wastefully. Here a great deal can be done as mentioned above (cf. pp. 128-130), and rising prices should push in this direction. However, this price effect will be slow to force adaptation and it would seem desirable that public policy assist in the development of a less wasteful transportation system, and so forth. Another source of relief, of course, is to increase and encourage prospecting for oil and natural gas all over the world. This the oil companies can be relied upon to do. A third remedy is to stockpile fuel reserves for short term emergencies. A fourth possibility, with very large resource potential, is the gasification of coal, now believed to cost between 55 to 79 cents per million Btu. A fifth possibility, but one not looking very hopeful, is to continue exploring the technological possibilities of exploiting coal tars and shale. A sixth contribution could come from the speedy construction of nuclear fast-breeder reactors.

But obviously the most important means toward getting safely through the transition period of increasing scarcity of petroleum is by developing the production of coal (requiring large investments), and also by developing new technologies of deriving energy from coal, including the production of fuel for motor vehicles. Most urgent from this point of view is immediate and vigorous support of research and development. The basic reason why coal can play this vital role is that the United States—like the Soviet Union and China—possesses vast reserves of it. Unfortunately, as we have seen, Western Europe, and even more so Japan, are very deficient in this fossil fuel.

The costs of developing a modern coal technology—one which meets pollution standards—will no doubt be huge. But the amounts will look far from inhibiting if one takes into account the vast amounts that will have to be paid for foreign oil in the future. Why, then, is so little being done in this direction? There can be no doubt that the coming world energy squeeze will tend to result in a vast redistribution of international power and influence—to the detriment of the United States, the other democratic and affluent countries with which this country is allied, and also to a large number of less developed countries.

LIMITS OF PRICE ADJUSTMENT

It is a widespread belief in Western countries that shortages can be made up by price adjustments. This means that price increases will occur and they will cause production to rise and at the same time substitutes will be offered at lower prices. Together these two forces will reestablish an equilibrium and the economy will proceed.

This need not be true at all. Surely if the price of oil and gasoline goes up in the United States—and if government regulations do not work to the contrary—new wells will be brought home, drilling will be made more efficient, production will increase, and the greater demand will be satisfied, perhaps at a permanently higher price. But the hidden implication in that conventional economic argument is that there indeed exists an elastic supply, that there are untapped reserves that can be mobilized. Such may not be the case—which then means that the higher prices merely check demand and reorient it toward other directions. Also, there simply may not exist any substitutes, at least not at a given level of technology, and sometimes even not at *any* other technology, now only dimly on the horizon.

Examples for the latter two cases is *first* the situation of oil consumption in Japan. No amount of price increase will lead to mobilization of Japanese oil drilling (except off-shore), for the simple reason that there is no oil in Japan (prospecting might possibly be activated, however). One hundred percent of oil consumption is imported, as was discussed above. Neither are there now any substitutes. A conversion to electric power for heating, motor cars, etc., also will not work, since there are no sufficient alternative energy sources available at the present time. And even if they did exist, the transformation of, say, motor cars to electrical drive would take a long time. Many other examples could be mentioned for different countries and materials.

The *second* case relates to air traffic. This is now universally dependent on oil. If in the future (say in 100-200 years) the oil supply should be exhausted, given the present oil-dependent technology, air travel and air transportation would come to a total halt the world over. Long before then it would become increasingly expensive, forcing a reduction in total traffic, since substitutes (conversion of coal to gas, etc.) will not be cheaper, if available at all, and then certainly demand enormous capital investments.

At any rate, it is easy to see that the life style to which the advanced nations have become adjusted would be completely changed, reverting to the speeds and inconveniences of a past age. It is immaterial whether that is good or bad; all that matters is to see that without change in technology, even the present level of certain activities as found in the developed nations cannot be maintained. From these remarks it follows, incidentally, that it is not enough to discuss the future of total energy supplies; rather, it is necessary to examine the composition of the whole and to understand that vital activities are inextricably tied to specific *kinds* of energy and its availability in particular countries.

These considerations make it clear that nations so dependent on particulars would do well to direct major research efforts toward overcoming expected difficulties of the above kind. This should be done soon. *First*, it is not predictable whether and when the necessary basic discoveries will be made; *second*, even if "available," it may be decades before they become available in practical form on a massive scale. Nuclear energy offers a good illustration; it is obvious that it will play an increasing role for energy supply, even in its conventional form of making electricity only via steam (rather than the conversion of nuclear energy directly into electricity). Yet in spite of government support and investments of sizable amounts, little progress has been made in over 25 years. The (immediate) energy crisis apparently has to become far more severe before industry and governments move. This must be taken as a sign of how other at first slowly evolving (but nevertheless inexorable) crises will be dealt with.

We see from these considerations how contemporary economics of whatever blend, relying on individual and government action (as experienced so far), cannot cope with situations of this character. Both are tied to systems which will break down when they are challenged by such fundamentally new situations. New systems will have to be invented, and be invented and accepted in time.

These considerations show that one cannot rely on "free market forces" and private initiative, if only because the time scales transcend an individual's active life span by orders of magnitude. Furthermore, there is no incentive for private interests to begin work at this scale and to carry it through. Neither is there assurance that governments will act in time, even when the signs of the future are clear and strong. It is curious that in modern times there is little dedication to very long run projects.

In antiquity this was quite different; even in prehistoric times. Stonehenge took certainly 100 years or more to build. The pyramids required decades for construction, and the great Gothic cathedrals were continuously being built, added to, and transformed. In terms of the wealth of those times, these efforts dwarf most modern public investments, not even excepting the military budgets of the super powers.

As the time of true shortages approaches, endangering not only whole industries but the very life of nations, the world will have to adopt entirely new attitudes, invent new organizations, and be forced to cooperate beyond all present or future frontiers. However, these extreme situations will not arise within the next 30 years or so, although they will cast shadows ahead. We mention this complex of problems to indicate the need for contemplation of a more distant future, lest the human race be surprised by a fate it can do something to avoid. Differences in ideologies, which now keep nations apart or even hostile to each other, will become less and less important. Signs of this development are now apparent.

Part IV

Suggestions on a Constructive
Approach

Chapter Seven

The Dynamic Simultaneous
Equation Approach, by Sector

The quantitative analysis of short, medium, and long term trends and forecasts in economics and in social systems cannot ignore the vast amount and considerable refinement of techniques developed in econometrics and mathematical economics. Yet it is the field most widely ignored in the literature on long term forecasting, even to the extent of open or implicit admission of ignorance of the discipline. "Feedback systems" and control theory are not such new concepts to economists: since the advent of at least Walras, even economists realize the complexity of economic and social processes. Any claim to the contrary is just a display of ignorance in economic matters.[1] It is not possible for us to review here either the state of the art of mathematical economics, nor that of econometrics. However we do strongly suggest that both topics are of fundamental importance in coming to an understanding of the true capacity and the true magnitude (or absence) of problems in the long term for economic and social systems—and hence military and political power—as far as these have to be based on economic and social achievements.

In this chapter we will review very simply the types of quantitative analyses and forecasts made based on empirical evidence. As a case study we show a typical sector analysis, in this case the communications sector of the United States. The results show the great flexibility of technical and economic systems to price changes, income changes, R&D expenditures, and the role of technical change. We will then continue in Chapter 8 with suggestions of additional analyses to suggest whatever quantitative work is possible or desirable.

ALTERNATIVE APPROACHES TO QUANTITATIVE
PROJECTIONS OF ECONOMIC SECTORS

The types of projections used in quantitative economics for sector analysis can be grouped into two broad approaches: the single equation approach and the simultaneous equation approach.

The Single Equation Approach

The variety of economic information used in single equation approaches differs greatly.

1. *Fixed Incremental Changes.* In these cases the projected activity level of an economic sector is simply projected on the basis of constant additions (decreases) in each time period. Typical of these projections are equations of the type

$$Q_t = \alpha + \beta t \tag{1.1}$$

where Q_t is the activity (output) level at time t, α a constant (initial) quantity, β the fixed increment in activity level per time period, and t denotes the time period.

2. Similar to (1) are projections of *fixed proportional changes* (growth rates) per time period. Projections of this type reflect typically "exponential growth curves," which since at least the time of Giovanni Botero (ca. 1533-1617) have led to predictions of impending collapse.[2] The equations typical of this approach are of the form

$$Q_t = (1 + r)Q_{t-1}$$
$$Q_t = (1 + r)^t Q_0 \tag{2.1}$$

where Q_t is the activity (output) level of the economic sector in time t, r the percentage rate increase per time period, and Q_0 the initial level at time zero. Again the information used in these approaches uses time as an explanatory variable, or some other single valued quantity.

3. *Static Structural Equations.* Equations of this type include explanatory variables of the same time period. The activity (output) level of the economic sector is explained as a function of any number of economic variables, such as number of households, income, prices, location, activity levels in other sectors. Some most important economic indicators can be calculated from such statistical estimates as income elasticities or price elasticities. Typical equations of this type are (using actual statistical estimates)

$$Q_t = -14,924 + .8025H_t + 42.3366Y_t \tag{3.1}$$
$$(8.58) \qquad (8.25)$$

where

$$Q_t \quad = \quad \text{activity (output) level, e.g., residential telephones in millions}$$

H_t = households in thousands
Y_t = disposable income in billions of constant dollars.

The numbers in parentheses are the t values, measuring whether the estimated parameters are statistically significant or not. The income elasticity $[\,(\partial Q_t/Q_t)\,/\,(\partial Y_t/Y_t)\,]$ is approximately 4.2. Another example is

$$Q_t = -12{,}043 + .9259\,L_t + 13.5311\,Y_t \qquad (3.2)$$
$$\phantom{Q_t = -12{,}043 +} (7.81) \qquad (3.34)$$

where

Q_t = business telephones in millions
L_t = white collar workers in thousands
Y_t = GNP in billions of constant dollars
Income elasticity: approximately 0.7

4. *Dynamic Structural Equations.* Single equations of this type include explanatory variables of the same time period as well as other (past) time periods. Again, the economic variables can include any quantity thought to explain the activity (output) level of the dependent variable. Typical of equations of this type are Equations (4.1) and (4.2), quantitative examples from the communications sector:

$$\Delta Q_t = -.0122 + .0038\,\Delta Y_t + .0013\,Y_{t-1} - .0366\,\Delta P_t \qquad (4.1)$$
$$ (3.5) \qquad (5.0) \qquad (4.0)$$

where

Q_t = consumer expenditures for telephone, etc.
Y_t = private consumption expenditures
P_t = relative price of telephone services.

From Equation (4.1) we can estimate short run price and income elasticities similar to those of static structural equations, now, however, with the further possible disaggregation into short run (within one time period) and long run effects. Equation (4.1) allows us only to estimate short term price and income elasticities. They are in our example:

	Income Elasticities	Price Elasticities
Short run	0.32	−0.26
Long run	?	?

If we were to include also past activity (output) levels of the explanatory variable in explaining the dependent variable in this year, then the single dynamic structural equation approach allows us to estimate short and long run elasticities. Equation (4.2) shows one such approach to explaining consumer expenditures for radio and television receivers:

$$Q_t = -12.03 + .6470\, Q_{t-1} + .0406\, \Delta Y_t + .0108\, Y_{t-1} \qquad (4.2)$$
$$(1.7) \quad (2.0) \qquad\qquad (4.8) \qquad\quad (1.6)$$

The short and long run income elasticities are

	Income Elasticities	Price Elasticities
Short run (1964)	2.97	0
Long run (1964)	2.12	0

Since Equation (4.2) does not include any prices as explanatory variables of expenditure levels, we cannot make any estimates of price elasticities.

The Simultaneous Equation Approach

The purpose of this part is simply to outline the scope of an empirical simultaneous equation approach to sectors of the economy in the context of long term forecasting, and problems therein. We think that this is best done by giving a typical quantitative example of such an approach, in this case the communications sector of the United States. In Chapter 5 we used the results of this approach in illustrating the inherent difficulties of long term structural forecasts, and possibly the lack of need for such forecasts, with the likely exception of the energy sector.

Typically, we may again distinguish between static and dynamic systems approaches, depending on whether allowance is made for time lags in the model over more than one time period. In the following, a system of first order difference equations is used to explain and estimate relations and dependencies of the U.S. communications sector. Any other sector of the economy could have been chosen.

The model described here has been designed to incorporate most of the major interrelationships among various components of the supply and demand factors so that the projections of future telecommunication may be appropriately generated. It was developed and estimated by Kan-Hua Young[3] in work for the National Aeronautics and Space Administration. In developing this econometric model, special attention has been directed to the potential applications of the model for policy considerations and to highlight the dependency of the forecasts on such policy decisions. For example, what is the rate of return to research and development in the telecommunications industry; what is the effect of research and development on the level of telecommunications technology;

what are the price and income elasticities in communications services—these are some of the important economic questions that can be answered by an econometric model. In addition, the effect of government regulation, such as the restriction of a "fair rate of return" is also an important economic problem that can be answered by an econometric model. The model to be described here has been developed to help answer some of these important economic questions.

The published studies of the telecommunications industry in the United States are surprisingly limited, in view of the important role of telecommunications in the national economy. In general, these studies examine either demand or supply separately. They attempt to analyze the demand function, the production function, and the investment function separately from one another. In contrast, this approach attempts to incorporate all of these interrelationships into a comprehensive econometric model by employing a system of simultaneous equations rather than several separate single equations. A recent study of the Canadian telecommunications industry appears to include most of the major components of an overview of the telecommunications industry. From the published condensed version of the report, it was not clear, however, that a cohesive model of a system of simultaneous equations has been developed. Furthermore, the role of research and development and the effect of government regulation do not appear to have received adequate attention.

The tentative model described below has been deliberately kept simple in order to demonstrate the main features and capabilities of an econometric model. Furthermore, the model is also designed to allow some flexibility for its several conceivable submodels to be examined separately. The model formulated here will be estimated empirically by using a set of consistent data. Most of the data required to implement the model are expected to be available from the national income account statistics published in *Survey of Current Business*[4] and the statistics compiled from the reports submitted by the common carriers of telecommunication published in *Statistics of Communications Common Carriers*.[5] The precise data sources will be mentioned, when they are known, for each variable separately. Some relevant empirical results of the past studies will also be provided to indicate what results seem to be most likely to emerge. It must be stressed, however, that these fragmentary results, being based on different data sources, cannot be used without extreme caution.

In order to facilitate our exposition, the discussion following this introduction is divided into five sections. Section 1 presents an overview of the tentative econometric model of telecommunications. Sections 2 and 3 consider demand and supply of telecommunications services separately. Section 4 discusses some supplementary relationships such as gross investment and new employment; these relationships, though they are not essential, are very important and thus deserve explicit consideration. The last section (5) offers a summary and some remarks.

1. Overview of the Model

The tentative econometric model of the telecommunications industry in the United States is a relatively simple one. As an initial step toward a more general study of the communications industry as a whole, the model is designed to examine the telephone and telegraph industry alone, though its extension to include radio and television broadcasting should pose very little difficulty. Rather than engaging in excessive detail, we have chosen to stress the interrelationships among the factors of supply and demand and the effects of government intervention through activities in research and development or profit regulation.

The model may be divided into three groups and has thirteen equations in all, including some definitions or accounting identities. The first group of equations involves the demand and revenue relationships, which include two demand functions for individual consumers and for business and government respectively. Other relationships in this group include the definitions of total demand, general price, and total revenue. The second group of equations contains the supply and cost relationships, which include a production function, two factor input demand functions and a cost function. In addition, a profit function and a price determination function are also included in this group. Finally, in the last group we consider some supplementary relationships such as gross investment and new employment. These relationships can be elaborated considerably; however, at present we have chosen to present only a relatively simple version in order to simplify our discussion. In the description of the formulation of the model we use the same notation as that used in Chapter 5, pp. 88-90 for endogenous and exogenous variables. We refer the reader to that chapter for the exact definition of the variables and the data sources used.

2. Demand and Revenue Relationships

In this section we shall briefly explain the demand functions for telecommunication services by individual consumers, and for business and government separately. In addition, several definitions on accounting identities providing the link to the supply and cost relationships to be considered in the next section will also be examined.

Residential Demand for Telecommunication. This portion of demand for telecommunication services includes what may be regarded as "final demand" by individual consumers. Using a model that has been widely employed by many empirical researchers, we may write the residential demand function as

$$q_{1t} = a_{10} + a_{11} q_{1(t-1)} + a_{12} \left[p_{1t} + p_{1(t-1)} \right] + a_{13} (y_t + y_{t-1}) \qquad (1)$$

where

$$q_{1t} = Q_{1t}/N_t$$

$$p_{1t} = P_{1t}/P_{yt}$$

and

$$y_t = Y_t/N_t$$

This is the so-called "flow-adjustment model" that has been frequently employed by Houthakker and Taylor[6] as supplement to the more familiar "state-adjustment model." Using private consumption expenditure instead of GNP, Houthakker and Taylor have obtained the following empirical results for the telephone, telegraph, and wireless category of private consumption expenditures.

$$q_{1_t} = -14.068 + .5497 q_{1(t-1)} -.0137 [p_{1_t} + p_{1(t-1)}]$$
$$\phantom{q_{1_t} = }(-3.96)\quad (5.94)\qquad\qquad (-1.18)$$

$$+ .00798 (y_t + y_{t-1})$$
$$(5.28)$$

$$R^2 = .999,\ S_e = .21$$

where the figures in the parentheses are t-values and S_e denotes standard error. From these results we can make the following inference

	Price Elasticities	Income Elasticities
Short run	−.30	2.82
Long run	−.51	4.85

Some striking results were obtained for the Canadian telecommunications industry by Dobell and others. Unlike the study by Houthakker and Taylor, GNP figures instead of private consumption expenditures were used in this Canadian Study. The results that most nearly correspond to (1), based on residence revenue of Bell Canada, may be summarized as

$$q_{1_t} = 2.96 + 0.8641 q_{1(t-1)} - 0.353 p_{1_t}$$
$$\phantom{q_{1_t} = }(0.74)\quad (7.95)\qquad\qquad (-1.87)$$

$$+ 0.00232 y_t$$
$$(1.10)$$

$$R^2 = .996,\ S_e = .27$$

From these results we can make the following inference regarding elasticities (at 1967 level)

	Price Elasticities	Income Elasticities
Short run	−0.09	0.12
Long run	−1.19	1.63

A comparison of these two sets of results shows that while the short run price elasticity in Canada appears to be lower than that in the United States; the long run price elasticity in Canada seems to be more elastic than that in the United States. On the other hand, both short run and long run income elasticities in Canada are considerably lower than those in the United States.

Business and Government Demand for Telecommunications. This portion of demand for telecommunication services includes all services that are not used by individual consumers directly, and thus may be regarded as "derived demand" used indirectly by individual consumers through business and government organizations. The chosen specification of the demand function is formally the same as that used for studying the residential demand for telecommunication. Thus we may write it as

$$q_{2t} = a_{20} + a_{21} q_{2(t-1)} + a_{22}\left[p_{2t} + p_{2(t-1)} \right] + a_{23}(y_t + y_{t-1}) \tag{2}$$

where

$$q_{2t} = Q_{2t}/N_t$$

and

$$p_{2t} = P_{2t}/P_{yt}$$

are defined similarly as the corresponding variables in Equation (1). Notice that in both Equations (1) and (2) we use deflated GNP per capita as an explanatory variable. Conceptually it may be argued that private consumption expenditure and gross corporate product, plus government receipts, should perhaps be used in Equations (1) and (2) respectively. For simplicity, however, we have used GNP in both of these equations.

Although the residential demand for telecommunication in the United States has been studied by Houthakker and Taylor jointly, and by Taylor separately, they did not examine the business and government demand for telecommunications which seems to be increasingly important during the more recent years. In a Canadian study[7], the data on total business revenue of Bell Canada were analyzed. Their results of the empirical demand function of business demand for telecommunication may be summarized as:

$$Q_{2t} = 185.53 + 0.5433\, Q_{2(t-1)} - 1.5370\, p_t + 0.00652\, Y_t$$
$$\quad\;\; (2.80) \quad\;\; (3.71) \qquad\qquad\; (-3.45) \qquad\;\; (2.88)$$

$$R^2 = 0.998, \quad S_e = 4.87$$

It must be pointed out that in this equation, Q_{2t} and Y_t are aggregate quantities, not expressed on a per capita basis. Furthermore, Y_t used is personal disposable income rather than GNP. From the empirical results given above, the elasticities (at the 1967 level) may be inferred as

	Price Elasticities	Income Elasticities
Short run	−0.39	0.27
Long run	−1.33	0.97

These results may be compared with the corresponding results for residential demand for telecommunication in Canada. It is interesting to note that while short run prices and income elasticities are higher for business and government than for individual consumers, the same is not necessarily true for long run elasticities, particularly income elasticity. These results are somewhat surprising, but not necessarily inconsistent with the fact of fast growing business and government demand for telecommunications if the price they are charged decreases rapidly.

Total Demand for Telecommunication Services. This is merely a definition stating that the total demand for telecommunications is the sum of residential demand and business and government demand. Thus we have

$$Q_t = Q_{1t} + Q_{2t} \qquad (3)$$

where the subscripts $_1$ and $_2$ of Q_{1t} and Q_{2t} indicate residential demand and business and government demand respectively. Notice that the quantities of telecommunication services are all expressed in 1958 constant dollars and thus may be regarded as an approximation of the number of "typical telephone calls."

General Price of Telecommunication Services. The price level of telecommunication services as a whole is defined as a weighted average of the prices charged to residential homes and to business and government, the weights being relative market shares. More explicitly, we have

$$P_t = (Q_{1t}/Q_t)P_{1t} + (Q_{2t}/Q_t)P_{2t} \qquad (4)$$

where Q_{1t}/Q_t and Q_{2t}/Q_t are simply market shares.

Total Revenue of Telecommunication Services. This represents a definition of total revenue in the telecommunications industry. Once the total quantity and general price level are determined, total revenue is simply

$$R_t = P_t Q_t (= P_{1t} Q_{1t} + P_{2t} Q_{2t}) \qquad (5)$$

where R_t is expressed in thousands of current dollars. This figure is important, since it is to be compared with the total cost to determine gross profit before indirect business taxes.

3. Supply and Cost Relationships

This section deals with the supply conditions, including the technological constraint on the telecommunication industry, factor input demands for capital and labor, and the resulting cost, profit, and price structures. There are three empirical relationships that must be estimated, including a production function and two factor input relationships. In addition, the cost function, the profit function, and the price determination function are also included.

Production Function. The production function describes technological constraint and expresses the relationship between the output and various inputs. At the level of aggregation that we are considering, it is customary to classify all inputs into capital and labor. Many specifications of the functional form have been proposed, including the widely used Cobb-Douglas form, the constant elasticity of substitution (CES) function, and the variable elasticity of substitution (VES) functions, etc.

It has been recognized in many recent studies that a careful examination of technological progress is essential to any study of a production function involving rapid technological change. The problem, however, is an extremely difficult one, since many types of technological progress are conceivable and frequently equally plausible (e.g., Hicks neutral or Solow neutral etc.). Because technological progress is obviously very important, our production function of the telecommunications industry must incorporate it explicitly. Furthermore, it is extremely desirable that the effect of research and development on technological progress can be assessed explicitly, since the rate of return to research and development expenditure has a very important policy implication. To fulfill this requirement, we have formulated a production function that can be estimated easily by introducing a small modification to the familiar Cobb-Douglas form. The production function proposed is

$$lnQ_t = a_{60} + a_{61}\, lnQ_{t-1} + a_{62}\, lnD_{t-1} + a_{63}\, ln(D_t/D_{t-1}) \qquad (6)$$
$$+ a_{64}\, ln(K_t/K_{t-1}) + a_{65}\, ln(L_t/L_{t-1})$$

where a logarithmic linear form is employed. It can be demonstrated that the coefficients shown in Equation (6) will enable us to derive the following estimates of the "structure parameters" which are of primary interest:

λ	$= a_{60}/(1-a_{61})$	constant term
α	$= a_{64}$	return to capital
β	$= a_{65}$	return to labor
γ	$= a_{62}/(1-a_{61})$	return to R & D
δ	$= 1 - a_{61}$	immediate distributed lag
θ	$= (1 - a_{61})a_{63}/a_{62}$	subsequent distributed lag

Note that the model assumes that the effects of research and development expenditures occur gradually. In fact, in terms of elasticities, it is explicitly assumed that the short run effect is δ (by the end of the first year) and the intermediate run effects (from the second year on) are assumed to be $[\delta + (1 - \delta) \theta \sum_{t=1}^{T} (1 - \delta)^{t-1}]$ (by the end of (T + 1) year). The long run effect is simply measured by γ, which may be compared with (α + β) measuring the return to scale of a proportional change of both capital and labor. Some of the special cases of Equation (6), for example, δ = θ or δ = 1 and θ = 0, may be useful.

The production function represented by Equation (6) is a completely new formulation. Therefore, no existing study can provide some indication regarding the magnitudes of the parameters involved. However, in a recent study by H.D. Vinod,[8] an alternative modification of the Cobb-Douglas form was employed to estimate the production function of the Bell System in the United States. His results can be summarized as

$$lnQ_t = 69.8541 - 6.40795\ lnK_t - 10.5900\ lnL_t$$
$$(8.50) \qquad (7.90) \qquad (8.67)$$

$$+ 1.09574\ (lnK_t lnL_t)$$
$$(9.13)$$

$$R^2 = 0.997$$

Notice that L_t used in this study is labor input in man hours rather than the number of employees. The only difference between the formulation above and the familiar Cobb-Douglas form is its addition of the last term which is the cross product term of lnK_t and lnL_t. Its presence, however, makes its interpretation much more difficult, since the elasticities now depend on the level of inputs. More specifically, the marginal elasticities of capital and labor now become

$$MEC = -6.40795 + 1.09574\ lnL_t$$

and

$$MEL = -10.5900 + 1.09574\ ln K_t$$

which vary from 0.80 to 1.28 and from −0.56 to 1.18 respectively, during the period from 1947 to 1970. In general, the negative marginal elasticities of labor in the early years are not plausible, and the marginal elasticities of both capital and labor are exceedingly high for the recent years.

In the Canadian study mentioned previously, an alternative modification of the familiar Cobb-Douglas form was made by introducing an index of

technological change (percent of direct dialing) as an additional explanatory
variable. Its results based on the data of Bell Canada can be summarized as

$$lnQ_t = -0.25 + 0.405lnK_t + 0.705lnL_t + 0.010D_t^*$$
$$(-0.81) \quad (6.8) \quad\quad (4.9) \quad\quad (9.5)$$

$$R^2 = 0.998, \quad S_e = 0.022$$

where D_t^* is the percentage of station-to-station toll calls dialed by the
customers.

These results may be contrasted with those of the Bell System in the
United States. While in both studies the return to scale seems to be greater than
one, the return to capital appears to be higher for the United States than for
Canada, and the reverse seems to be true for the return to labor.

Input Demand for Capital. In the production function, we have
explicitly considered two factor inputs, i.e., capital and labor. In general the
demands for these two factor inputs are determined by the prices of factor
inputs and the level of output. Thus a simple formulation of the input demand
for capital may be specified as

$$lnK_t = a_{70} + a_{71}ln\,r_t + a_{72}ln\,w_t + a_{73}lnQ_t \tag{7}$$

where a_{71} and a_{72} are own and cross price elasticities and r_t and w_t are the
prices of capital and labor. In our survey of the existing literature we found that
there seems to be no empirical study on the demand for capital following the
approach implied in Equation (7). If we assume that $a_{71} = -a_{72}$ and that the
price elasticities of the input demand for labor are negligible, then the price
elasticities of the demand for capital can be roughly derived from the following
results based on the data of Bell Canada

$$ln\,(K_t/L_t) = 1.75 + 0.13\,(w_t/r_t) + 0.23\,(w_{t-1}/r_{t-1})$$
$$(4.8) \quad (1.2)$$

$$+ \; 0.015\,D_t^*$$
$$(6.5)$$

$$R^2 = 0.991$$

The price elasticities inferred from these results and the assumption mentioned
above are

	Own Elasticities	Cross Elasticities
Short run	−0.13	0.13
Long run	−0.36	0.36

It appears, therefore, that the price elasticities of demand for capital in the communications industry are very low. This may not be unreasonable since the investment is mainly determined by the prospect of future revenue and profit. The results would probably not be very different for the United States.

Input Demand for Labor. Similar to the demand for capital input, we may examine the demand for labor input in the same manner. The input demand function for labor corresponding to (7) is

$$lnL_t = a_{80} + a_{81}lnw_t + a_{82}lnr_t + a_{83}ln Q_t \tag{8}$$

where the a_{81} and a_{82} are own and cross price elasticities. Like the demand for capital, there is no existing empirical study on the demand for labor input by the telecommunications industry in the United States. The Canadian study mentioned earlier provides some indication regarding the nature of the input demand function for labor. The relevant results can be summarized as

$$ln \ L_t = 2.90 + 0.002 \, (P_tQ_t \,) - 0.018 \, D_t^*$$
$$(38.0) \quad (8.1) \qquad\qquad (-7.4)$$

$$R^2 = 0.878$$

Thus, the elasticity of demand for labor input with respect to total output level is

$$\left(\frac{\partial L_t}{\partial Q_t}\right)\left(\frac{Q_t}{L_t}\right) = 0.002 \, P_tQ_t$$

where P_tQ_t is total revenue in millions of 1967 constant dollars (which is only 0.7 in 1967). Therefore, the labor input appears to be very inelastic with respect to output level.

Total Cost Function. The cost function usually expresses total cost as a function of the level of output, given a set of factor input prices. This type of cost function can be estimated directly from the empirical observations or derived from the production function with certain behavioral assumptions imposed. In fact, this is also true for input demands for capital and labor. In the present model, without introducing any behavioral assumption, we may simply write the cost function according to the definition. Thus we have

$$C_t = r_tK_t + w_tL_t \tag{9}$$

since total cost is simply the sum of expenditures for capital and labor.

Gross Profit Function. The gross profit function consists of two components, i.e., indirect business taxes and net profit. In a regulated industry such as the telecommunications industry both these components are determined by government policy. In order to demonstrate how government policy can affect gross profit, let us define t as the tax rate of indirect business taxes on gross profit and s as the "fair rate of return" on capital invested. By definition, we have net profit as

$$\pi_t = sK_t = (1 - t)\Pi_t$$

Therefore, we have

$$\Pi_t = [s/(1 - t)]K_t \tag{10}$$

where $s/(1 - t)$ is clearly the gross rate of return to capital, in contrast to s, which is the "fair rate of return."

Price Determination Function. Notice that the two major components which determine the price are average cost and unit gross profit. The cost of production is mainly determined by the technology employed and the gross profit in a regulated industry, as just shown, is determined by government policy. Therefore, once the technology and government policy are known the price to be charged is also determined. More explicitly, the price determination function can be written as

$$P_t = (C_t + \Pi_t)/Q_t \tag{11}$$

where P_t is the general price level of telecommunication service, which as defined earlier in Equation (4) is simply a weighted average of the prices of communications service charged to individual consumers and to business and government.

4. Supplementary Relationships on Investment and Employment

This section considers two important (but not really essential) relationships on investment and employment. At present we contemplate only relatively simple formulations, since an extensive investigation of these problems may be beyond the scope of our current effort, which concerns mainly the overall interrelationships.

Gross Investment Function. The existing econometric studies of the business investment function largely involve the empirical verification of the neoclassical theory of capital accumulation and investment. The main question naturally centers around how a desired level of capital stock is determined. In Equation (7) we have avoided this question by employing an empirically estimated demand function for capital stock. Since the capital stock generally depreciates as time goes by, this factor must be explicitly taken into account in considering the required level of gross investment. By definition, the gross investment function is

$$I_t = K_t - (1 - d_t) K_{t-1} \tag{12}$$

where δ_t is the depreciation factor, which is frequently assumed to be the same for all time periods. By a slight rearrangement it is easily seen that the net change of capital stock $K_t - K_{t-1}$ is simply the difference between gross investment I_t and the depreciation $d_t K_{t-1}$.

New Employment Function. Curiously this problem has received relatively little attention, despite its obvious important policy implications. The problem can be studied in a similar manner as we treat investment decision. Corresponding to (12), we may write the new employment function as

$$M_t = L_t - (1 - m_t) L_{t-1} \tag{13}$$

where m_t is the "retirement rate," which is defined to include all employees who leave the telecommunications industry. We can see, after a slight rearrangement, that the change in the number of employees in the industry $L_t - L_{t-1}$ is simply the difference between the number of new employees M_t and that of the employees who leave the industry.

5. Summary and Remarks

The purpose of this chapter was to formulate a quantitative economic model that allows an empirical (data oriented) estimation of economic relationships between "outside" variables (exogenous variables, not explained within the model) and "inside" variables (endogenous variables, explained within the model). Of course the very formulation of the model—the thirteen simultaneous equations—is an analytic exercise reflecting long experience and vast amounts of theoretical understanding, e.g., of demand-supply relationships, of production function alternatives, of capital and labor markets, of investment and employment functions, of price and cost functions, and so on.

The formulation process of the model also reflects a knowledge of statistical and mathematical estimation and solution techniques of such systems of equations. Thus in the context of our original list of forecasting approaches the quantitative analytic approach we suggest for studying individual sectors of economic systems is really an integrated approach limited only by the availability of data, and theoretical understanding.

At the same time we wanted to prove empirically the qualitative judgments made by us and others, based on a thorough study and understanding of economic and social systems—namely that first, such systems are very complex; second, such systems respond very actively to price and income changes; third, in the price and income adjustments one has to distinguish between short term and long term effects; and fourth, technological change and research and development expenditures have an often dominant impact on production and cost functions (i.e., the need for labor, capital, and other limited resource input requirements), potentially alleviating any foreseeable resources limitations, with the exception of energy (see Chapter 6).

The model presented here for the communications sector was specifically designed to evaluate the effect of research and development activities, and the effect of government regulation in setting the "fair rate of return" to capital.

The quantitative estimates for the telecommunications model are presented in the Appendix. The most significant, quantitative findings are:

1. *Price elasticities* of −0.34 (short run) and −1.51 (long run). That is, with an increase in prices for telecommunication services by 10 percent, the demand for these services in households would decrease by 3.4 percent and 15.1 percent respectively compared to the demand before the price change. For the business demand for telecommunications these elasticities are −0.01 in the short run, and as high as −3.17 in the long run!

2. *Income elasticities* of 0.57 and 2.56 for households, showing the relation between increases of household income and the demand for telecommunication services. For business demand for communication services, even higher elasticities were estimated.

3. *Marginal elasticities for capital, labor, and research and development* expenditures as well as the respective marginal products of these three factors. The long term marginal product of capital is 0.19 ($0.19 billion for $1 billion invested, discounted at a 10 percent social rate of interest), that of labor is 0.14 ($0.14 billion for every 1 million employees), that of R&D expenditures is 2.52 (!) ($2.52 billion for every $1 billion invested in R&D).

Other quantitative results are derived and shown in the Appendix, but those listed here are the significant findings for the evaluation of long term forecasting needs and capabilities.

Since the response of economic and social sectors to research and development expenditures is so large, the call to limit growth seems premature. Similarly long term forecasting tasks seem difficult since the incentives and budget decisions on R&D are not easily forecast, based on economic needs alone. They are to a substantial part enacted by the federal government ($16 billion out of a total $25 billion R&D expenditures in the United States in 1970). We recognize, of course, the danger of generalizing from the empirical results of one sector (communications) to all others. We think all the other sectors should be studied with equal care, using similar techniques. However, we did not find any intrinsic reason why the situation in the other sectors of the economy should be different, with one exception: *the energy sector.*

In concluding this chapter, it may be reiterated that the econometric model of the United States telecommunication industry was presented here mainly to illustrate that the pattern of an industry development is generally affected by many economic factors such as price and income as well as the R&D programs pursued by both government and industry. Since the political and military power of a nation is to a large extent dependent upon its industrial capacities, which may be predominantly either capital or labor intensive, it appears that our ability to perform long-term projections of political and military power will be greatly dependent upon our ability to project the complicated patterns of industrial development sector by sector. The econometric model described above was intended to demonstrate that an industry by industry study, though it may be exceedingly complex, can be useful, particularly in its explicit treatment of a given forecast and its underlying assumptions. Finally, the empirical estimates of price elasticities, income elasticities, and the responses of economic sectors to R&D expenditures are the most telling results in the context of long term projections.

Chapter Eight

Predictive Compatibilities and the Compressibility of Economic Systems

PREDICTIVE COMPATIBILITIES

As already intimated, while it is possible to project large aggregates such as population and GNP, the true interest in prediction, especially in government, lies in forecasting individual, more specific activities and tendencies. Macro projections usually hide a great variety of possible individual components and are therefore of limited value. But the greater the attempted detail, the more numerous become the sources—and sizes—of error. Yet the error usually cannot be determined until after the event, for the simple reason that in this whole field there is no theory on the basis of which one might argue. Neither is the past record of much value.

Illustrations of the two principal methods of making predictions are the following (taken from meteorology):

If weather has to be predicted, one can proceed as follows.

(1) Feed into the memory of a computer the daily data of weather maps for approximately the last 100 years by specifying temperature, barometric pressure, wind strength, humidity, etc. Then take the weather map for today, November 22, 1972, and instruct the computer to find the one most nearly identical with it. It may be the one for July 17, 1876. Then tell the computer to print out the map of July 18, 1876, and use this as the prediction for tomorrow, November 23, 1972. Or (2) disregard the past records; determine solely today's map and, on the basis of a firm theory, place these parameters into the proper equations and solve these with the help of a computer in a time interval which is significantly shorter than one day!

The first method has no theoretical basis, the second no historical one. Both are possible, the second one being obviously far superior—and, incidentally, the one on which most meteorologists are concentrating.

Now it is clear that there exists no firm theory to use in our case;

there are only rather vague surmises and a number of plausibility arguments. At present it is even unforeseeable how a suitable theory could be developed, and it is extremely difficult to form ideas about what such a theory should look like. Anyone familiar with the origin of new theories knows that, without such prior formulation of demands on a theory, none can ever be created.

Neither is there enough historical evidence which we could put into our hypothetical computer. What is available is mostly not quantitative (though in some cases, with extreme effort, this difficulty could be overcome). The main trouble is, of course, that while the weather series are mainly stationary, the prediction demanded here is for a nonstationary state, compounding all difficulties. The atmosphere and bodies of water, for example, have been changed as a result of worldwide industrialization. Past records could be used systematically only if an evolutionary principle were discovered that governs the changes of technology just as the Darwinian theory explains the evolution of life (but so far, with little predictive power!). Thus our experience has to be used in a common sense manner—and what is "common sense" in turn clearly depends upon the degree of sophistication of those examining the records!

With these limitations in mind, it is nevertheless possible to point to a principle that can be applied to predictions made largely on the basis of extrapolation of separate tendencies. This is the principle that the predicted values of different entities must be *compatible* with each other, given present technological and resource constraints and their expected developments. Consider that at the time t_0 we have a certain set of variables $x_1, x_2, x_3, \ldots$ which together describe the present politicoeconomical state of a country. If each of these variables has had a particular rate of change and if these rates are extrapolated separately to a point in time t_1 substantially removed from t_0, it does *not* follow that the state of the system thus postulated for t_1 is actually feasible. The structure of the system may be such that in many cases, rates of change of these variables have to change themselves in order to make a change of the whole *system* possible.

This idea is already reflected in some observations of Galileo when he showed that it would be impossible to double the size of a human being: the weight of the trunk would increase at such a rate that even the doubled size of the legs would not be able to support it, for strictly mechanical reasons. Hence the structure of the human being would have to be modified. When the child grows into an adult, the rates of change of the various organs adapt themselves to this principle. The emphasis on linear models for economic expansion obscures these relationships; but they cannot be overlooked in the present case even though one is far removed from being able to describe them in rigorous mathematical form.

While this can become fairly obvious if applied to a single country, it is another matter to apply these ideas to the interplay of several countries and regions of the world. The various predictions studied in this study fail completely on both counts. To carry these principles through in detail—as would be necessary for the Fucks case, for example—would involve major computations and statistical research beyond the scope of the present study. The "Limits to Growth" models may be seen as an attempt in this direction, albeit miscarried and misused.

Two major illustrations of the need and usefulness of *compatibility analysis* are given here on the basis of the chosen conjectures, one relating to China as a closed economic system (i.e., without major access to foreign resources and technology transfers), the other briefly concerning the interdependent projected expansions of the United States, the European Economic Community, and Japan.

Consider China. The projection by Fucks of 600×10^6 tons of steel produced by the year 2000 in that country is arrived at by extrapolation using appropriate differential equations for the purpose. At the same time, the population forecast is 1.6 billion inhabitants. Similarly, on the basis of our sector-by-sector analysis in Tables 6-2 and 6-3, we anticipate a Chinese steel production of about 400 million tons (consistent with Fucks's analysis). Two questions arise, apart from the basic one whether these two numbers are plausible and, if so, within what limits. The first, applying to steel, is whether sufficient raw material can be found within China or imported in competition with other countries. We shall assume that it can.[1] The other question concerns the *uses* of these large amounts of steel. There are at present no better indicators to go by than the uses of steel in countries highly industrialized now. (The United States has about a $30 billion annual rate of demand for iron and steel products.) There the largest consumers of steel are, in order, the steel industry itself ($6.6 billion in 1965); the automobile industry ($3.8 billion); structural metals, heating, and plumbing ($3.1 billion); metal containers ($1.5 billion); and other metal products ($2.1 billion). This is the distribution after a high level of industrialization had been reached in the United States, i.e., after railway construction, after the large absorption of previously produced steel in machinery, buildings, ships, etc.

China could reach the above mentioned figure of 400 million tons in 1990, and 600 million tons in 2000, only after a similar preceding industrialization. This is, by the way, the foremost reason for the failure of the "great leap forward" policy begun in China in 1958. Though steel, coal, and cement production, as well as production in other individual sectors, multiplied at a tremendous expense of energy and work, the effort finally collapsed because of the lack of *organization and coordination* of all the economic sectors, particularly the organization of the use of these primary products in second and third stage investment industries. The need for appropriate organizational and human capital was, is, and will be the main limiting factor of China's industrial expansion. One cannot dump hundreds of millions of tons of steel per year on a nonindustrialized country and sit back and expect economic growth. Therefore it is reasonable to assume that China will reach—at best in 2040—the current United States input coefficients of steel among industries, reflecting present United States technological demands on resources—*if such a resource-intensive technology is ever adopted by China.*

In the United States there are at present about 80 million motor cars in circulation. The corresponding number for the Chinese population and steel production would be about 250 million. It is obvious that the creation of a comparable Chinese automobile industry within about 30 years is most unlikely, since not only 250 million cars would have to be produced but perhaps 500 million or more because many would have become obsolete before the year 2000, assuming an age distribution of automobiles similar to the one prevailing in the United States.

In other words, around the year 2000, China would need an automobile industry producing about 30 million cars annually, approximately three times the present United States output, or larger than the combined automobile industries of the United States, Europe, and Japan in 1969! One must add to this the magnitude of the supporting industries and the need for road building in order to accommodate 250 million automobiles in order to form an idea of what is involved in summary forecasts of the kind criticized here.

On the other hand, one should recall that in the 1920s (and many times thereafter) when about 20 million motor vehicles were circulating in the United States, it was "proved" that this was the maximum attainable. However, tremendous investment, especially in road building, removed the barriers that seemed to support such conclusions. The above case of China is different only because of the short time span allotted and the magnitude of the implied industrialization.

Since it is difficult, if not impossible, given present day technology, to imagine a substantially different use pattern for steel than the one mentioned above for the United States, it follows that the two predictions are incompatible.[a] But it would be wrong to conclude from this that China will "collapse" or be stalled in its economic development drive—a conclusion the LTG modellers are all too quick to reach for the world as a whole. All that the proof of incompatibility means is that China will have to find fundamentally different economic, scientific, and social solutions in its economic development.

This example shows the limitation of simple extrapolation of single series or of arbitrary groups of series. The method of determining compatibility is widely applicable but it appears that little or no use has been made of it[2] in the various projections here under discussion. Since it is not our task to go into

---

[a]We regard it as quite probable that China will establish a different use pattern. She would be compelled to do so even if she wanted to imitate the United States model. But we have no way of knowing what the pattern will be.

an extensive, substantive analysis, but rather to describe methods, we shall not elaborate on this matter. Suffice it to say that considerable work has already gone into assembling the sources and figures for Tables 6-2, 6-3, and 6-5. In any case, the example given is adequate to point up a grave deficiency in most predictive attempts examined in Parts II and III.

The argument developed at the beginning of this section was essentially (though not wholly) static, but the possibility and need to make it dynamic are clearly given. It would be a task of major proportions, beyond the scope of the present work. The analysis of compatibility would have to be made sector by sector, for each major product. Balances of available resource flows of real capital, distribution systems, and balances of scientific, engineering, and industrial labor forces could be made. The major tool of such an analysis would then be sector specific econometric models, as examplified for communications in Chapter 7 and input-output models to study the interdependencies of economic processes and the implications of given final demand (production projections).[b] (See Table 8-1.)

One could first proceed from a priori fixed pattern of end products (e.g., amount of steel, cement, coal, fertilizer produced) and then check the resources, real capital, and labor requirements and their overall balance. If major bottlenecks were identified one could then proceed to see whether substitutes could be found or the requirements for the resources "compressed" without impairing the final demand production targets (introduction of more efficient production patterns with regard to the lagging resources—acceleration of technical innovation). If this analysis still demonstrated major shortcomings in the balance requirements, a serious problem about the further development of that economy would be indicated, which would require a completely different structure of production and technology—or possibly society—or else further economic, military, or political growth would be seriously impaired. But all we needed to do in this section is to identify the *need* for compatibility analysis in forecasting of this type. What in particular will happen in China is a different (substantive) problem.

---

[b]The interindustry relations are described by a system of linear equations

$$(E - A)X = Y$$

where Y is the vector of end products
             X is the intensity vector (input)
             A is the input-output coefficient matrix and
             E is an identity matrix

The input requirements can then be directly calculated by

$$X = (E - A)^{-1}Y$$

Since input-output tables are available for both the United States and the Soviet Union, one could study the potential Chinese development in stages, first to the Soviet levels, then to United States levels. Table 8-1 is an input-output table for the Soviet technology of 1959.

Table 8-1.   Main Indicators of the National Input-Output Table of the U.S.S.R. for 1959[a] (millions of rubles in end consumption prices)

	Transport and Communications[b]	Timber Wood and Paper	Trade, Purchasing and Supply of Material and Technical Goods	Fuels	Heat and Electricity	Other Industries Producing Material Goods
Transport and communications[b]	49.2	1698.9	116.5	2779.0	4.8	80.0
Timber, wood and paper	174.2	3120.3	787.1	417.1	3.1	165.5
Trade, purchasing and supply of material and technical goods	–	493.9	–	842.9	8.3	11.7
Fuels	1764.7	407.3	101.3	1982.3	1342.5	6.4
Heat and Electricity	150.2	90.4	42.0	336.8	4.4	2.7
Other industries producing material goods	–	78.1	–	–	–	–
Metals	125.0	131.3	94.7	71.4	6.7	4.5
Chemical	420.8	179.2	73.8	99.0	1.1	14.8
Metal-working and machine building	482.8	338.4	78.7	193.3	72.9	1.9
Building materials[c]	66.3	22.3	0.2	18.2	2.2	0.1
Agriculture and forestry	19.0	176.6	–	2.9	–	15.8
Foodstuffs	–	32.3	11.3	4.0	1.5	–
Light industry	145.0	371.8	487.8	161.1	10.4	24.3
Total	3397.2	7140.8	1793.4	6908.0	1457.9	327.7

[a]Source: M.P. Eydelman, *Mezhotraslevoy balans obshchestvennogo producta* (National Input-Output Table, Moscow, Statistika Press, 1966, pp. 284-285, 364-366; and N.P. Fedorenko, "Planning of Production and Consumption in the USSR," *Technological Forecasting*, Volume 1 (1969), pp. 87-96.

[b]The sector serving the production of material goods.

[c]Including glass and china.

THE COMPRESSIBILITY OF ECONOMIC SYSTEMS

The basic issue just discussed has never been studied sufficiently in economic theory or policy. However, history abounds in attempts, mostly unsuccessful, to bring a social system to a collapse by cutting its economy off from needed outside supplies. That this area of economics has drawn so little attention till now is surprising. There are two major issues, both related to the question of how much an economic system can be compressed without leading to a breakdown in its functions: *first*, how much of the existing economic activities

Metals	Chemical	Metal-Working and Machine Building	Building Materials	Agriculture and Forestry	Foodstuffs	Light Industry	Construction	Total
		Interindustry Production Relations						
757.7	604.9	823.4	1812.1	767.2	1212.3	443.3	38.9	11189.2
115.4	167.4	397.6	184.1	115.1	363.1	143.6	3015.0	9168.6
426.0	88.1	322.9	427.2	2858.6	3696.6	1404.0	–	10569.2
1811.6	250.4	407.3	499.8	1068.7	396.7	133.3	424.2	19606.9
397.6	193.8	330.4	237.2	88.3	111.5	161.1	200.6	2347.0
177.3	66.1	79.4	62.3	6.0	80.7	97.9	270.7	918.5
4718.5	280.7	4431.7	356.3	18.1	100.8	38.7	1619.3	11997.5
143.4	2216.2	1091.8	50.1	426.3	78.4	611.1	290.8	5701.8
368.2	102.5	3375.9	240.5	1428.6	330.9	139.1	2103.1	9256.8
18.8	36.9	127.1	1294.4	22.3	74.7	12.2	5680.1	7411.7
1.6	11.8	1.3	0.9	12447.2	16467.3	4470.8	77.7	33692.9
11.6	432.8	24.8	8.6	1582.4	13365.7	620.1	85.2	16180.3
145.6	508.6	359.7	67.3	146.2	194.4	15368.1	565.4	18555.6
9093.3	4960.2	11773.3	5240.8	20975.0	36473.1	23643.3	14371.0	

can be eliminated (by attack, scarcities, or catastrophe) without impairing the short or long term military and economic requirements, and *second*, how much can the "nongrowth" activities be constrained to allocate as much of the existing resources to the expansion of the investment goods sector (larger growth) and military production programs (greater security). Clearly, these issues go to the heart of compatibility analysis.

We cannot attempt here to fully derive a theory of economic growth; some basic concepts on the interrelation of consumption, investment, and savings were developed by J.M. Keynes. Some of his analytical framework may be used to illustrate the concept of compressibility of economic systems. In the following brief discussion we shall assume that the reader is familiar with the concepts of multiplier,[c] accelerator, induced investments, autonomous investments, and the concepts of Gross National Product (GNP), Net National Product (NNP), and National Income.

Figure 8-1 shows the relation between NNP and intended consumption by society in a market economy. The sloping line *CC* represents the consumption function which shows the amount of saving as a function of NNP. At *E*, where the intended consumption equals net national product (and no saving occurs beyond depreciation), the economy is in stationary equilibrium at 200. Without population growth, technological progress, or autonomous invest-

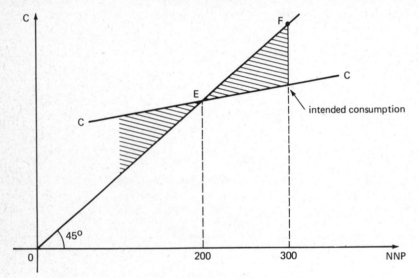

Figure 8-1. Net National Product and Intended Consumption

---

[c]The multiplier relates autonomous investment (e.g., government expenditures on military hardware) to increase in income (a multiple of the original investment) by the simple formula

$$k\,I = Y$$

where k is the multiplier. The multiplier can be related to the marginal propensity to save (*MPS*) by

$$(1/\,MPS\,)\,I = Y$$

and the marginal propensity to consume (*MPC*) by

$$(1/(1 - MPC\,)\,)I = Y$$

through the sum of the geometric series

$$I\,(1 + MPC + MPC^2 + \ldots MPC^{n-1}\,) = Y$$

where $O \leqslant MPC < 1$. Thus a higher *MPC* leads to larger increases in NNP for each unit of investment, and a larger *MPS* to a respectively smaller increase, in an economy with unemployed resources.

ment, the economy would remain at this level if left to itself. The full employment level of GNP or NNP may coincide with E, but most likely it will be somewhere to the right of E for historical and social reasons, or because of inefficiency. With some of the other factors present (technological progress, population growth) the industrial sector may invest a constant amount from year to year above and beyond depreciation values. Since the slope of $\overline{CC}$ reflects the marginal propensity to consume, we can add this investment to $\overline{CC}$ and directly determine the new NNP corresponding to $\overline{CC}$ and an investment I by industry. Figure 8-2 shows the new equilibrium point, E_1, where NNP equals consumption plus investment, again possibly below the full employment level of all resources, F. Figure 8-3 shows the same equilibrium point, now, however, as a function of investment saving equality.

The relation between intended savings and real investment made in a market economy is such as to insure the long term equilibrium of investments and savings. As long as the consumption and investment propensities in the economy do not assure a full employment of available resources, there exists room for autonomous (complementary) government investment in various projects of national interest.

For example, with a full employment level of 300 and intended consumption and investments as shown in Figure 8-2 and 8-3, the government

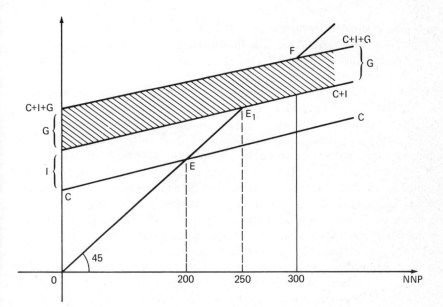

Figure 8-2. Net National Product and Intended Consumption, Autonomous Investment, and Government Project Opportunities

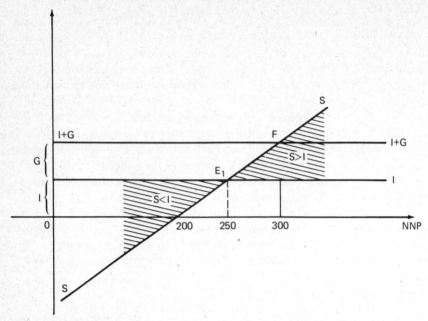

Figure 8-3. Savings, Autonomous Investments, and Government Project Opportunities

can initiate projects up to the amount G, which brings the economy to a full employment level, again through multiplier effects of the original expenditure G. The shaded area in Figure 8-2 may also be looked upon as the Government Project Opportunities (GPO).

It is easily seen that with a higher MPC and constant I (investment by industry for the market) the GPO is reduced. Though a high MPC is claimed to be very desirable in assuring full employment in a market economy (only a small increase in autonomous investments will lead to large increases in NNP through secondary effects), from the standpoint of compressibility of economic systems for maximum expected development and national defense expenditures quite the reverse is true. In this case, a low MPC and investment by industry will leave that much more opportunity for government to undertake programs of national priority in defense, science, education, health, transportation, resource exploration; this effect of compressing the consumption sector can come about in two ways—by reducing the absolute consumption level, with identical MPCs, or by a lower MPC. In both cases, the effect on the GPO area is similar in that it increases the possible level of government (deficit) spending from G to G_1 *at full employment* of all resources (see Figures 8-4 and 8-5).

The reason for this, in terms of Keynesian analysis, is that with a lower MPC the induced change in subsequent spending is proportionately less

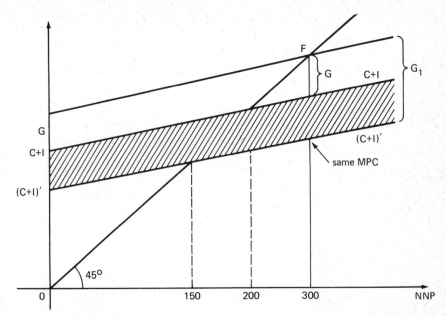

Figure 8-4. Shifts in Absolute Intended Consumption and Government Project Opportunities

and therefore also the resource requirement, in terms of employment, on the economy. This leaves room for additional projects of national priority to be accomplished in the period under consideration. For very similar reasons a balance of trade (payments) deficit is desirable, as it enlarges the GPO, and a surplus is undesirable—a fact all too often forgotten, particularly by policy makers. Population, technological progress, economic efficiency all have a bearing on the static and dynamic (growth) aspects of a nation. We cannot investigate these here. However, a lower limit to consumption does exist and this limit will differ (partly due to technology) from country to country and from time to time. Also the actual $\overline{CC}$ line in different economies varies greatly.

To what extent the consumption sector can be compressed even in a developed country is shown by the performance of the United States economy in World Wars I and II (see Figure 8-6). In both cases government expenditures—partly consumption but mostly military procurement—jumped within a few months from their normal 15 to 20 percent to levels around 80 percent for the duration of one to two years. These high levels of government expenditures were in part achieved by disinvestment (negative saving), and in large part just by a contraction of all other economic activities, mainly consumption and other business investments. This goes to show how low, potentially, the consumption level can be, and it helps explain the large resources a country like China can

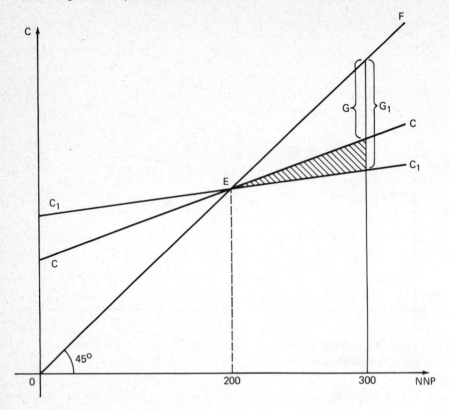

Figure 8-5. Change in Marginal Propensity to Consumer and Government Project Opportunities

allocate to programs of national defense and development and still provide for basic consumption.

There exist limits to the compressibility of the consumer sector and of any one industrial sector within an economic system. Input-output tables show many of the interconnections between different industrial activities. Not all these activities are equally important to the fulfillment of others, both as to their quantity and their substitutability. This brings up the need for completely new concepts, which should be pursued further.[d]

A system will be said to be totally connected if the destruction of any of its parts destroys the whole system, i.e., deprives it of all of its functions. There is thus a discrete drop from a given level of activity to zero. This is the characteristic of a kernel or core, when this system is embedded in a larger one whose essential functions are those of the kernel. The connectedness of any part not in the kernel to any other part also not in the kernel is of a lesser degree than that prevailing among parts within the kernel; the same applies to the connectedness of elements inside with elements outside the kernel. This statement can only be made in this form if the kernel can always be identified in

---

[d]For the following see Oskar Morgenstern, op. cit. p. 217 below.

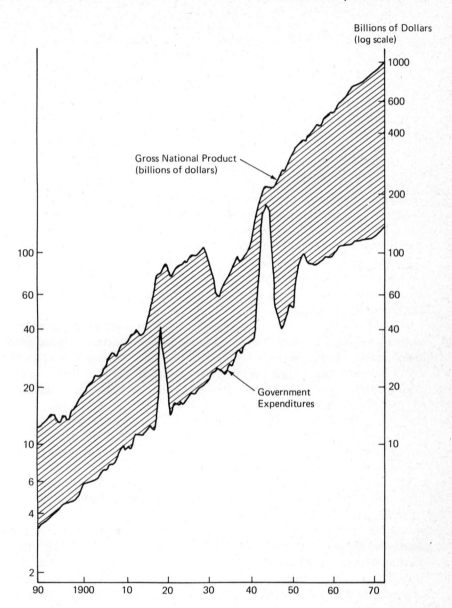

Figure 8-6. U.S. Gross National Product and Government Expenditures 1890-1965

the whole system. If there is more than one kernel, these relationships hold alternatively to each other; i.e., they become effective only with the actual formation of a particular kernel.

An example of a totally connected system—one where the system is identical with the kernel—is offered by an input-output coefficient matrix. Here the destruction of any one cell suffices to destroy the whole economy; this is necessarily true for any size of the matrix. This is clearly not a correct description of reality since we know that the economy is far more resilient and much less vulnerable. Therefore the input-output model can at best only describe one of the kernels of the entire economy.

This may be realistic for the case when the description is highly aggregated. For example, when only five or ten groups of industries or activities are distinguished, it is not implausible that each cell contains some transactions which also, in any other representation, might be called "vital" in the sense that their destruction collapses the whole economy. But if one of the five to ten industries is a very specific one, and if a cell involving it is destroyed, the conclusion that the whole economy would collapse is doubtful, unless techno-logical reasons are brought to bear upon the case, justifying the purely mathematical conclusions.[3]

Another model—that of the expanding economy developed by von Neumann—while apparently describing a totally connected economy (because of the assumption in the original model that all processes use some amounts of all goods produced again as inputs), describes more than the kernel, because the destruction of a process will merely slow down the rate of expansion. It is even possible that this model contains no kernel at all.

The first of these two systems cannot be compressed by omission of some of its function; the second can be gradually reduced in its expansion rate (which may even become negative) until it vanishes. The first system can also be reduced by operating through the bill of goods; in the second it is possible to do this by the direct removal of a good (i.e., without operating via the consumer), for example, by destruction, severe scarcity, or elimination of a process, provided technology permits this operation.

It is possible, however, to conceive of the economy as possessing at least one kernel surrounded by outer layers that support less "essential" functions. These, however, are very desirable since they improve or enrich the performance of the whole system. The simplest case would be where the kernel is physically identifiable together with the outer layers. We then have essentially two basic types i.e., (α) a *chain* connectivity or (β) a *star* connectivity. In both cases the system is totally vulnerable, inasmuch as a destruction of any one part of the kernel collapses the kernel and a fortiori the whole system, while the destruction of an outer layer does not destroy the kernel. In (α) destruction of L_1 would lead to the destruction of L_2, but not vice versa. But the destruction (or diminution) of neither nor of both would imply the same for the kernel. If

Chain

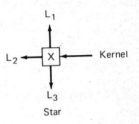

Star

the arrangement (β) exists, the outer layers are left independent of each other, though they all depend directly on the kernel.

These two types, with the ability of physically identifying the kernel, probably correspond little to large economic setups per se, but they can be observed in military and business organizations. In most organizations, such as the economic system, the kernel cannot be physically identified when viewing the entire system. We then have a *redundant system*, which has to be compressed in order to find at least one kernel. In the two cases (α) and (β) compression is also possible—i.e., one can knock off some or all layers and still retain the services performed by the kernel. But it may not be necessary to do this in order to discover the kernel. In the present case of redundancy, a reduction is necessary. It can be made experimentally (i.e., physically) or by application of some method of calculation (if one can be found).

A kernel begins to appear if further compression in the same direction brings about a *discontinuous* contraction of the performance of the remaining part of the system. The approaches to these points, made from several directions, delineate the kernel that the particular combined pressures identify. Other pressures may produce different points indicating different kernels. The various kernels will, of course, for technological reasons, have points in common, but we shall not pursue this matter further at this juncture.

The elimination of outer layers is due to the possibility of dropping activities not deemed "essential" according to some political or other determination. This process typically produces substitutions on a broad scale; but the critical points are those where no further substitution is possible without losing essential functions of the system. The vulnerability of a redundant system, as described in the preceding paragraph, thus does not rest in a particular component, but in the relation of components to each other. It increases as the substitution prospects decrease in number and deteriorate in yield. When all layers have been eliminated and the kernel has been reached, total vulnerability of the remaining type of organization prevails. Compressibility of economic systems arises also when resource endowments of our economy are such that they seriously impair the development of one of its sectors, or of the economy as a whole. In open economic systems—i.e., economies that engage substantially in world trade—such scarcities may cancel each other out or they may have a cumulative effect on the demand for a few limited raw material resources. This "interplay" between nations becomes increasingly important with further economic growth and expanding populations.

We now observe that the growth predicted for the U.S., Japan, and Western Europe has to be viewed in its entirety for its effects on the rest of the world producing raw materials. Even at present, these three countries or regions are far from being self-sufficient. The United States imports 30% of its needed copper, 25% of the oil consumed, etc. Japan relies on imports for 97% of its iron ore, 99% of its oil consumption (which provides 75% of its *total* energy base), 30% of its consumption of coal, 100% of natural rubber ($\approx$ 50% of its requirements), 100% of cotton, 100% of bauxite ores. The Soviet Union, because of its immense size, is in a wholly different position, being largely self-sufficient and remaining so even when a large growth factor is applied to its economy. This is because the Soviet Union, relative to its resources, is still less developed than Western Europe, Japan, and the United States.

The point of the "interplay" is that the different countries are competing—and will compete even more in the future—with each other for resources, many of which come from underdeveloped parts of the world. Such competition may lead to political conflicts not now evident that will strengthen the position of the raw material producing (but militarily weak) areas of the world. The most serious conflict of interest which we can anticipate now will be in the energy resources field. Both Europe (excluding the Soviet Union) and Japan as of 1970 imported more than *50 percent* of their energy resources from the outside world. In the case of Japan this figure was as high as 83 percent.

By 1990, on the basis of only a *proportional* expansion of energy needs with growth of GNP (past experience was a much larger than proportional expansion), we can anticipate deficits in the energy balance of the European Economic Community on the order of 1,300 million tons of coal equivalent *per year*, nearly equal to all of the United States energy production in 1965. Japan shows a similar deficit of about 600 million tons per year.[e]

Though very substantial energy resources do exist—particularly in the nuclear field if breeder reactors are developed (and possibly controlled fusion), which would take several decades to accomplish—the present outlook

[e]For other, more elaborate, estimates of this emerging situation, see Chapter 6.

lets one anticipate very substantial increases in the cost of energy in world markets in the next decades and of efforts to develop completely new sources, at a very intensified and accelerated scale. Substantial progress can be expected, but any failure in this field may have a serious impact on the economic development of these regions and on international relations. This will probably give more political power to the poor countries—a reversal of past and present trends—or encourage the development of new political units and associations with corresponding shifts in the international power structure. But the question remains whether the advanced countries will be able to secure, in one way or another, the amounts and kinds of energy and raw materials they will need to sustain the growth that is often predicted for them.

If the question is raised of developing and substituting other raw materials for those used, we are entering the realm of *technological* prediction. Here the following considerations apply.

1. The industrial countries may need more of the *same* raw materials that are in use today (iron ore, bauxite, oil, etc.) in order to sustain the predicted growth.

2. They may need other materials, in short supply at home, due to technological progress that will cause shifts in demand for raw materials and, in particular, forms of energy resources.

3. Research and development of minor efficient processes may alleviate the growing demands, at least for a time. Statements about these possibilities involve technological predictions of a most uncertain kind. In general, in a market economy, shortages express themselves by price rises. These then cause a search for new sources of supply.

This method has worked very well. Time and again, oil resources were said to be nearly exhausted; but a persistent growth of the demand for oil, coupled with a slight rise in oil prices and a considerable rise in profits, have led to intensive explorations resulting in new supplies that exceeded the previous ones. The present development of off-shore oil and the opening up of the North Slope in Alaska are excellent illustrations. *But certainly this process must at some time come to an end*, first in some country's own territory, then elsewhere.

Shortages, real or impending, lead to intensified search for substitutes. Of course, the need for substitutes may also appear for reasons unconnected with shortages, as in the case where scientific discoveries have been made. But substitutes also require raw materials.

The upshot of these observations is that the combination of population growth and shift, coupled with technological developments unevenly distributed throughout the world, will give rise to many new conflict situations and to the development of patterns of common and conflicting interest which cannot be simple projections from those of the present. It should be considered, for example, that population growth can mean very different things. For the Soviet Union, a country of high technology but largely underdeveloped in domestically available resources, population increase is tantamount to increased power. For Japan and the European Economic Community, it has other implications that will force these countries to reach out beyond their boundaries, either by trade or force, in order merely to keep going. Further population increase for India and similar countries is nothing but a calamity. Finally, population growth in the United States, Europe, and Japan—though on a much smaller scale than for most other countries—will pit these nations against each other in competition for those world resources not indigenous to their areas (oil, gas, copper).

The cumulative impact may produce trouble between them. It should be recalled that the fiercest conflicts and the cruelest wars have often been among those who were most similar to each other, economically or ideologically (e.g., civil wars and religious differences which today have turned into ideological confrontations). A dominating position in the energy sector by one country could potentially lead to a new form of effective economic and military domination.

While the projections give some idea of possible conflicts arising by necessity from basic, underlying economic-technical tendencies, the picture would be incomplete without also considering organizational possibilities and requirements.[4] Considering the latter first, it is conceivable that supranational organizations or authorities will spring up with power to allocate scarce resources all over the world: e.g., how much (and whether) iron ore from Australia is to go to Japan and China, or copper to the United States versus Europe. If this can be done peacefully, then we have one kind of development— though it is at present difficult to see how such authorities could evolve in the short time before 2000. The history of the League of Nations and the United Nations does not support optimism. For reasons given above, the Soviet Union would at least need to be a member of such arrangements, since she might be asked to give up raw materials she might covet for herself!

The analysis of the workings, advantages, and disadvantages of such organizations, for the United States as well as for the world in general, does not belong here. The matter is mentioned as one that properly belongs in any analysis of future developments—yet it is not found in the writings we have examined. This is a grave deficiency. The following will serve as an illustration of a tendency that may precipitate conflict.

Instead of measuring the development of a country merely by such items as population, GNP, and a few specific outputs, it has been suggested that a "power index" be formed. Such an index would be a measure of an interlocking array of activities that may be controlled by a government and used to foster military and other warlike endeavors (e.g., for economic warfare). This can be achieved by internal changes of an economy such that those activities are fostered which help to give suitable power to the country in question. Such efforts may also take into account particular regional situations and location. This implies that an economy can be seen as consisting of a core or kernel which, within limits, can be arbitrarily arranged for maximum military strength (given a certain technology).[5] Although some countries may choose to move in this direction while others will not, indicators used in aggregative prediction may not differ nearly as much as the evolving differences in their structural makeup.

This, therefore, is another illustration of the limited value of on the one hand using large aggregates, and on the other using isolated activities without connecting them into structures.

Part V

Conclusion

Chapter Nine

Some Major Conclusions on Forecasting

We will organize our conclusions in terms of several themes that were developed in the course of the foregoing analysis. The central theme is this: *for various reasons we downgrade the value of forecasts but uphold the value of forecasting.* Paradoxical as this statement seems at first sight, it reconciles our beliefs that the kinds of forecasting we have examined inspire little confidence, but that, nevertheless, something can be learned from attempts at forecasting in terms of broadening and otherwise educating the perspective of planners. For this reason we feel that the art of forecasting should be developed further, without utopian expectations, and the scope of forecasting activities extended to problem areas where they are badly needed, but which have been neglected by the practitioners of the art. This relative neglect results from the absence of suitable quantitative data.

Many forecasters have naturally been attracted to problem areas where such data exist or can be procured. But the availability of quantitative data is not nearly as much of an advantage as is generally believed. Excepting some obvious problem areas related to economic and demographic matters, this advantage is more deceptive than real; and there is no good reason why qualitative forecasting cannot do as well (which is, absolutely speaking, not good at all)—or even better. We will briefly explain these overall conclusions, although they are based on findings distributed over the entire study.

SOURCES OF DIFFICULTY

There are two major sources of difficulty with all quantitative forecasting. We will explain these with reference to econometric forecasting, which has been developed more than forecasting in any other problem area. One difficulty relates to the predictive model, and the other to the data needed to work the model. A model identifies the variable conditions that produce types of events (e.g., a business depression) and specifies their interaction. The classical model tends to be parsimonious in the selection of variables: the fewer the variables required to account for outcomes, the more elegant is the model. This disposition proved reasonably satisfactory in certain problem areas (demographic and economic), but not really very good even there.

For example, we may derive an explanatory scheme from the study of twenty past business depressions; but while it fits the aggregate, it may not fit well every single past depression, and we cannot assume that it will do well in forecasting the twenty-first slump. This is so because some *excluded* variable turns out to be very important in producing the next depression. Moreover, since parametric changes—in technology, level of industrial development, government intervention in the economy—will affect the operation of the variables included in the model, we cannot assume that the scheme derived from the study of the *last* twenty business slumps will do well to forecast the *next* twenty.

Much quantitative forecasting, of course, is neither importantly based on a model, nor proceeds without one altogether. If we simply identify a trend in order to project it into the future, we need not know how the trend was produced. But, as we have concluded repeatedly in our study, the choice of time periods over which a trend is identified, and hence of the trend itself, is a tricky problem which cannot be accommodated without the major injection of judgment. Moreover, if we do not know how a trend is produced, we are all the more subject to surprise as far as the future is concerned.

Data availability is the second source of trouble with quantitative forecasting. As we have noted in many passages of the preceding study, the quality of data is generally poor, although there are here again quality differences between problem areas. Data tend to be inaccurate, ambiguous, inconsistent over time, and obsolete.

If these twin difficulties have rendered econometric forecasting far less than a resounding success, how can we honestly expect good results from forecasting in problem areas—especially political—where the variable determinants cannot be reduced to a small number, where the social sciences have not so far achieved an adequate understanding of how these variables interact, where neglected variables often produce events (which we then call chance events and surprises), and where quantitative data either cannot be procured at all or are only most dubiously representative of reality? The art of finding new quantitative indicators of imponderables has attracted many eager practitioners in recent years, but any cool perusal of the relevant literature impresses one by the large element of judgment—often based on little substantive knowledge—involved in the construction and use of indicators.[1]

It is essentially for these reasons that we found the types of quantitative forecasting represented by Fucks, and by Forrester and Meadows, critically wanting. The former uses a very simple model—too simple, as we demonstrated—while the latters' model, basically ingenious in attempting to work with a large number of variables, requires a depth of knowledge about factor relationships that we are plainly far from possessing.

As we point out, the systematic introduction of dynamic compatibility checks would constitute a refinement of the quantitative technique. But though this is methodologically desirable—and certainly worth a determined exploratory effort—the difficulties of application are usually enormous, if not prohibitive. The most direct criticism, however, of the Forrester and Meadows approaches to long term forecasting is one of empirical evidence: the flexibility of social and economic systems to adapt to anticipated or actual problems in each major economic sector is so large as to shed much doubt on the factual usefulness of such forecasts. We found, in the example of the communications sector, very large price and income elasticities and, most important, a somewhat unexpected large responsiveness of that economic sector to R&D expenditures and policy.

Not all problem areas, however, are forbidding of useful results. This is shown in our own forecast regarding the world's future energy supply. Here the basic variables are firmly anchored in the nature of modern industrialization, the consumption habits of the affluent societies, population growth, and the fact that nature's store of fossil fuels is finite. Only the surprise of a technological miracle can keep the world from experiencing an increasing shortage of oil—and of fuel in general—at least for some decades. This is an example of a problem which governments should have attacked and used forecasts on some time ago, in order to adopt remedial action—as, for example, large scale R&D on coal technology—for the dominant trends were as visible ten years ago as they are now.

This exception is based mainly, on a qualitative judgment. If unlimited energy were available at zero cost (obviously an impossibility) then all other resource and growth problems are amenable to technical solutions; and, in the reverse, there exists no physical substitute for energy, although considerable possibilities of substitution exist among alternative energy sources. Given these qualitative statements, and the actual uneven distribution of energy sources, we do anticipate serious economic, political, and military interdependencies for the major world regions in the next decades.

The qualitative forecasting techniques we have sampled have various defects of their own, although their results are not stated with the pretentious accuracy of numbers. In principle, of course, if we could do qualitative conjecturing with perfection, we could do so also quantitatively. Our low and fragmentary knowledge about human affairs is the obstacle in both cases. Yet, as the example of Kahn and Wiener exhibits (when they are not indulging in simple trend projection, even using multiple assumptions), the design of future scenarios is less discouraged by lack of data, and able practitioners can roam rather far, and do so imaginatively. But no confidence-inspiring forecasts can be expected.

Surprises are bound to occur, and the things that will surprise us are largely the ones which will press future history into unanticipated directions. As someone once said regarding these turning point events, we cannot even imagine what we should exert our imagination on. But if done with a well stocked mind and good judgment, the sort of enterprise pursued by Kahn and Wiener is educational in that it alerts consumers to the rich interconnectedness of things; and this should help us, as we move into the future, in spotting problem areas which call for more specific forecasting efforts.

Delphi seems to us a dubious improvement over consultation in expert committees, or the traditional method of consulting individuals. Not that the technique is worthless—especially not when we are interested chiefly in aggregating current knowledge at the frontiers of certain developments like technology; but Delphi is expensive to use and will probably fail to prove cost-effective, regarding more difficult problems, and particularly those where we must rely, for want of a superior alternative, on the imagination of the single gifted individual.

POWER

If one is interested in future international configurations of national military power, and hence in forecasting in this problem area, it seems to us critically important that one does not operate with a simplistic notion of what power is, and of what power is based on. This point, which we have elaborated on several times in our study, constitutes our second theme. The simple assumptions that military forces equal military power, and that the international distribution of such power simply reflects national differences in economic and technological capacity, are apt to be seriously misleading, and to generate faulty forecasts.

Regarding the first assumption, we urge recognition of the conceptual distinction between putative and actualized power, and of the consequent need to study the variable conditions that govern the extent to which putative power can be transformed into actualized power in particular types of conflict situations. Regarding the second assumption, we pointed to administrative skill and political will as crucial bases of putative military power. A failure to understand these realities caused Americans to be surprised, for instance, by the speed with which China developed strategic nuclear weapons, and by the strength which North Vietnam displayed in the Vietnamese war. Unless our understanding becomes more refined, we will most certainly experience similar surprises in the future—which means more surprises than are necessary.

TECHNOLOGICAL INNOVATION

The importance of paying more systematic attention to political (and cultural) factors in attempts to forecast future shifts in international power does not mean that technological innovation will not play an important part as well. We observed that technological advance is also a very difficult problem area in which to make forecasts.

Two specific difficulties seem worth stressing in our conclusions. One relates to the future discovery of unanticipated technologies, of true breakthroughs, which are naturally unpredictable. The other relates to the exploitation of known and marginally improvable technologies. One form of innovation is the discovery of entirely new uses of already known technological ingredients which are combined in a new way. But perhaps still more important in this problem area—and here again we are noting the effects of administrative skill and political will—is comparative national ability to recognize that the capital structure (for example, of armed forces) is always obsolescing. This fact calls for ceaseless and prompt adaptations. This flexibility is far from easy to sustain since the people who are in charge of operating a particular part of the capital structure (e.g., a major weapons system) are naturally reluctant to see their established skills, positions, and identifications depreciate or even vanish.

USES OF FORECASTING

It is our fourth theme that, despite the grave weaknesses of available forecasting techniques, national planners continue to support and utilize the forecasting enterprise. Indeed, as we have pointed out, we are astonished that forecasting has not been pushed in various problem areas which seem to call for it, some quite urgently. We mentioned the belated discovery of the impending world energy problem. This is an example of what we have in mind.

There are other examples which suggest themselves readily. One is the possible effect of the impending world energy crisis on the distribution and uses of military, political, and economic power. How will states react when the indispensable basis of modern life becomes subject to severe restriction and threats? Will they cooperate to solve the problem as best they can—surely the only intelligent solution—or will they compete and fight in one form or another? We are also impressed by the fact that both China and Japan *could* become great military powers before long: Japan because of her rapidly expanding technological and economic resources, and China because even steady industrial progress at a modest rate will have great effects as a result of her huge population base. Yet this *potential* has to be modified very substantially in the case of Japan with its nearly total dependence on outside energy sources; thus even if Japan is allowed to build up a military power force structure, this power is subject to drastic cut-offs from the outside in a strategic confrontation.

The effects of foreign military aid and sales, particularly to the less developed parts of the world, on the probability and form of future military and political conflicts is another subject which, it seems to us, has been neglected. The recent upsurge of international violence committed by small terrorist groups demands imaginative research.

The very utility of national military power has undergone considerable decline in recent years. Is this trend likely to persist, and if so, which will be the probable consequences on future international relationships? These are only examples of subjects which merit study and the intelligent use of forecasting.

Finally—and this is our last theme—we repeat that planners should not only employ forecasting techniques, but should also *use the results* with principled skepticism. To expect firm forecasts on which action can be based, with confidence, is foolish in most problem areas. It is the more modest educational value of having one's mind sensitized to the complexity of evolving realities, and to some of the future possibilities, which make this orientation worthwhile. Attributing to forecasting the low posture which is its due means also, however, that planners must rid themselves of the desire for forecasts on which decisions about the future can be firmly based. Instead, they should cultivate the capability of remaining flexible, preserving options, and remaining constantly on the alert for new developments and surprises.

Appendix

Appendix: The Demand and Supply of Telecommunication Services in the United States: Empirical Results

Kan-Hua Young

INTRODUCTION

The purpose of this Appendix is to report some of the preliminary empirical findings of our study of the U.S. telecommunications industry. In the text we have outlined a system of simultaneous equations describing the demand and supply relationships of the U.S. telecommunications industry. The Appendix reports the results of our estimation of the parameters that appear in the specified system of equations.

The empirical relationships that were estimated can be grouped into two broad categories: demands for telecommunication, and its production, including derived demands for capital and labor. The following two sections present an evaluation of our preliminary empirical findings. In order to provide the readers with sufficient information for their independent judgment of the significance of our findings, the compilation of our complete set of data (1947 to 1970) is documented in a technical note following this Appendix, even though portions of these data are not necessary for the estimation of the demand and supply relationships.

RESIDENTIAL AND BUSINESS DEMANDS FOR TELECOMMUNICATION SERVICES

The U.S. telecommunications model we have specified is a relatively simple one. On the demand side we treat the demands for telecommunication services for residential and business uses separately. Further disaggregations into local and long distance telephone calls or telegraph messages may be desirable in future studies. In addition, a more detailed study of data communication may be called for. At present, since our emphasis has been the interactions between demand and supply, not the detail of individual components, we have limited our investigation to a fairly aggregate level.

Residential Demands for Telecommunication Services

This is the portion of telecommunication services that is directly purchased by individual consumers. Both the "state adjustment model" and the "flow adjustment model" as described by Houthakker and Taylor[1] have been employed in our statistical analysis. Some of the special cases of these models were also examined. Table A-1 summarizes our preliminary findings. It indicates that the choice of the flow adjustment model (designated as Specification II) seems to be most successful. In fact, the general form of the state adjustment

Table A-1.   Regression Coefficients and Associated Statistics of Residential Demand Functions for Telecommunications, 1947-70

Explanatory Variables	I	II	III	IV	V
			Dependent variable: Q_1/N Alternative Specifications		
Constant	–	0.0011 (0.41)	−0.0005 (−2.21)	−0.0019 (−0.55)	0.0027 (1.25)
$(Q_1/N)_{-1}$	–	0.7984 (14.94)	1.0732 (106.85)	0.9346 (12.08)	0.8381 (25.64)
$\Delta(P_1/P_y)$	–		−0.0070 (−2.16)		
$(P_1/P_y)_{-1}$	–			−0.0027 (−0.86)	
$\Delta(Y/N)$	–		0.0027 (2.75)		
$(Y/N)_{-1}$	–			0.0028 (2.08)	
$\Sigma(P_1/P_y)$	–	−0.0039 (−3.21)			
$\Sigma(Y/N)$	–	0.0023 (5.38)			
P_1/P_y	–				−0.0078 (−4.43)
Y/N	–				0.0037 (7.17)
R − SQ	–	0.9991	0.9986	0.9980	0.9994
Stand. Error	–	0.0003	0.0004	0.0004	0.0002

1. The following notation is used for explanatory variables:

$$\Delta(P_1/P_y) = (P_1/P_y)_t - (P_1/P_y)_{t-1}$$
$$\Sigma(P_1/P_y) = (P_1/P_y)_t + (P_1/P_y)_{t-1}.$$

Similarly for $\Delta(Y/N)$ and $\Sigma(Y/N)$.

2. Figures in parentheses are t-values.

model, designated as Specification I, was not computationally feasible when the least squares estimation procedure was adopted to estimate its parameters. (The cross product matrix that has to be inverted is nearly singular).

The derivation and interpretation of the state adjustment model and the flow adjustment model may be found in Houthakker and Taylor. As was pointed out by them, the flow adjustment model actually corresponds to a special case of the state adjustment model (p. 27). Other Specifications, including III to V, are clearly special cases of the state adjustment model. It must be pointed out, however, that the last specification may be regarded as a simplified version of the flow adjustment model where the specific finite approximation of a continuous variable suggested by Houthakker and Taylor is substituted by a procedure which simply ignores the distinction between *within* period and *between* period changes. In fact, this is an earlier version of the flow adjustment model, and the flow adjustment model employed by Houthakker and Taylor may be considered as its refinement. In the following discussion we shall treat it as a special case of the state adjustment model rather than a less refined version of the flow adjustment model.

A careful evaluation of the empirical results shown in Table A-1 clearly reveals that the flow adjustment model designated as Specification II is preferable to the state adjustment model, including Specifications I, III, and IV. The special case of the state adjustment model designated as Specification V is satisfactory since it implies reasonable price and income elasticities (at the mean values of prices and quantities). When it is interpreted as a simplified version of the flow adjustment model, its implications on price and income elasticities are also very reasonable and are approximately the same as those implied by its more refined version, designated as Specification II. The other special cases of the state adjustment model are not satisfactory, either because no estimates of long run elasticities can be derived or the signs of the implied price and income elasticities are contrary to our expectations. We have, therefore, selected the flow adjustment model designated as Specification II as the best formulation of the residential demand function for telecommunication services.

According to the empirical results of Specification II, the implied short run and long run price and income elasticities are

	Price Elasticities	Income Elasticities
Short run	−0.34	0.57
Long run	−1.51	2.56

These elasticities are calculated at the mean values of the observed prices and quantities during the sample period (1947-70). In the existing literature, there are two similar studies by Houthakker and Taylor and by Dobell et al., using the U.S. and the Canadian data respectively. Comparing with these earlier results, we found that our results seem to be very reasonable. It appears that Houthakker and Taylor might have underestimated the price elasticities and yet overestimated the income elasticities. On the other hand, the estimated elasticities made by Dobell et al. seem to be somewhat lower than what we expect, especially regarding the short run elasticities. For comparisoin, the elasticities implied by their estimates are presented below.

	Price Elasticities	Income Elasticities
Houthakker and Taylor		
(U.S.)		
Short run	−0.30	2.82
Long run	−0.51	4.85
Dobell et al.		
(Canada, 1967)		
Short run	−0.09	0.12
Long run	−1.19	1.63

We conclude that our own estimation of the residential demand function for telecommunication services as represented by Specification II is very satisfactory. The estimated values of the parameters are not only statistically very significant but also economically meaningful. Finally, it may be pointed out that the difference between our results and those of Houthakker and Taylor might have been due to their use of total personal consumption expenditures as a measure of "income." Our use of constant value GNP as a measure of income, though it may not be as desirable as disposable income, appears to provide more satisfactory results than those obtained by Houthakker and Taylor.[a]

Business Demands for
Telecommunication Services

This portion of telecommunication demands consists of all demands that are not purchased by individual consumers directly. Therefore, it actually includes both business and government demands for telecommunication services. The alternative specifications that are employed for empirical applications are essentially the same as those employed for studying residential demands. The only difference lies in the fact that the aggregate demand furtction rather than per capita demand function is being estimated for business demands.

As in the study of residential demands, both the state adjustment model and the flow adjustment model were examined. Several special cases of these models were also estimated. The results of the empirical estimation are summarized in Table A-2. In general, these results are not as satisfactory as those of the residential demands, though $R-SQ$ (the coefficients of determination) are very high. According to the state adjustment model designated as Specification I, the estimated short run and long run price elasticities are −0.35 and −2.47

---

[a]In a subsequent study we found that the estimated income elasticities are somewhat higher and price elasticities somewhat lower as a result of substituting disposable personal income for GNP.

Table A-2. Regression Coefficients and Associated Statistics of Business Demand Functions for Telecommunications, 1947-70

					Dependent Variable: Q_2
			Alternative Specifications		
Explanatory Variables	*I*	*II*	*III*	*IV*	*V*
Constant	−0.0352 (−0.05)	−0.3371 (−0.33)	0.0789 (0.72)	−0.7884 (−0.86)	0.3897 (0.40)
$Q_{2(t-1)}$	0.9554 (11.60)	0.9970 (9.29)	1.0927 (64.42)	0.9657 (9.77)	1.0459 (10.54)
$\Delta (P_2/P_y)$	−1.4608 (−3.78)		−0.5100 (−1.76)		
$(P_2/P_y)_{-1}$	−0.4058 (−2.77)			0.0300 (0.25)	
ΔY	−0.0022 (−0.80)		−0.0030 (−0.96)		
Y_{-1}	0.0023 (1.11)			0.0028 (1.11)	
$\Sigma (P_2/P_y)$		−0.0174 (−0.24)			
ΣY		0.0009 (0.64)			
P_2/P_y					−0.1529 (−0.93)
Y					0.0002 (0.06)
R − SQ	0.9973	0.9954	0.9961	0.9955	0.9955
Stand. Error	0.1664	0.2189	0.2017	0.2158	0.2169

1. The following notation is used for explanatory variables.

$$\Delta (P_2/P_y) = (P_2/P_y)_t - (P_2/P_y)_{t-1}$$

$$\Sigma (P_2/P_y) = (P_2/P_y)_t + (P_2/P_y)_{t-1}.$$

Similarly for ΔY and ΣY.

2. Figures in parentheses are t-values.

respectively, which is not unreasonable. But the implied income elasticities turn out to be negative, which is unreasonable. On the other hand, according to the flow adjustment model designated as Specification II, the estimated price and income elasticities of business demands for telecommunication services are (at means)

	Price Elasticities	*Income Elasticities*
Short run	−0.01	0.20
Long run	−3.17	65.74

Clearly the short run elasticities appear to be somewhat low and the long run elasticities appear to be too high, especially for income elasticity.[b] Because the results of other specifications are perhaps even less plausible, these tentative estimates are used for preliminary simulation. The results of Specifications III and V are judged to be unreasonable because the estimated coefficients associated with the lagged dependent variable are greater than one, and the results of Specification IV are considered not plausible because it implies positive price elasticity. Our preference of the flow adjustment model over the state adjustment model is not very strong, because it may be possible that the state adjustment model will provide reasonable results if we simply omit the statistically insignificant variables from Specification I. In addition, instead of using GNP as an explanatory variable, gross corporate product or corporate profit may be more appropriate.

Earlier we cited a study by Dobell et al. on Canadian telecommunications. Their results on business demands appear to be more plausible, though the specification employed is precisely the same as our Specification V, except disposable personal income is used instead of GNP. For comparison, we reproduce their estimated price and income elasticities as follows (1967)

	Price Elasticities	Income Elasticities
Short run	−0.39	0.27
Long run	−1.33	0.97

These results, though they are not implausible, appear to have underestimated the income elasticities, and possibly even the price elasticities, especially for the long run. Furthermore, as pointed out earlier, the same specification when applied to the U.S. data does not provide satisfactory results.

PRODUCTION FUNCTION AND INPUT REQUIREMENTS

We now turn to an evaluation of some of the empirical results related to production function and input requirements, including the derived demands for capital and labor by the telecommunications industry. The production function as formulated is a modfication of the familiar Cobb-Douglas production function, which is designed to evaluate the significance of research and development in the telecommunications industry. Technological progress in the telecommunications industry is assumed to be gradually developed as the research and development funds are expended. On the other hand, in the derived demand functions for capital and labor, our formulations discussed below do not take this factor into account. Therefore, further refinements may be necessary.

Production Function of Telecommunication Services

Using the notation explained in the text, we can write the production function in the following form

---

[b]This implies that the adjustment process is very slow. Therefore, it would perhaps take an extremely long period to realize such a large long term effect.

$$\ln Q_t \;=\; A\,(D_{t-\nu}) + \alpha \ln K_t + \beta \ln L_t$$

where

$$A\,(D_{t-\nu}) \;=\; \lambda + \gamma\,[\,\delta \ln D_t + (1-\delta)\,\Sigma_1^\infty\,\theta\,(1-\theta)^{\nu-1}\,\ln D_{t-\nu}]$$

represents the level of technology which is assumed to be a function of present as well as all past research and development efforts given as $D_{t-\nu}$. From this basic formulation, it can be shown that the following equation can be used for estimating the parameters

$$
\begin{aligned}
\ln Q_t \;=\;& \lambda\theta + (1-\theta)\ln Q_{t-1} + \gamma\delta \ln(D_t/D_{t-1}) + \gamma\theta \ln D_{t-1} \\
&+ \alpha\,[\,\ln(K_t/K_{t-1})\,] + \alpha\theta \ln K_{t-1} \\
&+ \beta\,[\,\ln(L_t/L_{t-1})\,] + \beta\theta \ln L_{t-1}
\end{aligned}
$$

Since we expect $\alpha\theta$ and $\beta\theta$ to be very small, as a first approximation we may omit $\ln K_{t-1}$ and $\ln K_{t-1}$ as explanatory variables. If we can assume θ is indeed zero, then the specification can be simplified as

$$
\begin{aligned}
(\ln Q_t - \ln Q_{t-1}) \;=\;& \gamma\delta \ln(D_t/D_{t-1}) \\
&+ \alpha\,[\,\ln(K_t/K_{t-1})\,] + \beta[\,\ln(L_t/L_{t-1})\,]
\end{aligned}
$$

In our empirical analysis, instead of using this model we have assumed that $\theta = \delta$, because $\theta = 0$ implies $\delta = 1$, which does not seem to be acceptable.[c]

By assuming $\theta = \delta$ and dropping $\ln K_{t-1}$ and $\ln L_{t-1}$, an alternative estimating equation may be derived as

$$
\begin{aligned}
[\ln Q_t - \ln(L_t/L_{t-1})] \;=\;& \lambda\delta + (1-\delta)\ln Q_{t-1} + \gamma\delta \ln D_t \\
&+ \alpha\,[\,\ln(K_t/K_{t-1}) - \ln(L_t/L_{t-1})\,] \\
&+ [(\alpha+\beta)-1]\,[\,\ln(L_t/L_{t-1})\,]
\end{aligned}
$$

---

[c]Our main conclusions derived from the empirical results obtained for this specification are supported by an alternative specification which assumes $\delta = 0$.

200 Long Term Projections of Power

which is sometimes more desirable because it is less likely to involve serious multicollinearity among explanatory variables. It is important to note that if constant return to scale, i.e., $\alpha + \beta = 1$ is further assumed, the last explanatory variable may be dropped. The empirical results of some of the specifications of the production function we have just discussed, together with others which do not explicitly specify the effect of research and development on technological progress, are summarized in Table A-3.

    Among various specifications that have been examined, Specification V appears to be the most satisfactory. Specification I is not satisfactory

Table A-3. Regression Coefficients and Associated Statistics of Production Functions of Telecommunications, 1947-70

Explanatory Variables	Explanatory Variable: lnQ_t Alternative Specifications					
	I	II	III	IV	V	VI
Constant	0.2538 (2.12)	0.9959 (0.04)	−2.8142 (−9.86)	−0.1841 (−0.12)	0.1613 (1.91)	0.1030 (1.14)
lnQ_{t-1}	0.8850 (10.28)				0.9488 (15.03)	0.9475 (13.48)
lnD_{t-1}	0.1213 (1.15)					
$ln(D_t/D_{t-1})$	−0.0108 (−0.11)					
$ln(K_t/K_{t-1})$	−0.0632 (−0.14)					
$ln(L_t/L_{t-1})$	0.1561 (0.63)				−0.8839 (−2.36)	
lnK_t		1.5989 (46.32)	1.4334 (19.75)	0.3676 (0.62)		
lnL_t		−0.1042 (−0.72)	1.8850 (2.35)	−0.1297 (−0.96)		
$lnK_t\,lnL_t$			−0.5206 (−2.51)			
Trend				0.0724 (2.07)		
lnD_t					0.0459 (0.57)	0.0546 (0.61)
$ln(K_t/K_{t-1})$					0.0667	0.9904
$-ln(L_t/L_{t-1})$					(0.15)	(3.89)
R − 5Q	0.9980	0.9965	0.9968	0.9965	0.9980	0.9975
Stand. error	0.0280	0.0372	0.0357	0.0372	0.0281	0.0313

1. Specifications V and VI use $lnQ_t - ln(L_t/L_{t-1})$ as the dependent variables. In Specification VI, constant return to scale is assumed, but not in Specification V.

2. Figures in parentheses are t-values.

because its estimated values of $\gamma \delta = -0.0108$ and $\alpha = -0.0632$ are contrary to our expectation that they should take positive values. Specification VI is not as preferable as Specification V since it assumes constant return to scale, which appears to be unjustifiable in view of the result that $(\alpha + \beta) - 1 = -0.8839$ is statistically significantly different from zero in Specification V. The other specifications, including II to IV, do not explicitly specify the effect of research and technology. In addition, some of the estimates are not in accordance with our expectations, e.g., the return to labor is negative according to Specifications II and IV as well as Specification III for some values of capital.

We may now examine the implication of the estimates of Specification V more closely. It can be verified without very much difficulty that our estimates imply the following marginal elasticities and marginal returns.

	Short Run	Long Run
Marginal Elasticities (= average elasticities)		
Capital	0.0667	0.0667
Labor	0.0494	0.0494
R & D expenditure	0.0459	0.8965
Marginal Products (at means, billions of 1958 dollars)		
Capital (per billion of 1958 dollars)	0.3325	0.3325 (0.1870)*
Labor (per million employees)	0.2463	0.2463 (0.1375)*
R & D expenditure		
(per billion of 1958 dollars)	0.2288	4.4694 (2.5168)*

*Discounted at 10% annually.

These results appear to be reasonable, though some of the estimates are not statistically significant. The results above show that the returns to capital and labor in direct production of telecommunication services, with a given technology, are relatively low. On the other hand, the return to R & D expenditure in the telecommunications industry seems to be very high. Although according to our estimates 1% increase in R & D expenditure for telecommunications technology will lead to only about 0.05% increase in output (with a given level of inputs), its ultimate effect will be approximately 0.90%, which is quite substantial. In terms of marginal products, we find that a $1.00 increase of R & D expenditure (for communication and electronic equipments) will bring about a $0.23 increase of output of telecommunication services in the short run, and eventually accumulate up to $4.47 which, as is shown in the parentheses, is equivalent to $2.52 in present value, using 10% discount rate.

Input Requirements: Capital and Labor

As pointed out earlier, our empirical results on the input requirement functions do not take into account technological progress. Furthermore, what we have estimated are at present limited to static formulations, therefore no attempt has been made to incorporate any dynamic consideration. For both factor demands for capital and labor we estimated several alternative specifications, using factor prices and output level as explanatory variables. These results are summarized in Table A-4.

As shown in the table, among the factors determining the demand for capital, the level of output is clearly the most significant factor. The sign of the estimated coefficients associated with capital price and relative prices is contrary to our expectation. On the other hand, the level of wage rate seems to

Table A-4. Regression Coefficients and Associated Statistics of Capital and Labor Input Demand Functions by Telecommunications Industry, 1947-70

Explanatory Variables	*Alternative Specifications*				
	I	*II*	*III*	*IV*	*V*
Demand for Capital					
Constant	−1.9887	2.6074	2.6065	1.7741	2.1296
	(−5.08)	(8.05)	(10.83)	(14.22)	(116.70)
lnQ_t	0.3098	0.6401	0.5762	0.2754	0.6307
	(2.21)	(60.99)	(20.20)	(2.22)	(73.90)
lnr_t	0.0401		0.1181		
	(0.58)		(1.99)		
lnw_t	0.5486			0.6445	
	(1.94)			(2.87)	
$ln\,(r/w)_t$		0.1041			
		(1.48)			
R − SQ	0.9969	0.9962	0.9965	0.9970	0.9960
Stand. Error	0.0222	0.0246	0.0235	0.0216	0.0251
Demand for Labor					
Constant	−2.3255	−1.5073	−1.0982	−0.6993	−0.4989
	(−2.19)	(−1.88)	(−1.74)	(−1.94)	(−11.18)
lnQ_t	−0.3454	0.0958	0.1841	−0.0846	0.1157
	(−0.91)	(3.70)	(2.46)	(−0.24)	(5.54)
lnr_t	−0.3035		−0.1484		
	(−1.62)		(−0.95)		
lnw_t	1.0901			0.3633	
	(1.42)			(0.56)	
$ln\,(r/w)_t$		−0.2197			
		(−1.26)			
R − SQ	0.5937	0.5864	0.5729	0.5604	0.5747
Stand. Error	0.0601	0.0606	0.0616	0.0625	0.0614

1. Technological progress has not yet been adequately treated in these equations. Furthermo: these equations are not formulated to take into account of dynamic considerations.

2. Figures in parentheses are *t*-values.

have some effect on the level of capital requirements. For these reasons, Specification IV is chosen for the preliminary simulation of the telecommunications model.

Regarding the demand for labor, our empirical results do not seem to be very satisfactory. None of the estimated values reflecting the price effects of either wage rate or capital price has the expected sign. The only explanatory variable that seems to be relevant is the level of output, therefore we have selected Specification V as the best among all alternative specifications.

SUMMARY AND REMARKS

This Appendix provides an evaluation of the empirical results on some of the equations of a telecommunications model described in the text. The empirical results evaluated include the residential and business demands for telecommunication services, the production function of telecommunication services, and the derived demands for capital and labor by the communications industry.

In general, on the demand side, the empirical results obtained for residential demand for telecommunication services is very satisfactory, and the corresponding results obtained for business demand appear to be less satisfactory. There are some possibilities for improving these results. They were considered promising and should be taken into account in the future work. On the supply side, our empirical results show that the return to R & D expenditure in the telecommunications industry appear to be very high, and the returns to capital and labor in direct production seem to be very low. These results are plausible and have important policy implications. Finally, our empirical results obtained for capital and labor requirements are less satisfactory. This aspect needs to be investigated more closely in future work.

Technical Note: Basic Data on U.S. Telecommunications

This technical note presents the sources of the basic data, including endogenous and exogenous variables, that appear in the telecommunications model specified in the text. The major sources of data and the definitions of the variables have been provided on pp. 80-90. The sample period included in this basic data covers 1947 to 1970. Some of the data are readily available, but others must be derived with varying degrees of reliabilities. The derivation of the basic data set presented in the following pages may be briefly described in order to indicate the quality of these data.

Residential Demand for Telecommunication Services: Data on $P_1 Q_1$ and P_1 are obtained from Tables 2.5 and 8.6 of *National Income Accounts*[1] and Q_1 is computed by $Q_1 = P_1 Q_1 / P_1$.

Business Demand for Telecommunication Services: They are calculated as residuals by using $Q_2 = Q - Q_1$ and $P_2 = (PQ - P_1 Q_1)/(Q - Q_1)$.

Total Demand for Telecommunication Services: Data on $R = PQ$ and P are obtained from Tables 1.22 and 1.21 for 1965 to 1970. For 1947 to 1964, $R = PQ$ are estimated from the data on Tables 1.12, 6.1, 6.11, 6.14, 6.15 et al. of *National Income Accounts*[2] and P is constructed on the basis of New York to Los Angeles telephone rates obtained from *Statistical Abstracts* (various issues). The data on Q are computed by using $Q = PQ/P$.

Capital and Labor Input Requirements: The estimation of capital stock is based on Tables 9 and 20 of *Statistics of Common Communications Carrier.*[3] The current dollar capital stock $(P_K K)_t$ of telecommunications industry is computed by summing the stocks of telephone and telegraph carriers that filed the reports to FCC, and then adjusted upward by multiplying 1.115 to include those carriers that did not file the reports. The constant dollar capital stock is calculated by applying $K_t = \Sigma_0^t [(P_k K)_t - (P_k K)_{t-1}]/P_{kt}$. The particular deflator P_{kt} used is that for gross private domestic investment obtained from *National Income Accounts*. The data on labor employment are obtained from Table 6.4 of *National Income Accounts*.

Cost and Profit of Telecommunication Industry: Data on cost and profit of telecommunications industry are obtained from Table 1.22 of *National Income Accounts* for the period 1965 to 1970. For the period 1947 to 1964, the comparable figures are estimated from Tables 6.1 and 6.11, 6.14, 6.15, et al.

New Investment and New Employment: Data are generated from $I_t = K_t - (1 - 0.05)K_{t-1}$ and $M_t = L_t - (1 - 0.025)L_{t-1}$, except M_t for 1950, 1958 and 1959. These data are largely hypothetical and are not used in any estimation of the parameters.

Population and Income: Data on population are obtained from *Statistical Abstracts*, and those on GNP and its deflator from *National Income Accounts*.

Prices of Capital and Labor: Price of capital is computed by dividing the sum of capital consumption allowance and interest by the capital stock. Similarly, the wage rate is computed by dividing employee compensation by the number of employees. The sources of data are the same as those for cost and profit.

Research and Development Expenditure: Data are obtained from various issues of *Statistical Abstracts* directly for the period 1957 to 1970. For earlier years, estimates were obtained by adjusting the data with slightly different coverage. In some cases, crude extrapolations were made. These research and development expenditures include funds provided by both industry and government in the communications and electronic equipment industries.

Tax Rate and Profit Regulations: Data on indirect business taxes are obtained from Table 6.14 of *National Income Accounts*, and those on gross profit is simply the sum of indirect business taxes and net profit obtained from Table 6.15 of *National Income Accounts*. The tax rates are calculated according to the definition as the ratio of indirect business taxes to gross profit. Profit rate is calculated simply as the ratio of net profit to the capital stock.

The complete data set for the econometric model of U.S. telecommunication industry is presented below.

Notes

Notes

Chapter 1

1. Manley St. Denis, "On the Evaluation of Naval Weapons Systems," unpublished draft, May 1969, Chapter 2.4.

2. Claude Shannon, *Mathematical Theory of Communications*, Urbana, Ill.: the University of Illinois Press, 1949.

3. Daniel Slotnick, "Unconventional Systems," *Computer Design*, 6(12): 47-52, 1967; and Institute of Electrical and Electronics Engineers, Inc., *1968 IEEE Computer Conference Digest*, 1968.

4. In one of the early English writings, *Reign of George VI, 1900-1925* (anonymous, 1763), the author projected eighteenth century England to 1900-1925, with no other technical innovation but channels, and North America still under British rule. In 1835 T.S. Mackintosh proposed aerial ships drawn by trained eagles. A more accurate, though still, ex post, completely off-side prediction on future economies was made in 1827 by Jane Webb, for the twenty-first century. Man had conquered nature, steam and electricity were major power sources, balloons transported passengers across the Atlantic, and waste places of the Earth had become major industrial centers with "macadamised turnpike roads supplied their place, over which post-chaises with anti-attritioned wheels bowled at the rate of fifteen miles an hour." For further references, see I.F. Clark, "The First Forecast of the Future," *Futures*, 1(4): 325-330, 1969.

Chapter 2

1. Ian I. Mitroff and Murray Turoff, "The Whys Behind the Hows," *IEEE Spectrum*, 10(3): 62-71, 1973.

2. T.J. Gordon and Olaf Helmer, *Report on a Long Range Forecasting Study*, Santa Monica, Cal.: The RAND Corporation, P-2982, 1964.

3. C.P. Snow, "Science and Government," *Science and Technology* (January 1969), pp. 36-37.

4. G.B. Bernstein and Marvin J. Cetron, "SEER: A Delphic Approach Applied to Information Processing," *Technological Forecasting*, 1(1): 33-54, 1969.

5. Olaf Helmer, "Analysis of the Future: The Delphi Method," Santa Monica, Cal.: RAND Corporation, P-3558, March 1967; Olaf Helmer, "Prospects of the Future: The Delphi Method," Santa Monica, Cal.: RAND Corporation, P-3558, March 1967; B. Brown and Olaf Helmer, "Improving the Reliability of Estimates Obtained From a Consensus of Experts," Santa Monica, Cal.: RAND Corporation, P-2986, September 1967.

6. H.Q. North, "A Probe of TRW's Future," TRW Systems, Redondo Beach, Calif., July 1966.

7. H.Q. North, "Technological Forecasting in Industry," presented at a Seminar to the NATO Defense Research Group, Teddington, Middlesex, England, November 1968.

8. T.J. Gordon, "New Approaches to Delphi," in *Technological Forecasting for Industry and Government*, J.R. Bright (Ed.), Englewood Cliffs, N.J.: Prentice-Hall, 1968.

9. B. Brown and Olaf Helmer, "Improving the Reliability of Estimates Obtained from a Consensus of Experts," Santa Monica, Cal.: RAND Corporation, P-2986, September 1967.

10. Norman C. Dalkey, "Delphi," Santa Monica, Cal.: RAND Corporation, P-3704, October 1967.

11. G.B. Bernstein and Marvin J. Cetron, "SEER: A Delphic Approach Applied to Information Processing," *Technological Forecasting*, 1(1): 33-54, 1969.

12. Joseph P. Martino, "An Experiment with the Delphi Procedure for Long-Range Forecasting," Institute for Electrical and Electronic Engineers, *Transactions on Engineering Management*, Vol. EM-15 (September 1968), pp. 138-144.

13. T.J. Gordon and H. Hayward, "Initial Experiments with the Cross Impact Matrix, Method of Forecasting," *Futures*, 1(1): 100, 1968.

14. A.D. Bender, A.E. Strack, G.W. Ebright, and G. von Haunalter, "Delphic Study Examines Developments in Medicine," *Futures*, 1(4): 289-303, 1969.

15. C.A. Bjerrum, "Forecast of Computer Developments and Applications, 1968-2000," *Futures*, 1(4): 331-338, 1969.

16. Erich Jantsch, *Technological Forecasting in Perspective*, Paris: Organization for Economic Cooperation and Development, 1967, p. 226.

17. H.Q. North, "Technological Forecasting in Industry," paper presented at NATO Defense Research Group Seminar, Teddington, England, November 12, 1968, p. 9.

18. Marvin J. Cetron and D.N. Dick, "Producing the First Navy Technological Forecast," *Technological Forecasting*, 1(2): 185, 1969.

Chapter 3

1. Wilhelm Fucks, *Formeln zur Macht*, Stuttgart: Deutsche Verlags-Anstalt, 1965.

2. V. Volterra, "Leggi delle fluttuazioni biologiche," *Rendiconti della R. Accademia dei Lincei*, Series 6, Vol. 5, 1927, p. 3; Volterra, *Leçons sur*

la théorie mathématique de la lutte pour la vie, Paris: Gauthier-Villers, 1931. The model itself is not explicitly described in Fucks's book; only its results are given.

3. Raymond Pearl, *The Biology of Death*, Philadelphia-London, 1922; R. Pearl and L.J. Reed, "On the Rate of Growth of the Population of the United States Since 1790 and Its Mathematical Representation," *Proceedings National Academy of Sciences*, Vol. 6, 1920, pp. 275ff.

4. V. Volterra, and H. Hadwiger, "Über die Integralgleichungen der Bevölkerungstheorie, *Mitteilungen der Vereinigung Schweizerischer Versicherungsmathematiker*, Vol. 38, 1939; A. Lotka, "Contribution to the Theory of Self-Renewing Aggregates with Special Reference to Industrial Replacement," *Annals of Mathematical Statistics*, 100: 11ff., 1939; A. Lopez, *Problems in Stable Population Theory*, Princeton, N.J., 1961.

5. It is very difficult, if not impossible at present, to estimate accurately or measure China's population; the latest official figures go back to the 1950s. In 1949 China gave its population officially with 475 million (transmitted by Chou En-lai to the United Nations in 1950; see *Hsin hua yueh pao*, 3(1): 24), 1950. In 1951 China's population was given at 500 million, in 1953 at 531 million. The population census of 1953-1954 gave a surprisingly high estimate of 600 million for June 1954 (Teng Hsiao-ping, "Census and General Election Completed in China. Population of China over 600 million." National Chinese News Agency, June 19, 1954; translated in American Consulate General, Survey of China Mainland Press, Hong Kong, June 19-21, 1954, No. 832, pp. 2-4); see also Irene B. Taeubner, Nai-chi Wang, "Population Trends in Eastern Europe, the USSR and Mainland China," *Proceedings of a Round Table at the 1959 Arsenal Conference*, pp. 263-302. Between 1955-1972 no official estimates of China's population have been made public. As to the present population of China, population analysts are at a loss. Estimates by outsiders vary by over 200 million, equivalent to the total U.S. population in 1969. UN estimates put the 1970 population at 760 million since confirmed by China.

6. Klaus Knorr, *Military Power and Potential*, Lexington, Mass.: D.C. Heath, 1970, Chapters 2, 4, and 5.

7. O. Morgenstern, *On the Accuracy of Economic Observations*, (2nd ed.), Princeton, J.J.: Princeton University Press, 1963, especially Chapter XV; as well as, by the same author, "Thirteen Critical Points in Contemporary Economic Theory," *Journal of Economic Literature* (December 1972): 1163-1189.

Chapter 4

1. Herman Kahn and Anthony J. Wiener, *The Year 2000: A Framework for Speculation on the Next Thirty-Three Years*, New York: Macmillan, 1967.

2. Donnella H. Meadows, Dennis L. Meadows, Jørgen Randers, William W. Behrens III, *The Limits to Growth*, New York: Universe Books, 1972. Jay W. Forrester, *World Dynamics*, Cambridge, Mass.: Wright-Allan Press, 1971. Jay W. Forrester, *Principles of Systems*, Cambridge, Mass.: Wright-Allen Press, 1968.

3. For example, Carl Kaysen, "The Computer That Printed Out WOLF," *Foreign Affairs* (July 1972), pp. 660-668. For a particularly pointed and appropriate review see Martin Shubik in *Science*, 174 (4013): 1014-1015, 1971.

4. Problems and questions of this nature can be raised with most other dire long term forecasts, e.g., "A Blueprint for Survival," *The Ecologist*, 2 (1), 1972.

5. Op. cit. (see Note 3).

6. For example, Clive W.J. Granger and M. Hatanaka, *Spectral Analysis of Economic Time Series*, Princeton, N.J.: Princeton University Press, 1964.

7. Clive W.J. Granger and Oskar Morgenstern, *Predictability of Stock Market Prices*, Lexington, Mass.: D.C. Heath, 1971.

8. A.Cournand and M. Lévy (Eds.), *Shaping the Future: Gaston Berger and the Concept of Prospective*, New York: 1973.

9. The report is discussed in a paper by P. Massé in Chapter 6 of the book cited above.

10. Erich Jantsch, *Technological Forecasting in Perspective*, Paris: Organization for Economic Cooperation and Development, 1967, Part II.

11. Bertrand de Jouvenel, *The Art of Conjecture*, translated from the French by Nikita Lavy, New York: Basic Books, 1967, p. 277.

Chapter 5

1. For a detailed analysis, see Klaus Knorr, *Military Power and Potential, op. cit.* Chapters 2-5.

2. U.S. Department of Commerce, "National Income and Product Accounts," *Survey of Current Business*, Washington, D.C.: U.S. Government Printing Office, July issue of each year.

3. For example, the just published work by the University of Sussex Science Policy Research Unit, U.D., *The Limits to Growth Controversy*, Guildford, Surrey: IPC Science and Technology Press, 1973.

Chapter 6

1. The figures are based on M. King Hubbert, "Energy Resources," in *Resources and Man*, Committee on Resources and Man, National Academy of Sciences, National Research Council, San Francisco: W.H. Freeman, 1969.

2. Klaus P. Heiss, "Nuclear Waste Disposal in Space, Space Shuttle System Economic Advantages: 1985-2000," ECON, E-2001-R1, September, 1973.

3. Lawrence M. Lidsky, "The Quest for Fusion Power," *Technology Review*, (January 1972), pp. 10-21. The first *tokamak*, the T-3 device at the Kurchato Institute of Technology, dates back to 1962 is the prototypical example of toroidal confinement by means of a large circulating current induced around the torus. The Princeton Plasma Physics Laboratory stellarator, also a toroidal device, supplies the plasma equilibrium by externally imposed twisted multiple magnetic fields.

4. Keith Boyer, "Laser-Initiated Fusion—Key Experiments Looming," *Astronautics and Aeronautics*, 11 (1): 28-38, 1973.

5. Peter Glaser, "Power from the Sun: Its Future," *Science*, 162 (November 1968): 857-861. See also Peter Glaser, "The Use of the Space Shuttle to Support Large Space Power Generation Systems," AAS Annual Meeting, Washington, D.C., December 26-31, 1972.

Chapter 7

1. E.g., Donnella Meadows, Dennis L. Meadows, Jørgen Randers, William W. Behrens III, "A Response to Sussex," in *Futures*, special issue, *The Limits to Growth Controversy*, IPC Science and Technology Press UK (February 1973), pp. 135-152; to quote, among others (p. 137): "System dynamics models are general and holistic. They are designed not for short-term predictions, but for exploration of the long-term dynamic properties of complex systems. A minimum level of training and experience in feedback systems and control theory is a prerequisite for the construction and analysis of system dynamic models. Without that training, it is possible to make elementary mistakes and to expend unnecessary energy analyzing irrelevant issues."

2. Giovanni Botero, *Della ragion di stato*, libri X, Venice, 1589, especially "Delle cause della grandezza e magnificenza delle città."

3. Kan-Hua Young, "An Econometric Model of U.S. Telecommunication Industry," Mathematica Working Paper, March 1973.

4. U.S. Department of Commerce, *Survey of Current Business*, Washington, D.C.: U.S. Government Printing Office, monthly publication.

5. Federal Communications Commission, *Statistics of Communications Common Carriers*, (year ended December 31, 1970), Washington, D.C.: U.S. Government Printing Office, 1972.

6. H.S. Houthakker and Lester Taylor, *Consumer Demand in the United States: Analyses and Projections*, Cambridge, Mass.: Harvard University Press, 1970.

7. A. Rodney Dobell, Lester D. Taylor, Leonard Waverman, Tsuang-Hua Liu, Michael D.G. Copeland, "Telephone Communications in Canada: Demand, Production, and Investment Decisions," *The Bell Journal of Economics and Management Science*, Vol. 3, No. 1 (Spring 1972), pp. 175-219.

8. H.D. Vinod, "Nonhomogeneous Production Functions and Applications to Telecommunications," *The Bell Journal of Economics and Management Science*, 3(2): 531-543.

Chapter 8

1. The 400 million tons of steel production could be sustained by China with regard to its resource base; China ranks *first* in world reserves and resources of iron ore. See K.P. Wang, "The Mineral Resource Base of Communist China," *An Economic Profile of Mainland China*, Washington, D.C.: U.S. Government Printing Office, 1967, Vol. 1, p. 170, Table 1.

2. It is developed in Oskar Morgenstern, "The Compressibility of Economic Systems and the Problem of Economic Constants," *Zeitschrift für Nationalökonomie* XXVI (1-3): 190-203.

3. An interesting demonstration of a discontinuous change in the stability of an input-output system of arbitrary size due to changes in the production levels of the individual industries is given by Y.K. Wong, "Some Mathematical Concepts for Linear Economic Models," in Oskar Morgenstern

(Ed.), *Economic Activity Analysis*, New York: Wiley, 1954, espec. p. 296. This interesting result has as yet not been absorbed in the literature.

4. United Nations Economic and Social Council, "Problems of the Human Environment," Report to the Secretary General, E-4667, New York, May 26, 1969.

5. There exists a theory of the expanding economy based on the original work of J. von Neumann which shows that an economic system may have subeconomies, each having a different rate of expansion but all expansion rates lying between determinable limits. These ideas have been further elaborated in J.G. Kemeny, O. Morgenstern, and G.L. Thompson, "A Generalization of the von Neumann Model of An Expanding Economy," *Econometrica*, 24: 115-135; and in a forthcoming book by O. Morgenstern and G.L. Thompson, *Expanding Linear Economic Systems* to be published, Spring, 1974.

Chapter 9

1. Robert Burrowes, "Theory Si, Data No!, A Decade of Cross National Research," and Gudmund R. Iversen, "Social Sciences and Statistics," both in *World Politics* XXV (Oct. 1972): 120-154.

Technical Note

1. U.S. Department of Commerce, "National Income and Product Accounts," *Survey of Current Business*, Washington, D.C.: U.S. Government Printing Office, July issue of each year.

2. Ibid.

3. Federal Communications Commission, *Statistics of Communications Common Carriers*, (Year ended December 31, 1970), Washington, D.C.: U.S. Government Printing Office, 1972.

Appendix A

1. H.S. Houthakker and Lester D. Taylor, *Consumer Demand in the United States: Analyses and Projections*, Cambridge, Mass.: Harvard University Press, 1970.

2. Ibid.

Selected Bibliography

Selected Bibliography

**Dealing with Works Primarily Concerned with
Prediction of Economic, Political and Military Power**

1. American Institute of Planners, *Environment and Policy; The Next Fifty Years*, William R. Ewald, Jr., (Ed.), Bloomington: Indiana University Press, 1968.

2. Ayres, Robert U., *Technological Forecasting and Long-Range Planning*, New York: McGraw-Hill, 1969.

3. Baier, Kurt and Nicholas Rescher (Eds.), *Values and the Future*, New York: Free Press, 1969.

4. Barach, A.B., *1975 and the Changes to Come*, New York: Harper & Brothers, 1962.

5. Bauer, Raymond A., et al., *Second-Order Consequences*, Cambridge, Mass.: M.I.T. Press, 1969.

6. Beckerman, W. and R. Bacon, "International Comparisons of Income Levels: A Suggested New Measure," *The Economic Journal*, September, 1966, pp. 519-536.

7. Bell, Daniel, "Twelve Modes of Prediction: A Preliminary Sorting of Approaches in the Social Sciences," *Daedalus*, Summer, 1964.

8. Bell, Daniel, *The Coming of the Post-Industrial Society*, New York: Basic Books, 1973.

9. Bender, A.D., A.E. Strack, G.W. Ebright, G. von Haunalter, "Delphic Study Examines Developments in Medicine," *Futures*, Vol. 1, No. 4, 1969, pp. 289-303.

10. Bernstein, G.B. and Marvin J. Cetron, "SEER: A Delphic Approach Applied to Information Processing," *Technological Forecasting*, Vol. 1, No. 1, June 1969, pp. 33-54. (Contains an annotated bibliography.)

11. Bjerrum, C.A., "Forecast of Computer Developments and Applications, 1968-2000," *Futures*, Vol. 1, No. 4, 1969, pp. 331-338.

12. Botero, Giovanni, *Della ragion di stato, libri dieci*, Venetia: Gioliti 1589, especially, "Delle cause della grandezza e magnificenza delle città."

13. Boyer, Keith, "Laser-Initiated Fusion—Key Experiments Looming," *Astronautics and Aeronautics*, Vol. II, No. 1, pp. 28-38, January, 1973.

14. Bright, James Rieser (Ed.), *Technological Forecasting for Industry and Government: Methods and Applications*, Englewood Cliffs, N.J.: Prentice-Hall, 1968.

15. Brown, B., and Olaf Helmer, *Improving the Reliability of Estimates Obtained from a Consensus of Experts*, Santa Monica, Cal., RAND Corporation, P-2986, September, 1967.

16. Brown, Harrison, *The Challenge of Man's Future*, New York: Viking Press, 1954.

17. Brown, Harrison, James Bonner and John Weir, *The Next Hundred Years*, New York: Viking Press, 1957.

18. Burrowes, Robert, "Theory Si, Data No! A Decade of Cross National Research," *World Politics*, October, 1972.

19. Calder, Ritchie, "Great Prospects for Geothermal Power," *New Scientist*, September, 1961.

20. Cetron, Marvin J., *Technological Forecasting: A Practical Approach*, New York: Gordon and Breach-Science Publishers, 1969.

21. Cetron, Marvin J., and Christine Ralph, *Industrial Applications of Technological Forecasting, Its Utilization in R & D Management*, New York: Wiley-Interscience, 1971.

22. Cetron, Marvin J., and D.N. Dick, "Producing the First Navy Technological Forecasts," *Technological Forecasting*, Vol. 1, No. 2, Fall, 1969.

23. Cheng, Chu-Yuan, "The Cultural Revolution and China's Economy," *Current History*, September, 1967, pp. 148-177.

24. Clark, I.F., "The First Forecast of the Future," *Futures*, Vol. 1, No. 4, June 1969, pp. 325-330.

25. Clarke, Arthur C., *Profiles of the Future: An Enquiry into the Limits of the Possible*, London, 1962, rev. ed. New York: Harper & Row, 1973.

26. Cohn, S., "Soviet Growth Retardation: Trends in Resource Availability and Efficiency," *New Directions in the Soviet Economy*, Part II-A, Washington, D.C., 1966.

27. Cole, Dandridge, *Beyond Tomorrow: The Next 50 Years in Space*, Amherst, Wis.: Amherst Press, 1965.

28. Commoner, B., *The Closing Circle*, New York: Knopf, 1971 & London: Cape, 1972.

29. Cournand, A., and M. Lévy (Eds.), *Shaping the Future: Gaston Berger and the Concept of Prospective* to appear, New York, 1973.

30. Dalkey, Norman C., *Delphi*, Santa Monica, Cal.: RAND Corporation, P-3704, October 1967.

31. Dalkey, Norman C. (Ed.), *Studies in the Quality of Life: Delphi and Decision-Making*, Santa Monica, Cal.: RAND Corporation, 1972.

32. Darmstädter, Joel, Perry D. Teitelbaum and Jaroslaw G. Polach, *Energy in the World Economy*, Resources for the Future, Baltimore-London: The Johns Hopkins Press, 1971.

33. Darwin, Charles Galton, *The Next Million Years*, New York: Doubleday & Co., 1953.

34. Denison, Edward F., "The Sources of Economic Growth in the United States and the Alternatives Before Us," Committee for Economic Development, Supplementary Paper No. 13, New York, 1962.

35. Dewhurst, J. Frederick, et al., *America's Needs and Resources*, New York: The Twentieth Century Fund, 1954.

36. Eckstein, Alexander, Walter Galenson and Ta-Chung Liu (Eds.), *Economic Trends in Communist China*, Chicago: Aldine, 1968.

37. Ernst, Morris L., *Utopia 1976*, New York: Rinehart, 1955.

38. Fedorenko, N.P., "Planning of Production and Consumption in the USSR," *Technological Forecasting*, Vol. 1, No. 1, June 1969, pp. 87-96.

39. Floyd, Acey, "Trend Forecasting: A Methodology for Figures of Merit," in J.R. Bright (Ed.), 1st Annual Technology and Management Conference, Englewood Cliffs, New Jersey, 1968.

40. Forrester, Jay W., *Principles of Systems*, Cambridge, Mass.: Wright-Allen Press, 1968.

41. Forrester, Jay W., *World Dynamics*, Cambridge, Mass.: Wright-Allen Press, 1971.

42. Fucks, Wilhelm, *Formeln zur Macht*, Stuttgart: Deutsche Verlagsanstalt, 1965.

43. Furnas, Clifford C., *The Next Hundred Years: The Unfinished Business of Science*, New York: Reynal, 1936.

44. Gabor, Dennis, *Investing the Future*, (1963), New York: Knopf, 1964.

45. Gabor, Dennis, "The Promise and the Threat of the Age of Leisure," Economic Research Council Lecture, March 3, 1966.

46. Gabor, Dennis, *Innovations: Scientific, Technological, and Social*, London: Oxford University Press, 1970.

47. Gabor, Dennis, *The Mature Society*, London: Secker and Warburg, 1972.

48. Gilbert and Kravis, *Comparative National Products and Price Levels, A Study of Western Europe and the United States*, Paris: Organization for Economic Cooperation and Development, 1958.

49. Gilfillan, S. Colum, "The Prediction of Inventions," *National Trends and National Policy*, U.S. Natural Resources Council, 1937.

50. Gilfillan, S. Colum, "The Prediction of Technical Change," *Review of Economics and Statistics*, Vol. 34, 1952, pp. 368-385.

51. Glaser, Peter, "Power from the Sun: Its Future," *Science*, Vol. 162, November, 1968, pp. 857-861. Also, P. Glaser, "The Use of the Space Shuttle to Support Large Space Power Generation Systems," AAS Annual Meeting, December 26-31, 1972, Washington, D.C.

52. Goldsmith, E., R. Allen, M. Allaby, J. Davoll, and S. Lawrence, "A Blueprint for Survival," *The Ecologist*, Vol. 2, No. 1, January 1972.

53. Gordon, T.J., and H. Hayward, "Initial Experiments with the Cross Impact Matrix, Method of Forecasting," *Futures*, Vol. 1, No. 1, 1968, p. 100.

54. Gordon, T.J., "New Approaches to Delphi," in *Technological Forecasting for Industry and Government: Methods and Applications*, J.R. Bright (Ed.), Englewood Cliffs, N.J.: Prentice Hall, 1968.

55. Gordon, T.J., and Olaf Helmer, *Report on a Long-Range Forecasting Study*, Santa Monica, Cal.: RAND Corporation, P-2982, 1964.

56. Granger, Clive W.J., and M. Hatanaka, *Spectral Analysis of Economic Time Series*, Princeton, N.J.: Princeton University Press, 1964.

57. Granger, Clive W.J., and Oskar Morgenstern, *Predictability of Stock Market Prices*, Lexington, Mass.: D.C. Heath & Co., 1970.

58. Heiss, Klaus P., Oskar Morgenstern, *Economic Analysis of the Space Shuttle System*, National Aeronautics and Space Administration (NASA), Washington, D.C.: U.S. Government Printing Office, January, 1972.

59. Heiss, Klaus P., "Nuclear Waste Disposal in Space, Space Shuttle Economic Advantages; 1985-2000," ECON, Princeton, N.J., September, 1973.

60. Helmer, Olaf, *Analysis of the Future: The Delphi Method*, Santa Monica, Cal.: RAND Corporation, P-3558, March 1967.

61. Helmer, Olaf, *Prospects of Technological Progress*, Santa Monica, Cal.: RAND Corporation, P-3643, August 1967.

62. Houthakker, H.S. and Lester D. Taylor, *Consumer Demand in the United States: Analyses and Projections*, Cambridge, Mass.: Harvard University Press, 1970.

63. Hubbert, M. King, "Energy Resources" in *Resources and Man*, Committee on Resources and Man, National Academy of Sciences, National Research Council, San Francisco: W.H. Freeman, 1969. (Chapter 8 contains an extensive bibliography.)

64. Hubbert, M. King, *Energy Resources: A Report to the Committee on Natural Resources*, National Academy of Sciences, National Research Council, Washington, D.C.: National Research Council, 1963.

65. Institute of Electrical and Electronics Engineers, Inc., *IEEE Computer Conference, Digest*, New York: IEEE, 1967.

66. International Bank for Reconstruction and Development, *World Bank Atlas of Per Capita Product and Population*, Washington, D.C., 1966.

67. International Institute for Strategic Studies, *The Military Balance, 1971-72*, London: IISS, 1972.

68. Inter-Technology Corporation, *The U.S. Energy Problem*, Warrenton, Virginia, November 1971, distributed by National Technical Information Services, U.S. Department of Commerce.

69. Iversen, Gudmund R., "Social Sciences and Statistics," *World Politics*, October 1972.

70. Jantsch, Erich, *Technological Forecasting in Perspective*, Paris: Organization for Economic Cooperation and Development, 1967. (Contains an annotated bibliography.)

71. Johnson, E.A., H.E. Striner, et al., "The Quantitative Effect of Research and Development on National Economic Growth," *Proceedings of the Second International Conference on Operations Research*, New York, 1961.

72. Jouvenel, Bertrand de, *The Art of Conjecture*, New York: Basic Books, 1967.

73. Jouvenel, Bertrand de, *Futuribles*, Paris: S E I D I S, 1965.

74. Jouvenel, Bertrand de, *On Power, Its Nature and the History of Its Growth*, New York: Viking Press, 1949.

75. Jungk, Robert and Johan Galtung (Eds.), *Mankind 2000*, London: Allen & Unwin, 1969.

76. Kahn, Herman and Anthony J. Wiener, *The Year 2000: A Framework for Speculation on the Next Thirty-Three Years*, New York: Macmillan, 1967.

77. Kaysen, Carl, "The Computer that Printed Out WOLF," *Foreign Affairs*, July, 1972, pp. 660-668.

78. Kemeny, J.G., Oskar Morgenstern and Gerald L. Thompson, "A Generalization of the von Neumann Model of An Expanding Economy," *Econometrica*, Vol. 24, pp. 115-135.

79. Knorr, Klaus, *Military Power and Potential*, Lexington, Mass.: D.C. Heath, 1970.

80. Knorr, Klaus, *Power and Wealth*, New York: Basic Books, 1973.

81. Kuhn, Thomas S., *The Structure of Scientific Revolutions*, Chicago: University of Chicago Press, 1962.

82. Landsberg, Hans H., Leonard L. Fischman, and Joseph L. Fisher, *Resources in America's Future*, Baltimore: Resources for the Future, Inc. and The Johns Hopkins Press, 1963.

83. Lenz, Ralph C., Jr., "Forecasting Exploding Technologies by Trend Extrapolation," J.R. Bright (Ed.), *1st Annual Technology and Management Conference*, Englewood Cliffs, N.J., 1968.

84. Lenz, Ralph C., Jr., "Technological Forecasting," ASD-TDR-62-414, Aeronautical Systems Division, Air Force Systems Command, June, 1962 (DDC Accession Number AD408, 085).

85. Lescarboura, A.C., "The Future as Suggested by the Developments of the Last 75 Years," *Scientific American*, Vol. 123, October 2, 1920, pp. 320-321.

86. Lidsky, L.M., "The Quest for Fusion Power," *Technology Review*, January, 1972, pp. 10-21.

87. Linstone, Harold A., and Murray, Turoff, *The Delphi Method and Its Application*, New York: American Elsevier, Fall, 1973 (to be published).

88. Lopez, Alvaro, *Problems in Stable Population Theory*, Office of Population Research, Princeton University, Princeton, 1961.

89. Lotka, A.J., "Contribution to the Theory of Self-Renewing Aggregates with Special Reference to Industrial Replacement," *Annals of Mathematical Statistics*, Vol. 100, 1939.

90. Low, Alfred M., *The Future*, New York, 1925.

91. Malthus, Thomas Robert, *An Essay on the Principles of Population*, (1798), republished as *On Population*, New York: Modern Library, 1960.

92. Martino, Joseph P., "An Experiment with the Delphi Procedure for Long-Range Forecasting," Institute for Electrical and Electronics Engineers, Transactions on Engineering Management, Vol. EM-15, September, 1968, pp. 138-144.

93. Martino, Joseph P., *Technological Forecasting for Decision-making*, New York: American Elsevier, 1972.

94. Mason, R.O., "A Dialectical Approach to Strategic Planning," *Management Science*, Vol. 15, No. 8, pp. B-403-B-414, April, 1969.

95. Meadows, Donnella H., Dennis L. Meadows, Jørgen Randers, William W. Behrens III, *The Limits to Growth*, New York: Universe Books, 1972.

96. Meadows, Donnella H., Dennis L. Meadows, Jørgen Randers, William W. Behrens III, "A Response to Sussex," in *Futures*, special issue *The Limits to Growth Controversy*, IPC Science and Technology Press UK, February 1973, pp. 135-172.

97. Mitroff, Ian I., "A Communication Model of Dialectical Inquir-

ing Systems—A Strategy for Strategic Planning," *Management Science*, Vol. 17, No. 10, pp. B-634-B-648, June 1971.

98. Mitroff, Ian I., and F. Betz, "Dialectical Decision Theory: A Meta-Theory of Decision Making," *Management Science*, to be published.

99. Mitroff, Ian I., and Murray Turoff, "The Whys Behind the Hows," *IEEE Spectrum*, Vol. 10, No. 3, March 1973, pp. 62-71.

100. Morgenstern, Oskar, "The Compressibility of Economic Systems and the Problem of Economic Constants," *Zeitschrift für National-ökonomie*, Vol. XXVI 1-3, pp. 190-203.

101. Morgenstern, Oskar, "Descriptive, Predictive, and Normative Theory," *Kyklos*, 1972.

102. Morgenstern, Oskar, *On the Accuracy of Economic Observations*, 2nd Edition, Princeton: Princeton University Press, 1963.

103. National Commission on Technology, Automation, and Economic Progress, *Technology and the American Economy*, Washington, D.C.: U.S. Government Printing Office, 1966.

104. National Petroleum Council, *U.S. Energy Outlook*, a report of the National Petroleum Council's Committee on U.S. Energy Outlook, Washington, D.C.: National Petroleum Council, December, 1972.

105. North, H.Q., "A Probe of TRW's Future," TRW Systems, Redondo Beach, Cal., July 1966.

106. North, H.Q., "Technological Forecasting in Industry," presented at a seminar to the NATO Defense Research Group, Teddington, Middlesex, England, November 1968.

107. Office of Aerospace Research, *Long-Range Forecasting and Planning*, A Symposium held at the U.S. Air Force Academy, Colorado, 16-17 August, 1966.

108. Osborn, Fairfield, *The Limits of the Earth*, Boston: Little, Brown & Co., 1953.

109. Pearl, Raymond, *The Biology of Death*, Philadelphia-London: J.B. Lippincott, 1922.

110. Pearl, Raymond, and L.J. Reed, "On the Rate of Growth of the Population of the United States since 1790 and its Mathematical Representation," *Proceedings National Academy of Sciences*, Vol. 6, 1920, pp. 275 ff.

111. Polak, Frederik L., *Prognostics*, Amsterdam: Elsevier 1971. (Contains a survey of existing literature.)

112. Popper, Karl R., *The Open Society and Its Enemies*, 2 Vols., (1945), 4th ed., rev., Princeton, N.J.: Princeton University Press, 1963.

113. *Report on India's Food Crisis and Steps to Meet It*, The Agricultural Production Team, sponsored by the Ford Foundation, issued by the Government of India, 1959.

114. Richman, Barry M., *Industrial Society in Communist China*, New York: Random House, 1969.

115. Rubin, Theodore J., "Technology, Policy and Forecasting," *Proceedings of the 1st Annual Technology and Management Conference*, Englewood Cliffs, N.J., 1968.

116. Schultze, Charles L., *The Politics and Economics of Public Spending*, Washington, D.C.: The Brookings Institution, 1964.

117. Shannon, Claude E., *The Mathematical Theory of Communications*, Urbana, Ill.: University of Illinois Press, 1949.

118. Shubik, Martin, *Science*, Vol. 174, No. 4013, December 3, 1971, pp. 1014-15.

119. Slotnick, Daniel L., "Unconventional Systems," *Computer Design*, Vol. 6, No. 12, December, 1967, pp. 47-52.

120. Snow, C.P., "Science and Government," *Science and Technology*, January, 1969, pp. 36-37.

121. Société d'Études et de Documentation Économiques, Industrielles et Sociales, Chroniques d' actualité, Paris. (Offers an extensive list of publications.)

122. Suchting, W.A., "Deductive Explanation and Production Revisited," *Philosophy of Science*, Vol. 34, March, 1967.

123. Taeubner, Irene B., and Nai-chi Wang, "Population Trends in Eastern Europe, the USSR and Mainland China," *Proceedings of a Round Table at the 1959 Arsenal Conference*, pp. 263-302.

124. Teng, Hsiao-ping, "Census and General Election Completed in China. Population of China over 600 Million." *National Chinese News Agency*, June 19, 1954; translated in American Consulate General, Survey of China Mainland Press, Hong Kong, June 19-21, 1954, No. 832, pp. 2-4.

125. Thomson, George, *The Foreseeable Future*, Cambridge, England: University Press, 1955.

126. United Nations, *Statistical Yearbooks*, New York: United Nations, 1959, 1965, 1968, and 1971.

127. United Nations, "World Energy Requirements in 1975 and 2000," United Nations International Conference on the Peaceful Uses of Atomic Energy, 1955, paper No. 8/P/902.

128. United Nations Economic and Social Council, "Problems of the Human Environment," Report to the Secretary General, E-4667, New York, May 26, 1969.

129. United States Arms Control and Disarmament Agency, *World Military Expenditures, 1966-67*, Washington, D.C.: U.S. Government Printing Office.

130. United States Office of Emergency Preparedness, *The Potential for Energy Conservation*, Washington, D.C.: U.S. Government Printing Office, October, 1972.

131. Vasilev, Mikhail V., Gushchev, Sergei Z., (eds.), *Life in the Twenty-First Century*, London: Souvenir Press, 1960.

132. Vinod, Hrishikesh D., "Nonhomogeneous Production Functions and Applications to Telecommunications," *The Bell Journal of Economics and Management Science*, Vol. 3, No. 2, pp. 531-543.

133. Volterra, V., Leçons sur la théorie mathématique de la lutte pour la vie, Paris: Gauthier, 1931.

134. Volterra, V., "Leggi delle fluttuazioni biologiche," *Rendiconti della R. Accademia dei Lincei*, Series 6, Vol. 5, 1927, p. 3.

135. Volterra, V., and H. Hadwiger, "Über die Integralgleichungen der Bevölkerungstheorie," *Mitteilungen der Vereinigung Schweizerischer Versicherungsmathematiker*, Vol. 38, 1939.

136. Wang, K.P., "The Mineral Resource Base of Communist China," *An Economic Profile of Mainland China*, Vol. 1, Washington, D.C., 1967.

137. Wong, Y.K., "Some Mathematical Concepts for Linear Economic Models," in Oskar Morgenstern (Ed.), *Economic Activity Analysis*, New York: Wiley, 1954.

138. Woytinsky, W.S., and E.S. Woytinsky, *World Population and Production*, New York: The Twentieth Century Fund, 1953.

139. Young, Kan-Hua, "An Econometric Model of U.S. Telecommunication Industry," Working Paper, Princeton, N.J., March 1973.

Index

Index

administration: competence in, 76; skill and power, 188
agriculture: and imports, 135; and managerial class, 85
Alaska: oil, 179
allocations, 169; concept of, 83; waste, 127, 128

Belgium: energy consumption, 108
Bell Canada, 151
Bender, A.D., 25
Berger, G., 9, 67
Bernstein, G.B. and Cetron, M.J., 24
Bjerrum, C.A., 25
Boltzmann, Ludwig, 4
Brown, B. and Dalkey, N.C., 24

Canada: and energy, 108; telecommunications and industry, 149-159
China: compatibility analysis, 165; energy and steel, 31, 22; foreign import, 135; and forecast problems, 71; and Fucks analysis, 27, 48; and GNP, 78, 117; iron ore, 217; petroleum, 137; politics and economic growth, 44-47; population, 215; resources, 114; and status, 126; threat, 189; and will, 81
communications: analysis, 61
compatibility: and analysis, 165
compressibility: concept of, 169-174
consumerism, 187
consumption: and input-output tables, 174; and net national product, 170-173; and resources, 59
connectivity: concept of, 176, 177
convergence: concept of, 23
Czechoslovakia: energy consumption, 108

data: transformation, 66
defense: and GNP, 78
Delphi, 188; method description, 13; interaction, 22; and Kahn and Wiener, 49; nature of work, 16
demand: concept in telecommunications model, 150
development: in China, 40
Dobell, A.R., 151; Canadian data, 195

East Germany: energy consumption, 108
Ebright, G.W., 25
E.E.C. (European Economic Community), 75; dependency, 178; energy consumption, 124; food import, 135; growth rate, 117; petroleum, 137; and scale, 86; and status, 126
energy: comparative production, 119-124; effect of war, 119; in Fucks, 31-36; fusion, 132; historic demand for, 103, 104; history of, 111; and industrialization, 187; and interplay, 178; nuclear, 140; production of and LTG, 60; size and distribution, 114-116; solar, 133, 134; squeeze, 134-136; supply, 80
environment: Fucks, 28; and recursiveness, 69
Europe: energy deficit, 4
expertise: and Delphi, 18-20

feedback: in Delphi, 33; in LTG, 56; necessity, 71; and systems dynamics models, 217; and systems generally, 145
flexibility, 189
forecasting: and approaches, 15; as art form, 185; and China, 44-47; and energy squeeze, 116; and expectations, 67; in Kahn and Wiener, 49-53; long-term, 87;

About the Authors

Klaus P. Heiss received his Ph.D. in economics from Hochschule for Walthandel, Vienna, Austria. He is with ECON, Inc., Princeton, N.J. Most recently, Dr. Heiss directed the study for the National Aeronautics and Space Administration on a U.S. space transportation system for the 1980s. Previously, he was director of Advanced Technology Economics and research associate and lecturer in economics for the Econometric Research Program at Princeton University. Dr. Heiss is the author of numerous publications including: *Economic Analysis of New Space Transportation Systems, Economic Analysis of the Space Shuttle System* with Professor Oskar Morgenstern, *Economic Analysis of Advanced Propulsion Systems* and *Benefit-Cost Analysis Principles for the North East Corridor Project.*

Klaus Knorr is a specialist on International Relations who received his LL.B. from the University of Tuebingen, Germany, and his Ph.D. in the International Relations at the University of Chicago. He has taught at Stanford, Yale and Princeton. From 1961 to 1968, he directed the Center of International Studies at Princeton. He has been a consultant of several government departments. At present, he is William Stewart Tod Professor of International and Public Affairs at the Woodrow Wilson School, Princeton University. Since 1953, he has been an Editor of *World Politics.* He is the author of numerous books and journal articles. Among his recent writings are: *On the Uses of Military Power in the Nuclear Age* (1966), *Military Power and Potential* (1970), and *Power and Wealth, The Political Economy of International Power* (1973).

Oskar Morgenstern is professor of economics at New York University. He was for a long time professor of economics at Princeton University where, in 1950, he founded and directed the Econometric Research Program. He is now organizing a new Center for Applied Economics at New York University. Author of many books and other publications in many languages, among which are: *Theory of Games and Economic Behavior* (with the late John von Neumann), *On the Accuracy of Economic Observations, International Financial Transactions and Business Cycles, Predictability of Stock Market Prices* (with C.W.J. Granger), etc. Professor Morgenstern is also Chairman of the Board of Mathematica, Inc. and Trustee of the Institute for Advanced Studies at Vienna, Austria, which he helped to establish ten years ago. He is a recipient of honorary degrees from the Universities of Munster, Basel, Vienna, and is a Correspondant de l'Institut de France.